DAY HIKER'S GUIDE
TO SOUTHERN CALIFORNIA

Cover photo: *Lupine, San Rafael Wilderness,* by David Muench

Book design and cartography by Mary Rose
Typography by Jim Cook
Map on page 10 by Susan Kuromiya

ACKNOWLEDGMENTS
For their cooperation, field and fact-checking, I'd like to thank the rangers of Los Padres, San Bernardino, Angeles, and Cleveland national forests; the rangers of Point Mugu, Malibu Creek, Topanga, Chino Hills, Mount San Jacinto, Palomar Mountain, Cuyamaca Rancho, and Border Field state parks; the rangers of Griffith, Elysian, O'Melveny Placerita Canyon, and Devil's Punchbowl parks. Thanks also to Noel Young, Capra Press editor-in-chief, who guided me over the perilous paths of publishing and whose skill and enthusiasm made possible the first edition of this book.

Portions of this manuscript have appeared in the Day Hike column in the *Los Angeles Times.*

PHOTO CREDITS
California State Department of Parks and Recreation, pp. 14, 68, 73, 80, 208, 220, 242, 252, 257; U.S. Forest Service, pp. 29, 32, 42, 106, 11, 116, 129, 130, 131; David M. Werk, pp. 39, 71, 82, 94, 160, 166, 168, 192, 196, 197, 227, 235, 261; Santa Barbara Historical Society, pp. 48, 54, 59, 170; E.R. Blakley Archives, p. 51; National Park Service, p. 60; Los Angeles Public Library, p. 115; Cristine Argyrakis, pp. 157-58; F.G. Hochberg, p. 163; all other photos by John McKinney.

LIBRARY OF CONGRESS CATALOGING IN PUBLICATION DATA
McKinney, John
Day Hiker's Guide to Southern California
1. Hiking—California, Southern—Guidebooks.
2. California, Southern—Descriptions and travel—
Guidebooks. I. Title
Includes Index.
GV199.42.C22S685   1987   917.94'9   87-5598
ISBN 0-934161-02-X

Published by
Olympus Press
Post Office Box 2397
Santa Barbara, California 93120

DAY HIKER'S GUIDE
TO SOUTHERN CALIFORNIA

John McKinney

Olympus Press

SANTA BARBARA, CALIFORNIA

CONTENTS

AS THEIR LAND IS

After all anybody is as their land and air is.
Anybody is as the sky is low or high,
the air heavy or clear
and anybody is as there is wind or no wind there.
It is that which makes them and the arts they make
and the work they do and the way they eat
and the way they drink
and the way they learn and everything.

—GERTRUDE STEIN

Chapter 1

UNDERSTANDING DAY HIKING
IN SOUTHERN CALIFORNIA

THE LAND WE CALL SOUTHERN CALIFORNIA is an island, ecologically isolated from the rest of the continent by a combination of geographic and climatic factors. Helen Hunt Jackson once said of Southern California: "It's an island on the land." Carey McWilliams popularized the phrase in his definitive history of the region, *Southern California: An Island on the Land*. The land's island nature is apparent when you enter it from the north or east. When you round Point Conception and the north-south orientation of California becomes east-west, it is obvious that you have entered a unique geographical province. If you come to Southern California from the east through Cajon Pass or San Gorgonio Pass, the change is immediately evident. Light is softer, the climate more temperate.

The land includes seven counties: Santa Barbara, Ventura, Los Angeles, Orange, Riverside, San Bernardino, and San Diego. Usually, only those parts of San Bernardino, Riverside and San Diego Counties "west of the mountains" are in Southern California, but a case can be made for including all of them and adding Imperial County as well. Some boosters insist Southern California's northern boundary is San Luis Obispo or even the Monterey County line, but geographically and ecologically it's at Point Conception. Southern California is the land south of the Transverse Range, which knifes across California toward the Pacific, just north of Santa Barbara.

Southern California is protected from the Mojave Desert by the San Bernardino and San Gabriel Mountain Ranges on the east and walled off from the San Joaquin Valley by other Transverse Ranges. The lowlands are covered with alluvial fans formed by earth washed down from the mountains. The coastal plain is "watered" by some of the driest rivers in the west: the Los Angeles, Mojave, San Gabriel and Santa Ana. Mark Twain may have been joking about them when he said he'd fallen into a California river and "come out all dusty."

7

Compass directions can be confusing to both newcomers and oldtimers. "Up the coast" in other parts of the world is usually taken to mean north, but it's not north in Southern California. To travel north from L.A., you head directly into the Mojave Desert, crossing our east-west trending mountains in the process. If you traveled a straight line, as the crow flies, from San Bernardino to Santa Barbara, you would travel 137 miles west and only 27 miles north.

Carey McWilliams has suggested that "The analyst of California is like a navigator who is trying to chart a course in a storm: the instruments will not work; the landmarks are lost; and the maps make little sense." California may be geographically cockeyed and Southern California even more so, but we day hikers before heading for the hills, ought to get our bearings. We need to find a few landmarks and consult a map. Orienting yourself to Southern California isn't *that* difficult. Try this:

SOUTHERN CALIFORNIA GEOGRAPHY MADE EASY

Get yourself an Auto Club map of California or one of those gas stations used to give out free. Spread it on the floor. (This is hands-on learning, so if you have small hands, you might want to borrow a friend with larger ones.) Put your right thumb on Santa Barbara, your right pinkie on San Diego and spread your fingers in as wide a fan as you can manage. One of the first things you may notice is that your palm covers the L.A. basin. Keep your palm firmly pressed down on L.A. to keep it from spreading into the wilderness. Look at your thumb. Above it is Point Conception, the northernmost point of Southern California. Above Santa Barbara are the Santa Ynez Mountains and beyond are those parts of the Los Padres National Forest we call the Santa Barbara Backcountry. Along your index finger are the San Gabriel Mountains and the Angeles National Forest. (Careful! Don't get your finger pinched in the San Andreas Fault.) Your middle finger is in the San Bernardino Mountains. Near the eastern terminus of this range is Mount San Gorgonio, the highest peak in Southern California. Between your middle and ring fingers, paralleling the coast in Orange County are the Santa Ana Mountains, protected by the Cleveland National Forest. At the tip of your ring finger at the north end of Anza Borrego Desert State Park lie the Santa Rosa Mountains. Take note of the Colorado Desert and farther to the north, the vast Mojave Desert. Due east from your pinkie is the southern part of the Cleveland National Forest, as well as the Palomar and Cuyamaca Mountain ranges. Now that you're oriented, raise that right hand of yours and pledge to preserve, protect, and enjoy these places.

HOW TO USE THIS BOOK

First decide where you want to hike. A palm oasis? An alpine meadow? A deserted beach? Consult map on p. 10 Pick a Trail Number in your geographical area of interest. Once you've selected a number, turn to the corresponding hike description in the main body of the book. Unsure of what to expect in the Santa Monica, San Bernadino or Cuyamaca Mountains? Read the appropriate chapter introduction.

There are 75 trails in this guide. Add the suggested options and you can design about two hundred different hikes. Beneath the name of the trail is the *trailhead* and one or more *destinations*. Every day hike in this book has a soul and a goal. You provide the soul; this guide will provide the goals. Let's face it, we're a goal-oriented society and we hikers are no exception. We hike for majestic views or for the best fishing spot, not just to be out there. Some day hikers collect peaks the way the motorhome driver collects decals.

MILEAGE, expressed in **ROUNDTRIP (RT)** figures, follows each destination. The hikes in this guide range from 2 to 17 miles, with the majority in the 5 to 10 mile range. **GAIN** or **LOSS** in elevation follows the mileage. In matching a hike to your ability, you'll want to consider both mileage and elevation as well as condition of the trail, terrain, and season. Hot exposed chaparral or miles of boulder-hopping can make a short hike seem long. I haven't graded the *Day Hiker's Guide* as to difficulty, because I believe day hikers vary too much in physical condition to make such an evaluation. However, you may wish to use the following guideline: A hike suitable for beginners and children would be less than five miles with an elevation gain of less than 700-800'. A moderate hike is considered a hike in the 5 to 10 mile range, with under a 2000' elevation gain. You should be reasonably physically fit for these. Preteens sometimes find the going difficult. Hikes over 10 miles and those with more than a 2000' gain are for experienced hikers in top form.

SEASON is the next item to consider. Although Southern California is one of the few places in the country which offers four-season hiking, there are still some seasonal restrictions. You can hike some of the trails in this guide all of the time, all of the trails some of the time, but not all of the trails all of the time. Season recommendations are based partly on hiker comfort and partly on legal restrictions. Those recommendations based on comfort can sometimes be disregarded by intrepid mountaineers. You can, if you so desire, hike to the top of Mount San Jacinto in the dead of winter, but you'd better bring snowshoes. It's possible to hike in the Colorado Desert in the middle of summer, but you'd better bring a water truck or a camel. Seasonal recommendations based on legal restrictions must not be disregarded. Closure for fire season is the chief

9

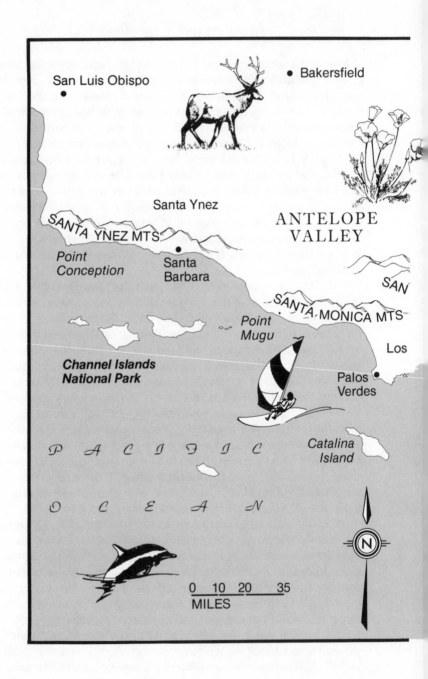

San Luis Obispo

Bakersfield

Santa Ynez

ANTELOPE
VALLEY

SANTA YNEZ MTS

Point
Conception

Santa
Barbara

SAN

SANTA MONICA MTS

Point
Mugu

Los

Channel Islands
National Park

Palos
Verdes

$\mathcal{P}$ $\mathcal{A}$ $\mathcal{C}$ $\mathcal{I}$ $\mathcal{F}$ $\mathcal{I}$ $\mathcal{C}$

Catalina
Island

$\mathcal{O}$ $\mathcal{C}$ $\mathcal{E}$ $\mathcal{A}$ $\mathcal{N}$

N

0 10 20   35
MILES

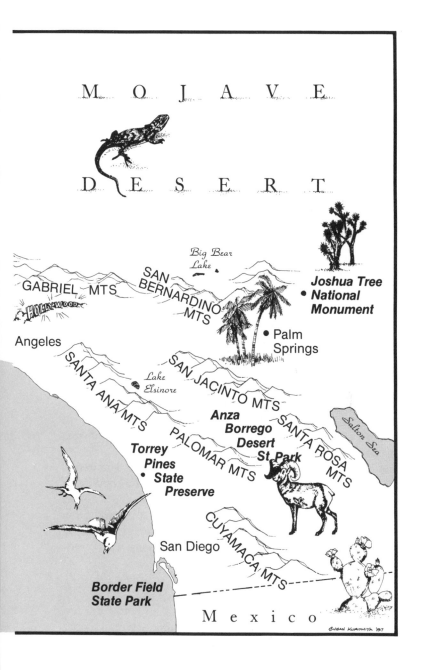

MOJAVE

DESERT

GABRIEL MTS
SAN BERNARDINO MTS
Big Bear Lake

Joshua Tree
• National
Monument

• Palm Springs

HOLLYWOOD

Angeles

SANTA ANA MTS

SAN JACINTO MTS

Lake Elsinore

Anza Borrego Desert St Park

SANTA ROSA MTS

Salton Sea

PALOMAR MTS

Torrey Pines
• State Preserve

San Diego

CUYAMACA MTS

Border Field State Park

Mexico

SUSAN KURASHIMA '87

restriction on day hiking in certain state park and national forest areas. Length of closure varies from area to area, depending on the year's rainfall. Some sections of national forest close automatically on July 1, and do not open up again until after the first heavy rain of winter. Others restrict entry for only a few weeks at the end of summer. A few trails in this guide may be impassable in winter and spring due to high water. Relevant fire and flood information has been noted below the season recommendation.

An introduction to each hike will describe what you'll see along the trail: plants, animals, panoramic views. You'll also learn about the geologic and human history of the region. This section will also tell you to "bring your fishing pole" or "check a tide table."

DIRECTIONS TO TRAILHEAD take you from the nearest major highway to trailhead parking. Alternative transportation, via bus or train where practical, has been suggested. For trails having two desirable trailheads, directions to each are given. A few trails can be hiked one way, with the possibility of a car shuttle. Suggested car shuttle points are noted. You may notice a slight L.A. bias to the directions when you proceed "up" to Santa Barbara or "down" to San Diego. For the sake of clarity and orientation, I've chosen downtown L.A. as a reference point. It seems to me, L.A. is as good a place to leave from as any. My apologies to Chula Vista, Pomona, Oxnard.

After the directions to the trailhead, you'll read a description of **THE HIKE.** Important junctions and major sights are pointed out, but I've let you to discover the multitude of little things that make a hike an adventure.

OPTIONS allow you to climb higher or farther or take a different route back to the trailhead.

It's not important that you follow the trail exactly as I've described it. Whether you hike the length of a trail and every one of its options or snooze under the first sycamore you find, is your decision and no one else's. There's enough regimentation in your life without me telling you where you *must* hike. This guide is for *you* to plan *your* day in the back country. Don't stick your nose in this guide; stick it in some wildflowers.

ON THE TRAIL

Choose the pace that's best for you. Rest once an hour for a few minutes. To keep your momentum and to avoid stiffness, several shorter rest periods are better than one long one. Set a steady pace, one you can keep up all day. Wear a watch, not because you have an appointment with a waterfall and you have to be punctual, but because a watch gives you some idea of pace and helps you get back to the trailhead before dark.

Hiking uphill takes energy. Hiking 2 miles an hour up a 10 percent grade requires as much energy as hiking 4 miles an hour on level trail. Climbing can be especially difficult in high altitude. Altitude sickness affects some hikers at about 8000 feet. Only a few hikes in this guide are above this elevation. Altitude can cause discomfort—headache and nausea above 5000 feet.

Hiking alone or with company is strictly a matter of personal preference. Most rangers warn you never to hike alone, primarily because they think most hikers are inexperienced, uncoordinated or both and they hate to make rescues. Having two or three in your party is a definite advantage if something goes wrong; someone can go for help. Hiking with a group is a good idea for first time hikers. Most inexperienced hikers are uncomfortable going solo. After a few hikes however, a craving for solitutde often develops—by which time you should be able to take care of yourself on the trail. There's a lot to be said for solitary hiking, as the writings of Thoreau, Whitman, and Muir would seem to indicate.

DAY HIKING THROUGH THE SEASONS

Many have sung praises of Southern California's Mediterranean climate. Relentless sunshine, winter and summer, is how the climate is usually stereotyped. But the semi-tropical stereotype holds true only in coastal regions and only at certain times of the year. There is nothing Mediterranean about the climate of the Mojave Desert or the San Jacinto high country. In Southern California's backcountry, seasons arrive with clarity and distinction. Day hikers can find trails that are "in season" in every month of the year.

WINTER brings snow to mountains in the Angeles, San Bernardino, and Los Padres National Forests. Rain visits the coastal lowlands. Deciduous trees and shrubs lose their leaves. Some animals become torpid or hibernate. But winter doesn't mean an end to all of nature's activities in Southern California, particularly in the lowland valleys and deserts. January is a fine time to take a beach hike, to visit shores laid bare by minus tides or to see what treasure winter storms have cast ashore. In February, the desert begins to bloom. February and March, last of the winter months, are often looked upon by many Southern Californians as the first months of spring. Day hikers are guaranteed solitude in these months. High country trails are covered with snow and those on the lower slopes are muddy going.

Wildflowers, Anza-Borrego Desert State Park

SPRING comes early to Southern California. Even the chaparral, so dull gray in other seasons, looks inviting. Ceanothus covers the lower slopes of the Santa Barbara Backcountry, the Santa Monica Mountains and San Gabriel Mountains with its dainty white and blue blossoms. Yellow violets and wild peony bloom amidst the chaparral. In March, the wild coreopsis on Anacapa Island grows wild. As spring temperatures increase, flowers in the hotter Colorado Desert diminish, but those in the higher Mojave Desert arrive with a flourish. In June, the flower show moves to the high country of the Transverse ranges. Lemon lilies appear streamside and lupine everywhere. Flocks of birds go about the business of building nests, laying eggs, raising young.

In SUMMER, snowmelt swollen creeks water emerald green meadows. Scarlet-stemmed snow plant emerges in the pine forests. By August, even the highest peaks have lost their mantle of snow and dayhikers can stand atop their summits and sign the hiker's register. A beach hike in the middle of summer is a pleasure. With the sun on your back, the surf at your feet and miles of beach in front of you, summer seems endless.

AUTUMN has its critics and its fans. Some say there's little use for a day that begins with frost, becomes hot enough to sunburn your nose by noon, and has you shivering by sunset. Wiser heads, those attached to day hikers no doubt, believe autumn is the best of all seasons. The high country is crisp, but still inviting and desert washes have cooled. Autumn colors oaks, dogwoods, willows and sycamores in the Cuyamaca and Palomar Mountains with red and scarlet pastels. There's enough color change to satisfy even the most homesick New Englander.

DAY HIKING HINTS

Many day hikes require little more equipment than comfortable shoes, yet hikers often overburden themselves with such nonessentials as hunting knives, hatchets, and propane stoves. The idea with equipment is to take only what you need. You want to get so comfortable with your equipment that you don't think about it; what little you need is on your back and what you don't need is far away.

FOOTWEAR: Day hiking begins and ends with the feet. You've no doubt seen hikers wearing everything from old sneakers to World War II combat boots. For the last two decades, lug-soled boots have been considered mandatory, but if you're carrying a day pack over easy terrain you don't need a heavy pair of boots. Jogging shoes can serve to get you started. But if you do much hiking over rough terrain, a good pair of boots is necessary and well worth the money. A lightweight pair with a vibram sole will do nicely. Don't buy more boot than you need. Blisters can ruin any hike, so be sure to break-in your boots before you hit the trail. Walk around town and be sure your feet develop a callous indifference to your boots.

A number of rubber soled boots have come on the market recently and you may find they fill the gap between running shoes and lug soled boots and give you miles of comfortable walking.

CLOTHING: You have most of what you need lying around the house.

• A T-shirt with a cotton shirt that buttons gives you a lot of temperature regulating possibilities. Add a wool shirt and a windbreaker with a hood and you'll be protected against sudden changes in temperatures.

- Shorts are useful much of the year in Southern California. Test your shorts to make sure they're not too tight. Step up on a chair and if they pull around the groin, butt, or thigh, they're too tight.

- For cooler days or walking through brush, a sturdy pair of long pants is necessary.

- Hats prevent the brain from frying and protect from heat loss when it is cold.

- Sunglasses are a big help when walking over snow or on hot, exposed slopes.

- Ponchos—a cheap vinyl one is okay unless you walk through brush with them. The Boy Scout ones aren't too bad.

FOOD: On a day hike, weight is no problem, so you can pack whatever you wish. Remember to pack out what you pack in. The day you hike is not the day to diet. There's a lot of calorie burning on a hike and quite an energy cost. You'll need all your strength, particularly on steep grades. Gorp, or trail mix, with fruit, nuts, raisins and M&M's is good high octane fuel. A sandwich, fruit and cookies make a good lunch. Sourdough bread, a fine cheese and a bottle of chablis is also nice. Avoid a big lunch. Exertion after a big lunch sets up a competition between your stomach and your legs and your legs lose, leading to weakness and indigestion.

WATER: It's still possible to drink from some backcountry streams and springs without ill effect, but each individual water source should be carefully scrutinized. Many hikers assume water is pure and 48 hours later have a queasy feeling that tells them their assumption was wrong. Water may harbor the organism *Giardia Lamblia,* one of the causes of "traveler's diarrhea." When you approach that stream, Sierra cup in hand, think about what may be upstream. A campground? Cows? High rushing mountain streams are usually safer than stagnant ponds. Bring purification tablets and use them if you have the slightest doubt about water quality. Purification tablets may be a bitter pill to swallow, but they beat intestinal discomfort any day.

FIRST AID KIT: A standard kit supplemented with an ace bandage in the event of hiker's knee or a sprained ankle. Take moleskin for blisters. Insect repellent won't stop mosquitos from buzzing around but it will inhibit their biting.

DAY PACK or "Summit Pack": A day pack is a soft frameless pack that attaches to your shoulders and sometimes includes a hip band or

16

waist belt for support. A good one will last a lifetime. Those bike bags or book bags of cotton or thin nylon won't hold up well. In picking a day pack, shoulder pads are a nice feature. You'll only be carrying five or ten pounds, but the pads are comfortable on a long hike. Get one with a tough covered zipper. Double-O rings slip and aren't the greatest shoulder strap adjusters. Get tabler buckles; they don't slip and they adjust quickly.

PRECAUTIONS

We still react in instinctive ways when we feel threatened by some aspect of the natural world. Don't let the few biters, stingers, and hazards mentioned in this chapter make you apprehensive about going into the backcountry.

BLISTERS: There's nothing worse than walking on feet that burn like hot coals. To avoid blisters, make sure your boots fit properly. Keep pulling up your socks and see to it that they don't bunch up. Act quickly if you feel a blister develop. Cut a hole in moleskin a little larger than your red spot and stick it in place with the blister poking through the hole. The idea is to surround it so the boot can't get at it. (If you covered it you could irritate it further and you'd have to peel the tape off the blister. Ouch!) Some hikers put a double layer of tissue paper over the blister and tape the tissue in place with surgical tape. If you get a full grown blister, pop it with a clean needle inserted under the edge and apply antiseptic, then put moleskin over the area.

POISON OAK: This infamous plant grows abundantly throughout Southern California mountains up to an elevation of 5,000 feet. It's a sneaky devil. It may lurk under other shrubs or take the form of a vine and climb up an oak tree. The leaves are one to four inches long and glossy, as if waxed.

Poison Oak

Effects of Poison Oak

All parts of the plant at all times of the year contain poisonous sap that can severely blister skin and mucous membranes. Its sap is most toxic during spring and summer. In fall, poison oak is particularly conspicuous; its leaves turn to flaming crimson or orange. However, its color change is more a response to heat and dryness than season; its "fall color" can occur anytime in Southern California. Leaves on some plants can be turning yellow or red while plants in most spots are putting out green leaves. In winter, poison oak is naked, its stalks blending into the dull hue of the forest.

Contrary to popular belief, you can't catch it from someone else's rash, nor from oozing blisters, but petting an animal or handling a piece of clothing that carries it can make you a victim.

There are a multitude of remedies. A bath with one-half cup sea salt and one-half cup of kelp helps dry the oozing. A dip in the ocean can help too. A few tablespoons of baking soda added to a tub of lukewarm water calms the itchies as well. Mugwort is also an effective panacea. Its fresh juice applied directly to the pained area relieves itching. Then, of course, there's always calamine lotion, and cortisone cream.

RATTLESNAKES: Like typical Southern Californians, rattlesnakes take to the trail to enjoy the sunshine, so keep an eye out. Despite the common fear of rattlers, few people see them and rarely is anyone bitten. An estimated 300 yearly snake envenomations occur in the Southland. Only a small percentage of these bites cause serious injury.

The red diamond rattlesnake is found in coastal, hill and desert regions, the sidewinder and western diamondback in the desert, and the southern pacific rattler lives in coastal regions between Malibu and San Juan Capistrano and in inland areas like remote sections of Griffith Park.

If you've been bitten, remain calm. Check to be sure you've actually been envenomated. Look for swelling around the wound within five minutes. If it doesn't swell, you've escaped and no hospital treatment is necessary. If swelling and other symptoms occur—numbness around the lips or hairline, a metallic taste in the mouth or twitching facial muscles, it got you.

Getting to a hospital emergency room is more important than any other first aid. Keep the site of the wound as immobilized as possible and relax. Cutting and suction treatments are now medically out of vogue and advised only as a last resort if you're absolutely sure you can't get to a hospital within four hours.

BEES: More fatalities occur from allergic reaction to insect strings than from rattlesnake bites. People allergic to bee stings can get a desensitization shot and a specially equipped bee kit from an allergist.

TICKS: They're ¼ to ½ inch long and about the same color as the ground, so they're hard to see. Ticks are usually picked up by brushing against low vegetation. When hiking in a tick area it's best to sit on rocks rather than fallen logs. Check your skin and clothing occasionally. You and your loved one can groom each other like monkeys at the zoo. If one is attached to the skin, it should be lifted off with a slow gentle pull. Before bathing, look for ticks on the body, particularly in the hair and pubic region.

GETTING LOST AND FOUND

No one expects to get lost in the Southern California backcountry. "After all," say novices, "the mountains aren't big and icy like the High Sierra and we're only out for the day and . . . " Even the experienced can get lost. Getting lost is usually the result of taking a "short cut" off an established trail. Danger is magnified if the hiker is alone or if he failed to tell anyone where he was hiking and when he planned to return.

Try to avoid getting lost in the first place. Know your physical condition and don't overtax yourself. Check your boots and clothing. Be prepared for bad weather. Inquire about trail conditions. Allow plenty of time for your hike and allow even more for your return to the trailhead.

When you're on the trail, keep your eyes open. If you're hiking so fast that all you see is your boots, you're not attentive to passing terrain—its charms or its layout. STOP once in a while. Sniff wildflowers, splash your face in a spring. LISTEN. Maybe the trail is paralleling a stream. Listen to the sound of mountain water. On your left? On your right? Look up at that fire lookout on the nearby ridge. Are you heading toward it or away from it? LOOK AROUND. That's the best insurance against getting lost.

Alright, but you're *really* lost. Stay calm. Don't worry about food. It takes weeks to starve to death. Besides, you've got that candy bar in your day pack. You have a canteen. And you have a poncho in case of rain. You're in no immediate danger, so don't run around in circles like a mindless chicken.

LOOK AROUND some more. Is there any familiar landmark in sight? Have you been gaining elevation or losing it? Where has the sun been shining? On your right cheek? Your back? Retrace your steps, if you can. Look for other footprints. If you're totally disoriented, keep walking laterally. Don't go deeper into the brush or woods. Go up slope to get a good view, but don't trek aimlessly here and there.

If it's near dark, get ready to spend the night. Don't try to find your way out in the dark. Don't worry. If you left your itinerary, your rescuers will begin looking for you in the morning. Try to stay warm by huddling against a tree or wrapping yourself in branches, pine needles or leaves. The universal distress signal is 3 visible or audible signals—3 shouts or whistles, 3 shiny objects placed on a bare summit. Don't start a fire! You could start a major conflagration.

Relax and think of your next hike. Think of the most beautiful place you know—that creek of snowmelt gushing down from that stony mountain, a place where the fish bite and the mosquitos don't . . . You'll make it, don't worry.

TRAILS THEN AND NOW

The first Southern California trailmakers were wild animals, breaking down the brush as they journeyed to and from water. Indians used these ready-made trails and fashioned new ones for trade and travel. Indian trails rarely climbed via switchbacks; instead, they took the steepest and most direct route. The Spaniards blazed few new trails, contenting themselves with Indian paths.

The restless Americans were tireless trailmakers. They hurried into the mountains to dig for metals, to graze their cattle, to cut timber. They needed trails and they needed them right away. Trees were felled and brush was cleared. Gunpowder was rammed in holes drilled into rock and the most immoveable granite was blown to smithereens.

Fortunately for Southern California backcountry, mountaineering became popular before the backcountry was wrecked. Day hikers can thank nineteenth century Englishmen for the "invention" of hiking. Between 1850 and 1870, Englishmen assaulted every Alp and established the lodge, the resort, and the picture postcard. Alpinism is what the English called their new sport. Americans on the East Coast imported alpinism, then brought it with them when they traveled west to Southern California. During the latter part of the nineteenth century, great tracts of land, stretching from San Bernardino to San Luis Obispo, were set aside as Timberland Reserves by the federal government. A flood of immigrants to Southern California and the few natives all headed into the timberland to enjoy the mountain life.

"Our Italy" and "Little Switzerland" is what tourist brochures called Southern California. Bragged one brochure of that era: "The Santa

Monica Mountains provide the hiker a paradise. Incomparable scenic panoramas are to be had by those willing to spend the effort. The combination of mountains, oceans and valleys, provide awe-inspiring landscapes when viewed from the promontories."

The years between 1890 and 1930 were a wonderful time to be a Southern California day hiker. "The Great Hiking Era," historians would later call it. Residents of the L.A. basin could take the electric red cars to the base of the San Gabriel Mountains and then hike trails up Arroyo Seco or Mount Wilson. The San Bernardino Mountains, the San Jacinto Mountains and the Santa Barbara Backcountry also experienced the clomp-clomp of hob-nailed boots. Trail camps, fishing camps, and resorts were established in local mountains. Soon Southern California was crisscrossed with trails leading to these resorts and camps and to the best fishing spots and highest peaks.

But alas, by 1930, Southern California took to wheels. As Southlanders learned to drive, they forgot how to hike. During the Depression, the CCC boys built a number of car campgrounds and highways into the mountains. Soon drive-in campgrounds and paved roads replaced trail camps and trails.

In the 1950s Southern California, perhaps realizing how autobound they had become, began re-discovering the joys of the local mountains. In the last three decades, hundreds of miles of trail have been overhauled and many more miles of new trail constructed. Today, thanks to local mountaineers, conservation organizations, and state and federal rangers, Southern California has more miles of trail than most states. There's a trail waiting to take you wherever you want to go.

MAPS

About one half of the hikes in this guide take place in one of the four Southern California national forests: Los Padres, Angeles, San Bernardino, and Cleveland. Forest Service maps are available at ranger stations for a small fee. They're general maps, showing roads, rivers, trails, and little else. You'll learn where the trailheads are located and where entry is restricted during fire season. The Forest Service keeps their maps fairly up-to-date, so they're useful for checking out-of-date topographic maps.

Each road and trail in the national forest system has a route number. A route number might look like this: 2S21. Wooden signs, inscribed with the route number, are placed at some trailheads and at the intersection of trails to supplement other directional signs. The route numbers on your map usually correspond to the route numbers on the trail, but be careful because the Forest Service periodically changes the numbers.

Trails on Forest Service maps are drawn in red and black. Red trails are usually maintained and are in good shape. Black trails are infrequently maintained and their condition ranges from okay to faint.

Some hikers have a love affair with topographic maps. Those blue rivers, green woods and labyrinthine contour lines are...well, artistic. Topos show terrain in great detail and are the best way to prevent getting lost. If, for example, you know absolutely there's a road one mile to the west that runs north and south, it can be quite a comfort. Topos show trails, elevations, waterways, brush cover, and man's improvements. Along with a compass, they're indispensable for cross-country travel.

Topos come in two scales, the 15' quadrangle and the 7½' quadrangle. The 15' series scale is approximately 1 inch to 1 mile and the contour interval (the gap between contour lines) is 80 feet. 7½' series maps have a scale of 2½ inches to a mile with a contour interval of 40 feet. For the day hiker, the 7½' series is preferable. Most of the hikes in this guide utilize 7½' topos.

Topos can be bought at many sporting goods and mountaineering backpack stores. Or write to: U.S. Geological Survey, Federal Center, Denver, CO 80225.

BACKCOUNTRY COURTESY

• Leave your radio and tape player at home.

• Dogs, depending on the personality of the individual pooch, can be a disruption to hikers and to native wildlife. Be warned, many state and county parks don't allow dogs, either on or off a leash.

- No smoking on trails.

- Resist the urge to collect flowers, rocks, or animals. It disrupts nature's balance and lessens the wilderness experience for future hikers.

- Litter detracts from even the most beautiful backcountry setting. If you packed it in, you can pack it out.

- You have a moral obligation to help a hiker in need. Give whatever first aid or comfort you can and hurry for help.

- Don't cut switchbacks.

DAY HIKING TO A NEW LAND ETHIC

In the Santa Ana Mountains, 200-year-old oaks are uprooted to make room for a suburb. The toppled oaks, their roots drying in the sun, provide mute testimony against a culture that is still searching for a meaningful land ethic. Santa Ynez Canyon in the Santa Monica Mountains is suffering a similar fate. The canyon's sandstone walls have been blasted away and terraced for hundreds of luxury homes. What was to be the jewel of Topanga State Park is now a tract of asphalt and stucco.

Environmentally unsound construction is evident all over Southern California. The forces of *Cut & Fill* and *Grade & Pave* each year engulf more and more open space. There are still places that remain inviolate from the earthmover and the cement mixer, but these places grow fewer each year. As the late twentieth century version of the good life creeps into Southern California's backcountry, it may be time to ask ourselves, "What color is paradise?"

I think it's green.

A change in our land ethic begins with a change in perception and a change in perception begins with you. It's not a difficult change to make; in fact, day hiking can provoke it. The change I'm suggesting requires only that you open your eyes a little wider and see the natural world from a different perspective.

Perception is a funny thing. Did you ever notice the change in pitch of a train whistle as it goes away from you? A nineteenth century Austrian physicist, Christian Doppler figured that sound waves varied with the relative velocity of the source and the observer. He applied his Doppler effect to light waves, as well. He saw that as the position of observer and light source change, the colors of light will shift. Day hikers can notice a Doppler effect of their own. Looking up at Mount San Gorgonio from the L.A. basin, the hiker sees a snowy peak rising above the smog. Atop the mountain, the hiker looks down on a thick brown inversion layer blanketing the Southland. Quite a difference in views between the bottom of the basin and the top of the mountain!

To day hike is to alter your perceptions, to see things in a new light. You see where you are and what you left behind and you realize that the two are closer together than you had imagined. The distinction between "out there" and "right here" blurs and when that happens you've become a conservationist. As a conservationist, you'll perceive that our boulevards, our wilderness, and we ourselves are part of a fragile island. The future of the island depends on your perceptions.

RIM OF WILDERNESS

Seen through the eyes of the wilderness, how stupid and insane it all seems. The mad eagerness of money-seeking men, the sham pleasures of conventional society, the insistence upon the importance of being in earnest over trifles, pall on you when you think of them.

—GEORGE S. EVANS
"The Wilderness," *Overland Monthly*, 1904.

To the delight of conservationists, Congress in 1984 approved the California Wilderness Act, which set aside as Wilderness nearly 2 million acres of state land from Sheep Mountain to the High Sierra to Mount Shasta. The legislation gave Wilderness status to a quarter million acres of wild lands situated within a 100-mile radius of Los Angeles and known collectively as the Rim of Wilderness.

Southern California day hikers can be enthused over Rim of Wilderness legislation because no other region in America has such scenic variety so near an urban center. Others—surely nonhikers—scoff at the notion of wilderness in Southern California and gripe that local mountains don't have the highest-deepest-widest anything. Skeptics insist, for example, that one can't expect to find wilderness in the San Gabriel Mountains. Nonsense! These doubters are the same people who see the well-dammed, well-visited lower East Fork of the San Gabriel River and never walk upstream to the Narrows, never see the monumental gorge this river has cut, never see the river in its wild and tumultuous majesty. Wilderness is where you find it; those who can't find it haven't looked very hard. Southern California mountaineers make no apologies for the wilderness near home. They know the vegetation is thick enough, the mountains rugged enough, the weather treacherous enough to meet anyone's wilderness criteria.

The 1984 California Wilderness Act added acreage to already existing wilderness areas including the San Rafael, San Gorgonio, and San Jacinto. The bill created the 64,000 acre Dick Smith Wilderness in the Los Padres National Forest, the 44,000 acre Sheep Mountain Wilderness in the Angeles National Forest and the 40,000 acre San Mateo Canyon Wilderness in the Cleveland National Forest.

Preserving large tracts of land is important, of course, but we need to look at the creation of Wilderness Areas not just in terms of gross acres locked up, but in terms of *wildness* preserved. Its wildness for those of us who wish to temporarily escape the comforts wrought by Alexander Graham Bell, Henry Ford, and Sir Thomas Crapper; for those of us who want to see slopes without scars, rivers without silt, backcountry places so quiet you can hear the beating of your heart. For these people, our Rim of Wilderness offers room—lots of it—to think of our planet, our place, ourselves.

While much Southern California wildland has been preserved, some remains in danger. Areas such as Sespe Creek in the Los Padres National Forest and Fish Canyon in the Angeles National Forest are slowly being shaped by Forest Service policy and the political process.

Now may be the last chance to preserve examples of Southern California close to the primitive conditions in which the Indians and Spaniards discovered them. We must preserve these fragile ecosystems, not just for our recreation, but as a way of honoring and respecting the evolutionary process and the natural rhythm of life.

For now, and I hope forever, you'll need to make a little extra effort to get to and through these wildlands. The trails are less used and more tentative than others in this book. Trailheads are harder to find. Comforts and services are few and far between. That's what a wilderness is. Ice House Canyon and San Mateo Creek, Manzana Narrows and Mount San Jacinto are all the more precious when you sweat a bit to reach their primordial joys. Day hikes through the wilderness are long hikes that take a long day. You wouldn't want it any other way.

Chapter 2

LOS PADRES NATIONAL FOREST
(Santa Barbara Backcountry)

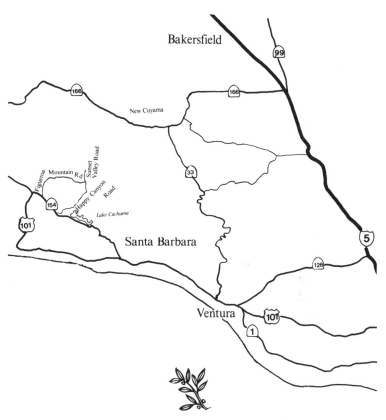

That anybody should undertake a jaunt of hundred and fifty miles or so on foot for the pleasure of walking was unthinkable by the conventional Western mind; but I was already familiar with the strong points of tripping afoot and the lure of that splendid chain of mountains back of Santa Barbara . . . To motor there seemed out of key with such a land, though thousands do it; and besides, motoring is expensive. No, for me "The footpath way" with kodak over my shoulder, a pocketful of dried figs, and freedom from care.

—CHARLES FRANCIS SAUNDERS
Under the Sky in California (1913)

Santa Barbara Backcountry

WILDERNESS-BOUND TRAVELERS have a difficult task in deciding what to call the rugged mountain terrain arranged in a wide semi-circle around Santa Barbara. The padres left behind many names, but none of them fit. Elsewhere in Southern California, wilderness areas were named for the dominant mountain range in the vicinity. But there isn't a dominant mountain range behind Santa Barbara. Instead, there are a number of smaller ones with names like Pine and Topatopa, Sierra Madre and Santa Ynez. So when we go, where do we say we're going? Hikers sometimes say they're "going up to the Los Padres," an imprecise term at best, because the Los Padres National Forest includes lands as far north as Big Sur. Geologists aren't much help either. They call the land the "Transverse Ranges Geomorphic Province." Until popular use gives map-makers new inspiration, the best name we have is the Santa Barbara Backcountry. Anyway, whatever this land of condors and great gorges, sandstone cliffs and wide blue sky is called, it's guaranteed to please.

Most of the Santa Barbara Backcountry is in the Los Padres National Forest. Together, Santa Barbara and Ventura Counties have more than a million acres of national forest land. The backcountry is under the jurisdiction of three forest districts. The Ojai District includes Sespe and Piru Creeks as well as Sespe Condor Sanctuary. The Santa Barbara District includes the Santa Ynez and San Rafael Mountain ranges. Mount Pinos District protects high conifer forest and includes the backcountry's highest peak, Mount Pinos (8831').

Archeological work in the backcountry has been extensive and has contributed much to our understanding of Chumash Indian culture. Several thousand years before the arrival of the Spanish, an estimated 10,000 to 18,000 Chumash lived in the coastal mountains from Malibu Canyon north to San Luis Obispo. Early Spanish explorers admired Chumash craftsmen, their fine houses and wood plank canoes. But the padres and soldiers of Spain who followed the explorers forced the Chumash to give up their ancient ways. Mission life broke the spirit of the Chumash and destroyed their culture. Living conditions were so desperate at the missions that a brief revolt took place at the Santa Barbara, Santa Ynez and La Purisima Missions in 1834. However, most Chumash were forcibly returned to the missions and suffered further enslavement.

Gold and grass brought Americans to the Santa Barbara Backcountry. From the time of the early padres, rumors of the lost Los Padres Mine lured prospectors. There was enough gold in the hills and streams to keep prospectors prospecting until well into the twentieth century, but no one ever found a big bonanza or the lost mine. Other

mining endeavors were more profitable. Near the turn of the century, U.S. Borax Company mined borax from Lockwood Valley. Lush grass on the San Joaquin side of the backcountry provided grazing for thousands of cattle. Cattle have grazed these hills since the era of the Spanish land grants and the hiker will often surprise a few cows.

Wild fire was a major problem in the late nineteenth and early twentieth centuries. Within a twenty year period, much of the backcountry burned, prompting the federal government to realize that the land needed protection. For fire prevention and watershed management purposes, large backcountry sections were set aside in the Pine Mountain and Zaca Lake Forest Reserve and the Santa Ynez Forest Reserve by decree of President Theodore Roosevelt and two years later the area became known as the Santa Barbara National Forest. In later years acreage was added and subtracted, with the backcountry finally coming under the jurisdiction of the Los Padres National Forest in 1938.

More than 1600 miles of trail range through the various districts of Los Padres National Forest. Nearly half of this trail system winds through the area we call the Santa Barbara Backcountry. Many of these trails have been used for centuries. Follow a trail to its end and you might be surprised at what you find. Remains of Indian camps may be found in the farthest reaches of the forest and in remote meadows are remnants of early homesteads. Backcountry trails take you over some rough terrain—slopes are unstable and steep. Geologists classify more than half the land as "extremely sensitive" or "highly sensitive" to slippage. But what is agony for the homeowner is a delight for the hiker. As you day hike through this folded and fractured land, you might conclude that the backcountry was made for hiking, not settling.

1

Santa Cruz Trail

Season: All year
Recommended map: Los Padres
National Forest
Topo: Little Pine Mountain,
San Marcos Pass

Upper Oso to Nineteen Oaks Camp
3½ miles RT; 600′ gain.
Upper Oso to Little Pine Saddle
10 miles RT; 3300′ gain.
Upper Oso to Happy Hollow Camp
13 miles RT; 3300′ gain.

Santa Cruz Trail presents a lengthy climb, but rewards the hiker with a superb view of the Channel Islands and the wide Pacific. Atop Little Pine Mountain is an ecological island of various conifers that one might expect to find only in the High Sierra. Happy Hollow Camp, tucked between Little Pine Mountain and a sister peak, shaded by tall ponderosa pine, is appropriately named.

In January you may find snow at the summit, but on most days the temperature should be comfortable. Summer hikes up the exposed slope of the mountain can be hot. Start hiking in the cool of the morning when the trail is in shadow and enjoy your lunch at the top beneath the boughs of a big cone spruce. An ocean breeze usually keeps the mountaintop cool.

Pack lots of water; the only dependable water source on this day hike is at the trailhead.

Directions to trailhead: From Highway 101 in Santa Barbara, take State Highway 154 over San Marcos Pass. Turn right onto Paradise Road and follow it east for five miles along the Santa Ynez River. After passing Los Prietos Boys Camp, and crossing the river, turn left on Oso Road and follow it a mile to Upper Oso Campground. Hiker parking is provided.

The Hike: The route begins at a locked gate beyond the campground and for the first mile follows Camuesa Fire Road (5N15), which was recently reopened by the Forest Service to motorcycle traffic. Pausing for an instant to consider the logic of this, continue up the road, staying just to the east of Oso Creek, where there are several fine swimming holes. When the road takes a sharp hairpin turn, leave the two-wheeled locusts behind and continue straight on Santa Cruz Trail.

For the next mile the trail is relatively flat, although it drops in and out of washes on the east side of Oso Creek. Soon the hiker sees a spur trail

on the right that leads 1/10 of a mile to Nineteen Oaks Camp. Oaks shade this camp, but not 19 of them. A few tables suggest a picnic. Geologically minded hikers will note the distinctive outcroppings of Franciscan strata and scars in the nearby hills where mercury, also known as cinnabar or quicksilver, was mined.

Option: To Little Pine Saddle. The trail heads north, crosses Oso Creek and begins switchbacking through grassy meadows. Dipping in and out of oak- and poison oak-smothered canyons, you ascend a hill to a saddle between the ridge you're traveling and Little Pine Mountain.

The trail soon switchbacks north, then west across the south face of Little Pine Mountain. The trail is steep and strenuous, but well constructed; it's chiseled into rock in places and stabilized by metal stakes and railroad ties. (No place for acrophobics!) In approximately 2½ miles you'll cross two large meadows, which in spring are smothered with purple lupine, poppies, and Indian paintbrush. They almost look landscaped. For most of the year, though, these meadows (called "Mellow Meadows" by laid-back Santa Barbarans) are tall dry grass—the habitat of deer and even an occasional mountain lion.

The trail climbs around the heads of half a dozen canyons before reaching Alexander Saddle. To the left a bulldozed road goes to Alexander Peak (4107'). To your right a trail leads to Happy Hollow Camp; you may follow this trail or continue on the Santa Cruz Trail and in a little less than a mile you'll pass a second connector trail leading to Happy Hollow Camp.

Option: Happy Hollow Camp from Little Pine Saddle. Follow the right-hand trail or make your own route over the ridgeline to camp. Weatherworn pines on the ridgeline offer shade and you'll catch fabulous views of the Channel Islands, Santa Ynez Valley, and Lake Cachuma.

Ranger Valentine on Santa Cruz Trail, 1926

Large sugar pines and a few live oaks cling to the north face of Little Pine peak. Farther along the trail you will be among Western yellow pine, spruce, and Douglas fir.

Happy Hollow, nestled among ponderosa pine, fir, and oak, has a few tables and stoves. Water is available at Little Pine Spring (see side trail). In the 1930s this camp was a recreation site for Civilian Conservation Corps workmen, who constructed Buckhorn Road. A handsome field station, resembling a chalet, stood here until razed in the mid-1970s. The name Happy Hollow is apt; the camp is indeed in a hollow, and hikers are no doubt happy after a 3300′ elevation gain in six miles. What hikers may not be so happy about in this north face camp is the lack of sunlight. The hollow traps the cold. Snow is often found here weeks after a storm, long after it has melted elsewhere.

From Happy Hollow, you may return to the Santa Cruz Trail the way you came or take that second connector trail mentioned above. This short steep trail leaves the hollow from West Big Pine Mountain Road on the northwestern edge of the campground. Follow the road 50 yards to the signed junction for the trail leading to Little Pine Spring. This trail ascends steeply through pines then descends one mile, rejoining the Santa Cruz Trail near the turnoff to Little Pine Spring.

Side trail: Santa Cruz Trail to Little Pine Spring. One half mile long. Little Pine Spring Trail, steep and primitive, leads steeply down canyon to the spring. Here you'll find a seldom used trail camp with a stove and table.

Season: All year
Topo: Peak Mountain,
Hurricane Deck
Recommended map: Los
Padres National Forest

 2

McPherson Peak Loop Trail

Aliso Park to Hog Pen Spring
5 miles RT; 900' gain.
Aliso Park to McPherson Peak
10 mile loop; 2900' gain.

The San Rafael Wilderness, heart of Santa Barbara backcountry, inspired the late Dick Smith, and several naturalists before him, to roam, explore and behold. This is condor country, where these survivors of the Pleistocene Age were given their last sanctuary.

Smith spent fifteen years roaming the backcountry. He crouched behind improvised blinds for days at a time to observe the great dark birds with 10-foot wingspans. Through his book, *CONDOR JOURNAL* (Capra Press), he alerted the public to the plight of this flying relic from the Stone Age. He saw the condor as a miner's canary, carried to test the air. (If the canary dies, the miner is in danger.) Smith regarded the condor as Southern California's environmental canary.

This day hike takes you into Smith's favorite backcountry, up to the potreros along the crest of the Sierra Madres where ravens swoop in the wind like dolphins of the sky over meadows sometimes blanketed by carpets of tidy tips and other spectacular displays of wildflowers. Here you will see the russet-colored Mountain Quail (larger and a stronger flyer than its lowland cousin), Cooper hawks and golden eagles. A breeze will blow glorious waves on slopes of lavendar Brome Grass, colonies of Owl's Clover and occasionally the nodding dark blooms of the Chocolate Lily. From McPherson Peak you will have a commanding view of the San Rafael Wilderness area to the south and the colorful badlands to the north.

Directions to the trailhead: From Highway 166, 2½ miles northwest of New Cuyama, turn south on Aliso Canyon Road. Bear right at the first fork and continue 4½ miles to the Aliso Campgrounds. Driving beyond this point is not recommended, particularly in the rainy season.

The Hike: Follow the jeep road which takes you from the shady Aliso Valley up through chaparral. The trail climbs for 2¼ miles to Hog Pen Spring Campground. Hog Pen was named by the McPhersons who once raised pigs at this spring. Although there is a faucet, water is often not available in the dry season.

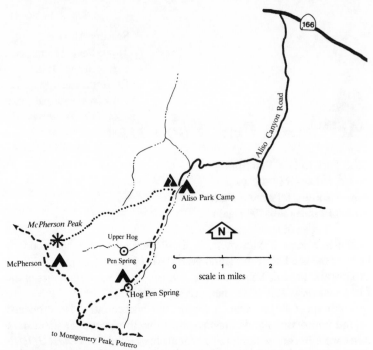

Option: To McPherson Peak. Now the real climbing begins as you follow many switchbacks on the climb to Sierra Madre Road in 2 miles. Much of the way follows along the edge of a brushy canyon where frequently are heard the rustlings and crashings of animals below. Perhaps they were caused by wild or feral pigs, known to roam the San Rafael Wilderness.

Turn west (right) on Sierra Madre Road and continue 2 miles to the McPherson Peak lookout. En route you are given magnificent views down into the Sisquoc River and the cliffs where condors have nested and roosted over the centuries. Watch for Columbia black-tail deer in the meadows, and the prints or scat of coyote, mountain lion, black bear or bobcat.

At McPherson Peak (5,749′) you have a commanding lookout view in all directions. Rest and watch the skies. Eat lunch and scrutinize the Sisquoc River canyon, the marvelous San Rafaels and Hurricane Deck. This was high country for the Chumash, where they hunted, worshipped and even practiced astronomy.

Instead of retracing your steps back down to Aliso Camp, search the slope just east below the lookout for the old McPherson Trail (27W02). It takes you down through chaparral along a rib of the peak. After a 2-mile descent you reach an unmarked junction with an overgrown trail. Bear right and follow it gently downhill 2 miles back to Aliso Camp. You may need to do a little bushwhacking, but the transforming views make it all worthwhile.

3

Manzana Creek Trail

Season: All year, except in
times of high water
Recommended map: Los
Padres National Forest
Topo: Bald Mountain,
Figueroa Mountain,
San Rafael Mountain

NIRA to Lost Valley Camp
   2 miles RT; 100' gain
NIRA to Fish Creek Camp
   6 miles RT; 400' gain
NIRA to Manzana Camp
   12 miles RT; 1100' gain
NIRA to Manzana Narrows
   14 miles RT; 1200' gain

The major entry point for the San Rafael Wilderness, NIRA is an acronym for the National Industrial Recovery Act, a federal program launched during the Depression. NIRA is an auto camp and popular day-use area.

San Rafael Wilderness was the first Wilderness Area in America set aside under the federal Wilderness Act of 1964. "San Rafael is rocky, rugged, wooded and lonely," remarked President Lyndon Johnson when he signed the San Rafael Wilderness bill on March 21, 1968. "I believe it will enrich the spirit of America."

Manzana Creek Trail passes tall thin alders and, in season, wildflowers. Four creekside camps beckon the picknicker. In addition to a few stocked trout that survive the legions of fishermen, you'll find frogs, crayfish, and turtles in the Manzana. Rewarding the hiker after numerous creek crossings is Manzana Narrows, a narrow part of the canyon where there are some fine pools for fishing and cooling off.

Directions to trailhead: From Santa Barbara, take Highway 154 past Cachuma Lake to Armour Ranch Road, making a right turn and continuing 2½ miles to Happy Canyon Road, then making another right and continuing 18 miles (Happy Canyon becomes Sunset Valley Road after passing an intersection with Figueroa Mt. Rd.) to NIRA Camp. Parking space for hikers is provided at the south end of the campground.

The Hike: Leaving NIRA Camp, the trail immediately crosses Manzana Creek and begins a gentle ascent along the north bank of the creek. The route switchbacks up a low ridge cloaked with digger pine and soon arrives at Lost Valley Camp, a small site tucked amongst oak and pine at the mouth of Lost Valley Canyon. This canyon reaches from Manzana

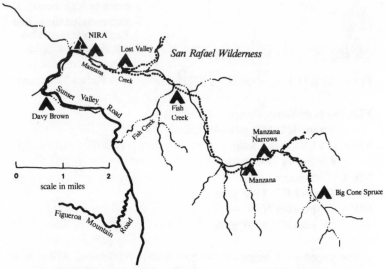

Creek up to Hurricane Deck, heart of the San Rafael Wilderness. Lost Valley Trail departs from camp and climbs up to the magnificent deck.

Option: To Fish Creek Camp. Manzana Creek Trail meanders along the north bank of the creek for the next two miles. The trail rises above the canyon, which each year shows fewer ill effects from the devastating Wellman Fire of two decades ago.

Look to your right across the creek and you'll soon see Fish Creek Camp on the far side of the Manzana flood plain, where Fish Creek Canyon meets Manzana Creek. Fishermen like the camp because the creeks here usually support a large trout population. The somewhat overused camp is set in an exposed area.

Option: To Manzana Camp. Past Fish Creek the trail at first stays on the north wall of the canyon, passing through low chaparral and dipping in and out of washes. Manzana Canyon begins to narrow and the trail heads down toward the creek, which is lined by tall thin alders. The trail crosses the Manzana, and a half mile later, crosses again. The canyon narrows even more and, after a few more creek crossings, reaches Manzana Camp. Located beneath picturesque live oak, the camp offers a dependable water supply, fishing, and swimming pools. The manzanita, which gave its name to half the geographical features around here, abounds.

Option: To Manzana Narrows. Beyond the camp, the trail switchbacks up onto the east wall of the canyon, then soon descends to Manzana Narrows Camp. Wedged in the narrow canyon, the oak- and willow-shaded camp offers pools for fishing and cooling off.

Return the same way.

36

4

Beartrap Trail

Season: All year
Recommended map: Los
    Padres National Forest
Topo: Reyes Peak
See map p. 41

Reyes Creek Trail to Upper Reyes Trail Camp
    6 miles RT; 800′ elevation gain
Reyes Creek Camp to Beartrap #1 Trail Camp
    10 miles RT; 1100′ elevation gain

Reyes and Beartrap Creeks are two of the many pretty watercourses that spill from the northern slopes of Pine Mountain in Los Padres National Forest. The creeks run full speed in the spring and even during a dry year, still have some water.

Upper Reyes is a cool, canyon trail camp named for a local pioneer family. Farther up the trail is Beartrap Camp, where the Reyes and other settlers established hunting camps. The fierce grizzly was lord and sovereign over these mountains until man eliminated him from the area with guns and traps.

Near the trailhead is Camp Scheideck Lodge, established in the 1890s as a hunting lodge. Now the establishment is a funky country bar, where hikers may gather post-hike to quench their thirst.

Directions to trailhead: From Interstate 5 just north of Gorman, take the Frazier Park exit and follow Frazier Mountain Road west for seven miles to Lockwood Valley Road. Turn left and proceed 24 miles to the signed turnoff for Reyes Creek Campground, Los Padres National Forest. A second sign advertising Camp Scheideck Lodge is also at this junction. Turn left and follow the paved road as it crosses the Cuyama River. Caution: crossing can be difficult during times of high water. Continue two miles to Reyes Creek Campground.

Between campsites 17 and 18, you will find a dirt road leading up a small hill. Walk up this road 150 yards to the signed trailhead.

The Hike: From the Reyes Creek trailhead, follow the Beartrap Trail (23W02) up canyon. It's a moderate climb, alternating between elfin forest and pine forest.

The trail switchbacks up a saddle. Behind you, to the northwest is a fine view of the tortured terrain of the Cuyama Badlands. In front of you, to the southeast is the much more inviting forested canyon cut by Reyes Creek. From the saddle, a half mile descent brings you to Upper Reyes Trail Camp. It's a pleasant streamside camp, a good place to cool your heels or to take a lunch stop.

Option: To Beartrap Trail Camp #1. Energetic hikers will assault the switchbacks above Upper Reyes Trail Camp and climb to the ridge separating Reyes Creek from Beartrap Creek. The trail then descends to an oak and pine-shaded camp on Beartrap Creek.

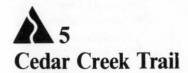 **5**

Cedar Creek Trail

Season: All year
Recommended map: Los
    Padres National Forest
Topo: Lockwood Valley,
    San Guillermo

Thorn Meadows to Cedar Camp
    5 miles RT; 300′ gain.
Thorn Meadows to Fishbowls
    9 miles RT; 1000′ gain.
Return via Piru Creek
    12 miles RT

The Fishbowls are a deep series of potholes, dredged out of the sedimentary rock creekbed by the erosive power of rushing water. You'll enjoy basking on nearby flat rocks and dreaming your life away. When you awake from your dreams, a plunge into the cold water of the Fishbowls will quickly clear your head. As brook trout nibble at your toes and water showers down upon you from above, you'll feel like you're swimming in an aquarium.

This hike is one of the nicest in the Mount Pinos area of the Los Padres. The trail climbs through an incense cedar and pine forest to the headwaters of Piru Creek. The creek springs from the slopes of Pine Mountain, which is not the same as Mount Pinos, and bubbles through a maze of mountains. Piru Creek pools were the site of some gold mining at the turn of the century. Even today, you can spot weekend prospectors looking for a flash in the pan.

Directions to trailhead: From Interstate Highway 5 just north of Gorman, take the Frazier Park exit and follow Frazier Mountain Road west to the Lake of the Woods "Y" intersection. Bear left here and continue 11 miles on the Lockwood-Ozena Road. Turn left on signed Grade Valley Road, a dirt road suitable for all but very low slung passenger cars. Proceed for 7½ miles, then turn right on signed Thorn Meadows Road (7N03), and proceed ½-mile to the beginning of the signed Cedar Creek Trail on the right.

The Hike: From the signed Thorn Meadows trailhead hike up the narrow, dirt road that is closed to vehicles. The timber appears to be second generation and the area seems to have been logged. After 2 miles of pleasant hiking through oak woodland and scattered pines, the road becomes a trail near a fork in Piru Creek. In another ½ mile you arrive at peaceful Cedar Camp on a south fork of the creek in a tiny basin ringed by incense cedar and big cone spruce. The camp is a wonderful place for a picnic and provides opportunity to soak up some shade for the hot climb ahead.

Fishbowls

When you're sufficiently cooled, return to the trail, which continues through the forest, climbs out onto the backbone of a ridge, and in a long mile reaches a sometimes-signed junction. To the left, the trail leads to Pine Mountain Lodge. Bear right (north) to the Fishbowls on Trail 22W05. It swoops up and down two more ridges and descends steeply to Fishbowls Trail Camp, 1½ miles from the trail junction. This camp occupies a quiet shady canyon cut by the headwaters of Piru Creek. From the camp, the Fishbowls are a scant ¼ mile upstream.

Return the same way or take the long, lazy loop along Piru Creek back to the trailhead.

Option: Return Via Piru Creek. This return route adds 3 miles to your trek, but it's easy hiking. From Fishbowls Camp, Trail 21W05 winds lazily along Piru Creek. Piru flows sometimes gently, sometimes frothily and collects the contributions of lesser and more transitory creeks. Fishing is fair in some of the deep quiet pools of Piru. After 6 miles and many winding turns, you reach Grade Valley Road, where you saw the cows on the drive to the trailhead. Turn right and follow it ½ mile to the Thorn Meadows Road. Another ½ mile along this road brings you back to your car and the trailhead.

▲ 6
Piedra Blanca Trail

Lion Campground to Piedra Blanca
    3 miles RT; 200′ gain.
Lion Campground to Twin Forks Camp
    6 miles RT; 600′ gain.
Lion Campground to Pine Mountain Lodge Camp
    11 miles RT; 3000′ gain.

Sparkling Piedra Blanca (White Rock) is the sort of place where Castaneda's Don Juan might lurk. The sandstone formation extends for miles between the upper reaches of the Sespe and the mountains to the north. Most of the sandstone in the Sespe area, called the Sespe Formation, is distinguished by its red color. It's a land-laid formation, deposited in layers of mud and sand on land. Unlike the red rock that guards the mouth of Sespe Creek, Piedra Blanca's thick sequences of sedimentary rock are of marine origin. These marine deposits are particularly notable in the Santa Barbara backcountry and are found in the Santa Ynez, Topatopa, Piru, and Pine Mountain Ranges. Perhaps the most spectacular formations are found at Piedra Blanca.

Piedra Blanca

This day hike takes you over chaparral-cloaked hillsides and visits mighty Piedra Blanca. The trail then follows Piedra Blanca Creek and climbs for some distance to Pine Mountain Lodge Camp, the site of a hunting and fishing lodge that once stood on the slopes of Pine Mountain.

Directions to trailhead: From Ojai, take Highway 33 north 14 miles. Turn right on Rose Valley Road (7N03) and continue 6 miles to Lion Campground. Park in the special day-use lot near the campground. The sometimes-signed trail begins across the creek.

The Hike: Cross the creek and pick up the trail (22W03) on the other side. The trail cuts through chaparral and wastes no time heading for Piedra Blanca. These jumbo rocks are in your sight most of the way. Like staring at clouds, the longer you gaze at the Piedra Blanca formations, the more they assume the shape of your imagination: dragons with missing teeth, white sandcastles with spires and turrets, the Washington Monument...

Pine Mountain Lodge, 1940

Option: To Twin Forks. From the rocks, the trail descends sharply to an unnamed tributary of Piedra Blanca Creek, finds the creek itself, and follows it up-canyon. The trail dips in and out of the narrow oak woodland lining the creek. You pass an attractive streamside trail camp named for the dominant sandstone, Piedra Blanca, and continue upcreek. Soon you come to Twin Forks Trail Camp, named for its location near the North and Middle Forks of Piedra Blanca Creek. Either Piedra Blanca or Twin Forks make nice picnicking spots.

If you want to spend more time staring at the great white rocks, return to Piedra Blanca and the trailhead the way you came. Otherwise, continue up the creek.

Option: To Pine Mountain Lodge. From Twin Forks, the trail twists along with the North Fork of Piedra Blanca Creek. It ascends steeply for about 2 miles, then leaves the creek and climbs chaparral-and pine-covered slopes. After cresting a ridge, the trail descends another mile to Pine Mountain Lodge Trail Camp, about 6,000 foot elevation. Sometimes snow falls here in winter. It's cool and green, a good place to take off your shoes and sit awhile.

7

Mount Pinos Trail

Mt. Abel to Sheep Camp
5 miles RT; 500' gain
Mt. Abel to Mt. Pinos
12 miles RT; 900' gain

This 6 mile peak-to-peak trail offers the peak bagger four opportunities to climb an 8,000-foot peak. Between Mount Abel and Mount Pinos there are easy cross-country climbs to Grouse Mountain and Sawmill Mountain. This trail passes through dense pine and fir hollows, visits Sheep Camp, and ascends Mount Pinos, a blustery peak that offers views of the San Joaquin Valley, the Mojave Desert and the sprawling Los Padres high country. Atop Mount Pinos is a condor observation site.

Directions to trailhead: Exit Interstate 5 at the Frazier Park turnoff and drive west on Frazier Mountain Park Road, then Cuddy Valley Road. About five miles past the hamlet of Lake of the Woods, you'll reach a junction. To reach the Mt. Pinos Trailhead, bear left and continue nine miles to the Chula Vista Picnic Area. One more mile on a dirt road (closed in winter) takes you to the Condor Observation Site near the top of Mt. Pinos and the beginning (or end) of the Mt. Pinos Trail.

To reach the Mt. Abel Trailhead, bear right at the above-mentioned junction and proceed eight miles on Mil Portrero Road to Cerro Noreste Road. Turn left and go seven miles to the signed trailhead ½-mile below the summit of Mt. Abel. Parking is not plentiful right at the trailhead, so park in a safe manner along the road.

The Hike: Leaving the trailhead behind, you descend a draw into a forested hollow, ½-mile from the start. Bear left at the signed junction here. The trail begins ascending the side of Grouse Mountain, named no doubt for the resident blue grouse population. You might flush a number of these dark, ground-dwelling birds out of the bush.

Soon the trail levels off and you'll come to a saddle on the east slope of the mountains. If you want to peak bag Grouse Mountain, you'll have to

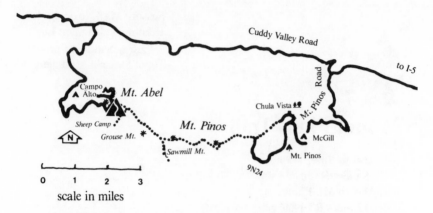

go cross-country to your right. The summit is designated by a pile of rocks. Sometimes there's a summit register for you to sign. A word about peak bagging: resist the urge to blaze trees, pile rocks, or otherwise disturb the landscape. Let the next person find his way, like you did.

Back on the main trail, continue following the saddle to a junction with North Fork Trail.

Sidetrip to Sheep Camp ½ mile. Bear right on the North Fork Trail and descend through waving wild iris, their petals ripple in the breeze like a miniature halftime show. Sheep Camp, ½ mile from the junction, was used as a base camp by San Joaquin Valley ranchers in the nineteenth century. Today Sheep Camp is one of the highest trail camps in the Los Padres. For the day hiker, it makes a pleasant picnic ground. A seasonal spring (purify before drinking) is at the camp. Cross-country skiers visit here in winter; it's the terminus of the Mount Pinos Skiway, which begins at the Chula Vista Parking Lot, 5½ miles away.

Return to the main trail, which soon passes close to the summit of Sawmill Mountain. Again, it's an easy cross-country climb to bag the peak. The summit, marked by a pile of rocks, is on the north side.

Back on the main trail, you'll descend the pine-covered slopes of Sawmill Mountain, then ascend an open slope via switchbacks up balding Mount Pinos. Every height you've ascended thus far has seemed the ultimate one, but they have been mere stepping stones to The Ultimate—Mount Pinos, the highest peak in the Los Padres. As you stand among the gnarled Ponderosa pine atop the summit, you'll have the whole Los Padres at your feet.

Pick up your car, or return the same way.

Season: All year
Topo: Matilija, Wheeler Springs
Recommended map: Los
Padres National Forest

▲▲8
Matilija Trail

Matilija Cyn. Rd. to Matilija Camp
  2 miles RT; 200′ gain
Matilija Cyn. Rd. to Middle Matilija Camp
  7 miles RT; 900′ gain
Matilija Cyn. Rd. to Forest Road 6N01
  15 miles RT; 3000′ gain

The meaning of "Matilija" is unknown, but it may have been the Chumash word to describe the showy Matilija poppy, prized by the Indians for its medicinal qualities. The poppy's botanical name, *Romneya coulteri,* honors two Irish scientists and longtime friends, astronomer Romney Robinson and botanist Thomas Coulter. Coulter first collected this outstanding flower in 1831. During the early years of this century, Ojai entrepreneurs dug up Matilija poppies by the thousands and sold them in Los Angeles.

The Matilija poppy is found along many an Ojai backcountry trail. It blooms from May to July, stands 3-7 feet tall, and is bushy at its base. The delicate flowers have six white crinkled petals and a golden center. Matilija poppies have a strong, sweet fragrance and the hiker who nears a stand may detect their presence with his nose before sighting them.

The Matilija area has the dubious distinction of being the flash point for some of the largest fires in Southern California history. In June of 1917 the Matilija-Wheeler Springs Fire burned for 5 days and nights and blackened more than 30,000 acres. The 1932 Matilija Fire burned nearly a quarter million acres. One of the fire lines was Highway 33, then under construction.

The 1985 Wheeler Fire scorched much of the Ojai backcountry, including the steep terrain watered by the many forks of the Matilija Creek. On the high chaparral-covered ridges, a holocaust took place. The canyon bottoms fared a little better in the firestorm, and are making a remarkable recovery.

Matilija Trail, at its lower end, offers an ideal family outing alongside the Upper North Fork of Matilija Creek. More experienced hikers will enjoy pushing on to the canyon's upper reaches for fine ocean and mountain views. The fire burned most of the facilities at the creekside camps, so they aren't the attractive destinations they were in previous years; however, many nice pools, cascades, and flat sunny rocks offer pleasant picnic spots. Except for times of very high water, creek crossings can be safely accomplished.

Directions to trailhead: Continue on Highway 33 four miles past Ojai, and past the leftward turnoff to Matilija Hot Springs. (Keep this hot springs resort and Wheeler Hot Springs Resort a few miles up the highway in mind for a post-hike soak.) A short mile past Matilija Hot springs, turn left on Matilija Canyon Road (Forest Service Road 5N13) and proceed 5 miles to a locked gate across the road. A parking area is located just before the gate. Note that Matilija Trail could suggest a one-way hike; you could utilize a car shuttle or have a friend drop you off at the upper trailhead located a few miles beyond Cherry Creek Camp (elevation 4,500 feet). To reach the upper trailhead, proceed 27 miles north of Ojai on Highway 33 and turn left on unimproved Cherry Creek Road (6NO1). The advantage of this one-way route is an all-downhill hike; the disadvantage is that the slopes traversed by the upper part of the trail were severely burned in the 1985 Wheeler Fire.

The Hike: Pass the locked gate and hike along the dirt road through Matilija Canyon Ranch and a private wildlife reserve. (Please stay on the road and respect private property.) After crossing two branches of Matilija Creek, the road turns left, but you'll follow the unmarked spur that turns right and follows the creek. Within 50 yards, cross the creek twice more and begin hiking along the creek bank. A mile of nearly level walking brings you to Matilija Camp.

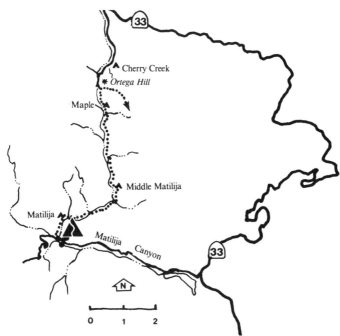

Matilija Camp, with its stoves, is a nice picnic spot. The geologically-inclined will note how stream erosion in this area has exposed areas of severe folding and faulting; past actions of the Santa Ynez Fault are very much in evidence.

Option: To Middle Camp. Past the camp, the trail fords several small tributary creeks that feed the Upper North Fork and crosses a wide meadowland. You'll observe abandoned Forest Service Trail 23W20, which leads to the jeep road that runs from Cherry Creek Camp to Highway 33, just north of Wheeler Gorge. The trail switchbacks above the creek for a while, then resumes again on the canyon bottom. Some level travel and a few more crossings bring you to a live oak-shaded Middle Matilija Camp. You can lunch here and call it a day, or push on up creek.

Option: To Forest Road 6N01. Beyond the camp, the trail fords and re-fords the creek a half dozen more times. The canyon floor is forested with big cone spruce, bay laurel and maple. You'll rise out of the canyon, then descend into the narrowing canyon and arrive at abandoned, but still serviceable Upper Matilija Camp.

From this camp, the trail continues upcreek another mile, then rises steeply north out of the canyon. Switchbacks offer the hiker fine views of Old Man Mountain, the Santa Ynez range and the Pacific. The upper canyon slopes were severely burned in 1985. Maples at Maple Camp were incinerated. Ghostly skeletons of chokecherry, manzanita and scrub oak line the trail, which after the fire suffered erosion and slide damage. A final steep climb brings you to the terminus of the trail at Forest Service Road 6N01 near Ortega Hill.

Tunnel Trail, La Cumbre Peak

Chapter 3

SANTA YNEZ MOUNTAINS

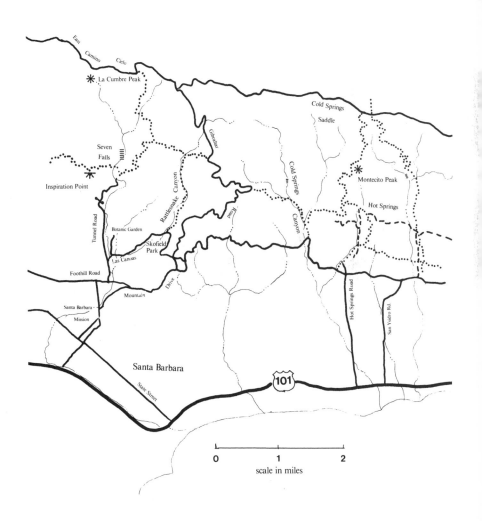

East Camino Cielo

La Cumbre Peak

Cold Springs
Saddle

Seven
Falls

Gibraltar

Inspiration Point

Rattlesnake Canyon

Cold Springs

Montecito Peak

Tunnel Road

Botanic Garden

Road

Cold Springs Canyon

Hot Springs

Skofield
Park

Las Canoas

Foothill Road

Drive

Santa Barbara
Mission

Mountain

Hot Springs Road

San Ysidro Rd.

Santa Barbara

State Street

101

```
0              1              2
        scale in miles
```

Santa Ynez Mountains

A FEW MILLION years ago, the Santa Ynez Mountains rose slowly from the sea. The mountains are not secretive about their origin and display their oceanic heritage in a number of ways. Tilted blocks of sedimentary rock, which have aggregated tens of thousands of feet in thickness, provide the first clue to the mountains' former undersea life. Fossils of sea animals give further testimony that the mountains were once many leagues under the sea. Even the vegetation betrays the mountains' origin. The mineral-poor sandstone slopes formed in the ocean deep can support little more than dense brush, so it's the chaparral community—buckthorn, mountain lilac and scrub oak—that predominates.

The Santa Ynez Mountains are part of a series of east/west trending ranges known as the Transverse Ranges, which encircle Southern California from San Diego to Point Conception. The backbone of the Transverse Range is the San Bernardino and San Gabriel Mountains, while the Santa Ynez Mountains form the uppermost or most westerly part of the Transverse Spine. The Santa Ynez extend almost fifty miles from Matilija Canyon on the east to Gaviota Canyon on the west. Compared to other ranges in the Transverse system, the Santa Ynez are quite small, ranging from 2,000 to 4,000 feet.

At first glance, the range seems smothered with a formless gray mass of tortured vegetation. On closer inspection, the Santa Ynez reveals more charm. Sycamores and bays line the canyons and a host of seasonal creeks wash the hillsides. In spring the chaparral blooms and adds frosty whites and blues to the gray-green plants. The backcountry looks particularly inviting after the first winter rains. On upper peaks, rain sometimes turns to snow.

Santa Ynez Mountain trails mainly follow the canyons above Santa Barbara and Montecito. The network of trails generally follows streams to the top of the range. They start in lush canyon bottoms, zig-zag up the hot, dry canyon walls, and follow rock ledges to the crest. Many of the trails intersect *El Camino Cielo* (the sky road), which follows the mountain crest. From the top, enjoy sweeping views of the Pacific, Channel Islands and coastal plain. Northward, row after row of shar mountains spread toward the horizon. These mountains were born beneath the sea and may some day return to their birthplace. In the meantime, say for the next million years or so, the mountains will continue to provide splendid hiking.

Packing in supplies to Ranger Station on Manzana Creek, 1905

9
Tunnel Trail

Tunnel Road to Seven Falls
   3 miles RT; 400′ gain
Tunnel Road via Jesusita Trail
to Inspiration Point
   5 miles RT; 800′ gain
Tunnel Road to East
Camino Cielo
   8 miles RT; 2350′ gain

*A pleasant party spent yesterday up Mission Canyon, visiting the
noted Seven Falls and afterwards eating a tempting picnic dinner
in a romantic spot on the creek's bank. To reach these falls
requires some active climbing, able bodied sliding and skillful
swinging . . .*

—SANTA BARBARA DAILY PRESS, 1887

Seven Falls has been a popular destination of Santa Barbarans since
before the turn of the century. The seven distinct little falls found in the
bed of Mission Creek are still welcoming hikers. While the falls are all
but dry in summer, water tumbles gracefully over the rocks in winter. In
spring, wildflowers bloom between the canyon walls, forming a perfect
picture.

Tunnel Trail and road were used by workers to gain access to a
difficult city waterworks project launched by the city of Santa Barbara.
Workmen burrowed a tunnel through the Santa Ynez Mountains to
connect the watershed on the backside of the mountains to the growing
little city. Braving floods, cave-ins and dangerous hydrogen gas, a crew
labored eight years and finished the project in 1912.

This hike passes near the tunnel and by the remains of the tunnel
keeper's house. It joins the Jesusita Trail for an exploration of the Seven
Falls along Mission Creek and a trip up to Inspiration Point. Continuing

on the Tunnel Trail rewards the hiker with inspiring views from "the sky road," East Camino Cielo.

Directions to trailhead: From the Santa Barbara Mission, drive up Mission Canyon Road, turning right for a block on Foothill Boulevard, then immediately turning left back onto Mission Canyon Road. At a distinct V-intersection, veer left onto Tunnel Road and drive to its end. Park along the road.

The Hike: From the end of Tunnel Road, hike past a locked gate onto a paved road, which soon turns to dirt as you leave the power lines behind and get increasingly grander views of Santa Barbara. Our route makes a sharp left and crosses a bridge over the West Fork of Mission Creek. Below the bridge little Fern Falls cascades into a handsome pool. This is where the tunnel from Gibraltar Dam exits the Santa Ynez Mountains to supply Santa Barbara with its water supply.

Beyond the bridge, you'll hike a short distance under some handsome oaks to a junction marked by a California Riding and Hiking Trail sign. To visit the falls, descend briefly but steeply on Jesusita Trail to Mission Creek.

At the canyon bottom, hike up creek into the steep gorge that's been cut from solid sandstone. Geologically minded hikers will recognize fossilized layers of oyster beds from the Oligocene Epoch. For thousands of winters, rain water has rushed from the shoulder of La Cumbre Peak and cut away at the sandstone layers, forming seven distinct falls and several deep pools. Be careful; the higher falls are difficult to climb.

Option: To Inspiration Point. The trail switchbacks steeply up the chaparral-cloaked canyon wall to a power line road located atop a knoll. Although the point is not all that inspiring, the view from the cluster of sandstone rocks is worth the climb. The coast, quite some distance north and south, Catalina, the Channel Islands, Santa Barbara and the Goleta Valley makes an inspiring picture.

Option: Tunnel Trail to East Camino Cielo. From the signed junction with Jesusita Trail, we begin our ascent toward La Cumbre Peak. In ½ mile the trail crosses the Southern California Edison Catway and rises above the power lines. The trail switchbacks up a ridge for a mile, traverses a knoll and in about ¼ mile meets the signed junction with the Rattlesnake Trail, which leads off to Gibraltar Road and Rattlesnake Canyon. At this junction continue on the Tunnel Trail, bearing left (north). The sign reads 2 miles to Camino Cielo. You follow the contours of a ridge for 1½ miles. The last ½ mile of trail levels out as it meanders through a small canyon to its intersection with paved Camino Cielo in the saddle near Angostura Pass. If you want to bag La Cumbre Peak (3985'), it's a ¾ mile hike west along the road.

Return the same way.

Mr. and Mrs. Lyman Pope at Tin Can Shack, 1916

10
Rattlesnake Canyon Trail

Skofield Park to Tin Can Meadow
4½ miles RT; 1000' gain
Skofield Park to Gibraltar Rd.
6 miles RT; 1500' gain

Rattlesnake Canyon Trail is serpentine, but otherwise far more inviting than its name suggests. Some say the name may have been prompted by the image of the winding trail etched on the canyon walls.

The joys of Rattlesnake Canyon were first officially promoted by none other than the Santa Barbara Chamber of Commerce. Many a turn-of-the-century visitor to Santa Barbara resorts enjoyed hiking and riding in the local mountains. Eager to keep the customers satisfied, in 1902 the chamber purchased easements from canyon homesteaders to develop a recreation trail. "Chamber of Commerce Trail," as the chamber called it, was an immediate success with both tourists and locals. However, to the chamber's consternation, both the trail and the canyon itself continued to be called Rattlesnake. Chamber of Commerce Canyon sounded a bit self-serving, so the chamber tried to compromise with an earlier name, Las Canoas Canyon, and adopted a 1902 resolution to that effect. "The name of Rattlesnake Canyon is unpleasantly suggestive of a reptile," it argued, "which is found no more plentifully there than elsewhere along the mountain range and may deter some nervous persons from visiting that most delightful locality."

In the 1960s, the city of Santa Barbara purchased the canyon as parkland. A handsome wooden sign at the foot of the canyon proudly proclaims: Rattlesnake Canyon Wilderness.

This trail explores Santa Barbara's little wilderness canyon. Red-berried toyon, manzanita with its white urn-shaped flowers, and purple hummingbird sage cloak the slopes and offer a variety of smells and textures. In early spring ceanothus blooms, adding frosty whites and blues to the gray-green thickets. Shooting stars, larkspur, and lupine also spread their color over the slopes and meadows.

Directions to trailhead: From Highway 101 in Santa Barbara, go uptown (toward the mountains) on State Stree to Los Olivos Street.

Turn right and proceed a half mile, passing by the Santa Barbara Mission and joining Mission Canyon Road. Follow Mission Canyon Road past its intersection with Foothill Road and make a right on Las Canoas Road. Follow Las Canoas Road to Skofield Park. Park on the road or in the large parking area just before the picnic grounds. The trail begins on Las Canoas Road near the handsome stone bridge that crosses Rattlesnake Creek.

The Hike: From the sandstone bridge across from Skofield Park, hike up a brief stretch of trail and join a narrow dirt road that parallels the east side of the creek. For lovely picnicking, take any of the steep side trails down to the creek. In the early nineteenth century the mission padres built a dam in the bottom of the canyon, which channeled water into a stone aqueduct and diverted it into the mission's waterwork system. Portions of the aqueduct still exist and can be seen by the careful observer.

The trail zigs and zags across the creek, finally continuing along the west bank to open, grassy Tin Can Meadow. The triangular-shaped meadow gets its name from a homesteader's cabin constructed of chaparral framing and kerosene can shingles and sidings. For the first quarter of this century, Tin Can Shack was an important canyon landmark and several guidebooks of that era mention it. It was a popular destination for picnickers who marveled at the inspired architecture and posed for pictures in front of it. In 1925, a brushfire destroyed the shack and it soon disintegrated into a pile of tin. Today, only faint traces of the shack's foundation can be seen in the meadow, although when the angle of the morning sun is just right, hikers swear they can see bits of tin glinting in the sunshine.

Option: To Gibraltar Road. At the apex of the triangular meadow is a junction; a side trail takes you ¾ mile and climbs 500 feet to its intersection with the Tunnel Trail. To the right, Rattlesnake Canyon Trail climbs about ¾ of a mile and 500 feet to its intersection with Gibraltar Road. There you will be greeted by an unobstructed view of the South Coast. Watch for strangely patterned triangular aircraft overhead. A favorite hang glider's launching peak is almost within reach.

Return the same way.

11
Cold Springs Trail

Season: All year
Recommended map: Los
   Padres National Forest
Topo: Santa Barbara
See map p. 49

Mountain Drive to Montecito Overlook
   3 miles RT; 900′ gain
Return via Hot Springs Canyon
   6 miles RT
Mountain Drive to Montecito Peak
   7½ miles RT; 2500′ gain
Mountain Drive to Camino Cielo
   9 miles RT; 2700′ gain

Our favorite route to the main ridge was by a way called the Cold Spring Trail. We used to enjoy taking visitors up it, mainly because you come on the top suddenly, without warning. Then we collected remarks. Everybody, even the most stolid, said something.
        —STEWARD EDWARD WHITE
        The Mountains, 1906

After the Santa Ynez Forest Reserve was established in 1899, rangers recognized the desirability of a trail crossing the Reserve from coast to desert. A trail up the West Fork of Cold Springs Canyon had historically been the way into the Santa Barbara backcountry, but the rangers realized that this tricky trail, which climbed around a waterfall and crossed shale slopes, would be difficult to maintain. In 1905, the Forest Service built a trail up the East Fork of Cold Springs Canyon.

And a lovely trail, it is. It begins by the alder-shaded year-around creek, then rises out of the canyon for fine coastal views.

Cold Springs Trail offers the hiker a choice of three delightful options. The century-old West Fork Trail leads to a 300-foot waterfall, the "newer" East Fork Trail climbs to well-named Montecito Overlook and ascends Montecito Peak, and a connector trail leads to historic Hot Springs Canyon and enables the hiker to make a loop trip.

Directions to trailhead: From Highway 101 in Montecito, a few miles south of Santa Barbara, exit on Hot Springs Road and proceed toward the foothills for 2½ miles to Mountain Drive. Turn left. (Note the signs pointing to the Hot Springs Trail. If you choose to take the loop trail option of this hike, you'll be descending via the Hot Springs Trail to

Mountain Drive and walking along this road back to your car.) A mile's travel on Mountain Drive brings you to the Cold Springs trailhead, which begins at a point where a creek flows over a cement drainage apron.

The Hike: The trail immediately crosses the creek to the east side of the canyon. It rises briefly through oak woodland, then returns to the creek. On your left, ¼ mile from the trailhead, is the easily-overlooked, unsigned West Fork Trail.

Sidetrip: West Fork Trail to Gibraltar Road. 3 miles RT; 1000' gain. Follow the trail across the creek. Just up-canyon from the crossing is the confluence of the two branches of Cold Spring Creek. The trail rises above the creek.

Alongside the trail are pipes, from past and present municipal water projects. Leakage from the pipes waters ferns and oxalis. California bay laurel also line the trail.

Three-quarters of a mile up the West Fork, you'll spot an unsigned trail on your right. A rough path leads to the waterfall. West Fork Trail itself continues past two seasonal creeks and climbs steeply to Gibraltar Road.

Continuing past the West Fork junction, East Fork Trail rises up the canyon wall and rejoins the creek a ½ mile later. Look for a fine swimming hole below you to the right. The trail then switchbacks moderately out of the canyon to Montecito Overlook.

Past the overlook, you'll cross a fire road leading down to Hot Springs Canyon, begin an uphill climb and soon encounter the Hot Springs connector trail.

Option: Return via Hot Springs Canyon. Follow the connector trail down into Hot Springs Canyon. Along the trail some exotic flora thrives—bamboo, huge agave, banana and palm trees—remnants of the landscaped gardens that surrounded Hot Springs Resort during its glory days. One hot pool, reconstructed by locals, offers an opportunity to take a soak. If this pool or others nearby look inviting, drop in.

Explore the ruins of Hot Springs Hotel, constructed in the early 1880s. Europeans and Americans from colder climes flocked here to "take the cure." A 1920 fire destroyed the hotel; it was rebuilt and burned again in 1964.

Follow the dirt road (once the carriage road leading to the resort) and join the trail that descends the canyon. You'll emerge from a residential area onto Mountain Drive, which you'll follow to the right one mile back to the Cold Springs trailhead.

Hot Springs Hotel

Option: To Montecito Peak. From the junction with the Hot Springs Connector Trail, Cold Springs Trail switchbacks up canyon and offers fine coastal views. A one mile climb brings you to two eucalyptus trees (about the only shade enroute!) and another ¾ mile of travel takes you to the unsigned junction with a side trail to Montecito Peak. A steep ¼ mile climb up this trail leads to the top of Montecito Peak (3214'). Enjoy the view and sign the summit register.

Option: To Camino Cielo. Cold Spring Trail continues a last mile to Camino Cielo. From the Sky Road, many trails lead into the far reaches of the Santa Barbara backcountry and grand views are your's. As author/ adventurer Stewart Edward White described the panorama:

> *"And from under your very feet rose, range after range, tier after tier, rank after rank, in increasing crescendo of wonderful tinted mountains to the main crest of the Coast Ranges, the blue distance, the mightiness of California's western systems. The eye followed them up and up, and farther and farther, with the accumulating emotion of a wild rush on a toboggan."*

Chapter 4

SANTA MONICA MOUNTAINS

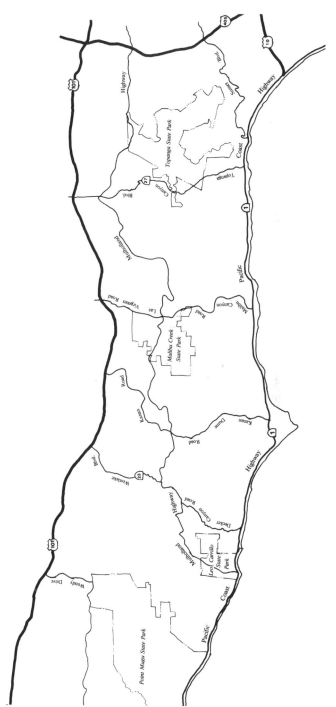

Santa Monica Mountains

The copper hued men who roamed these hills not so long ago were very likely better tenants than you and I will be. And when we are gone, as we will go, a few unnoticed centuries will wipe out our bravest scars, our most determined trails.

—JOHN RUSSELL MCCARTHY
Those Waiting Hills: The Santa Monicas, 1924

THE SANTA MONICAS are the only relatively undeveloped mountain range in the U.S. that bisects a major metropolitan area. They are a near-wilderness within an hour's drive of six million people, and stretch all the way from Griffith Park in the heart of Los Angeles to Point Mugu, 50 miles away. The mountains, which include the civilized Hollywood Hills and the oh-so-civilized Beverly Hills, run westward to the steep wildlands above Malibu.

The range is 12 miles wide at its broadest point and reaches an elevation of a little over 3,000 feet. Large stretches are open and natural, covered with chaparral and oak trees, bright in spring with wildflowers. Water from winter rains runs down steep slopes and fosters a wide variety of life on canyon floors. Oak woodland and fern glens shade gentle seasonal streams. Within the mountains is a variety of animal life, from the most sociable of frogs to the most reclusive of mountain lions. The coyote, mule deer, raccoon, rabbit, rattlesnake, skunk and fox find shelter in the Santa Monicas. Birdwatching is excellent. The wrentit, the brown towhee, red-tail hawk, quail, turkey vulture, and many, many more birds patrol the skies.

The hills and canyons used to be hiding places for bandits. The notorious highwayman Vasquez had a refuge here, but visited his sweetie once too often and fell into the sheriff's net. The fog-covered Santa Monicas, with few roads and trails, were a favorite haunt of the contrabandistas. Under Mexican rule, every sea trader had.to land in San Francisco or Monterey and pay duty. To avoid the drastic customs, the contrabandistas slipped their cargo ashore by moonlight at secret coves, then trekked the goods over the mountains to Los Angeles.

In the nineteenth century, the Santa Monicas were controlled by a few large holdings including the Rancho Malibu and the Rancho Guadalasca and used primarily for cattle raising. As the land holdings were broken up, ranchers supplemented their modest living by renting space to visiting horsemen and vacationers. At the turn of the century, eccentric oilman Colonel Griffith J. Griffith gave 3,000 acres of his ostrich farm to Los Angeles on the condition that it be forever maintained as a park. Thus Griffith Park was formed on the eastern terminus of the Santa Monicas. Throughout the past three decades, conservationists have made inch-by-inch progress to secure park lands.

The largest areas of open space are in the western part of the mountains. Point Mugu State Park holds the finest native tall grass prairie and the best sycamore grove in the state. The gorge cut by Malibu Creek is an unforgettable sight.

In the eastern part of the mountains, open space is harder to come by, but those little pockets that do exist are all the more valuable for being so close to the metropolis. Canyons such as Los Liones, Caballero, and Franklin are precious resources for the park-poor Los Angeles basin.

Southern California nature lovers put on their hiking boots and jumped for joy in 1978 when the bill creating the Santa Monica Mountains National Recreation Area was approved by congress. Eventually a larger park will be formed, to be overseen by the National Park Service. Allocations are slowly being made by the state and federal government to fund purchases of private land to supplement the four major holdings: Will Rogers, Topanga, Malibu Creek and Point Mugu State Parks.

The new park is the unfinished story of Southern Californians, aided by few meaningful laws for intelligent land use, defending the Santa Monicas on every government level. Southlanders have helped the Santa Monicas cope with natural disasters of fire and flood and unnatural disasters like the proposed Malibu and Mulholland Freeways.

The National Recreation Area is not one large area, but a patchwork of state parks, county parks, and private property still to be acquired. The network of trails through the Santa Monicas is a rich pastiche of nature walks, scenic overlooks, fire roads and horse trails leading through diverse ecosystems: meadowlands, savannas, yucca-covered slopes, handsome sandstone formations, and springs surrounded by lush ferns. The Backbone Trail, to run from Will Rogers State Historic Park to Point Mugu State Park, is slowly being completed and when finished will literally and symbolically link the scattered beauties of the Santa Monicas.

12
La Jolla Valley Loop Trail

Parking lot to La Jolla Valley Trail Camp
7 miles RT; 700′ gain
Return via Mugu Peak Trail
8 miles RT; 1000′ gain

Ringed by ridges, the native grassland of La Jolla Valley welcomes the hiker with its drifts of oaks and peaceful pond. This pastoral upland is unique: it has resisted the invasion of non-native vegetation. It's rare to find native grassland in Southern California because the Spanish introduced oats and a host of other foreign grasses for pasture for their cattle. In most cases, the imported grasses squeezed out the natives; but not in La Jolla Valley.

This trail passes a waterfall and tours the beautiful grasslands of the valley. A longer option offers superb views of the Pacific and Channel Islands.

Directions to trailhead: Drive about 30 miles upcoast on Pacific Coast Highway (21 miles past Malibu Canyon Road if you're coming from the Ventura Freeway and the San Fernando Valley). The turnoff is 1.5 miles north of Big Sycamore Canyon, which is part of Point Mugu State Park. From the turnoff, bear right to the parking area. The signed trailhead, near an interpretive display, is at a fire road that leads into the canyon.

The Hike: The fire road heads north up the canyon along the streambed. As the canyon narrows, some tiny waterfalls come into view.

At the first trail junction, bear right on the La Jolla Valley Loop Trail. In a little less than ½ mile, you'll arrive at another junction. Leave the main trail and you will descend the short distance to a lovely cattail pond. The pond is a nesting place for a variety of birds including the redwing blackbird. Above the pond is a picnic area with tables, running water, and a good view of the ducks and coots.

Returning to the main trail, you'll skirt the east end of La Jolla Valley, enjoy an overview of waving grasses and intersect a "T" junction. To the right, 0.7 mile away, is Deer Camp Junction (See Hike 13), which provides access to trails leading to Ranch Center, Wood Canyon and Sycamore Canyon. Bear left and in ½ mile you'll arrive at La Jolla Valley

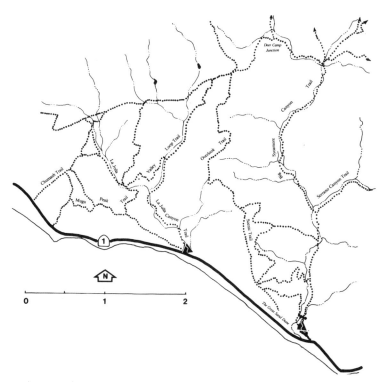

Camp. The camp, sheltered by oaks and equipped with piped water, is idea for picnicking. After leaving the camp, turn left on a short connector trail that skirts the pond to La Jolla Canyon Trail. Or continue on another ½ mile to a signed junction and a longer connecting trail back to the La Jolla Canyon Loop Trail.

Option: Return via Mugu Peak Trail. Continue past La Jolla Valley Camp and hike through the billowing grassland. Keep an eye out for speedy roadrunners, who dash through the grass. The trail heads toward the "spy in the sky," the missile-tracking disc atop Laguna Peak to the west. The trail crosses a number of branches of La Jolla Creek, following this watercourse and its oak copses as it cuts through the rolling grassland. You'll want to dawdle near here, perhaps do a little cross country thrashing on one of the deer trails or go off stalking wild chocolate lilies hidden in the grass.

You'll join the Chumash Trail heading southward toward the Pacific and soon climb to a low saddle where there are splendid views of the ocean and the Channel Islands. Bear left on the Mugu Peak Trail, which contours around the prickly pear and yucca covered slopes of Mugu Peak (1266′). After rounding the mountain, bear to the right on La Jolla Valley Loop Trail and return to the trailhead.

Season: All year
Recommended map: Trails of the
    Santa Monica Mountains
Topo: Point Mugu
See map p. 65

▲ 13
Sycamore Canyon Trail

Big Sycamore Canyon to Deer Camp Junction
    6½ miles RT; 200′ gain
Return via Overlook Trail
    10 miles RT; 1300′ gain

Every fall, millions of Monarch butterflies migrate south to the forests of Mexico's Transvolcanic Range and to the damp coastal woodlands of Central and Southern California. The Monarch's awe-inspiring migration and formation of what entomologists call over-wintering colonies are two of nature's most colorful autumn events.

All Monarch butterflies west of the Rockies head for California in the fall; one of the best places in Southern California to observe the arriving monarchs is near the campground in Big Sycamore Canyon at Point Mugu State Park.

The monarch's evolutionary success lies not only in its unique ability to migrate to warmer climes, but in its mastery of chemical warfare. The butterfly feeds on milkweed—the favored poison of assassins during the Roman Empire. This milkweed diet makes the monarch toxic to birds; after munching a monarch or two and becoming sick, they learn to leave the butterflies alone.

Monarch butterfly

The butterflies advertise their poisonous nature with their conspicuous coloring. They have brownish-red wings with black veins. The outer edge of the wings are dark brown with white and yellow spots. While one might assume the monarch's startling coloration would make them easy prey for predators, just the opposite is true; bright colors in nature are often a warning that a creature is toxic or distasteful.

Sycamore Canyon Trail takes you through a peaceful wooded canyon, where a multitude of monarchs dwell, and past some magnificent sycamores. The sycamores that shade the canyon bearing their name are incomparable. The lower branches, stout and crooked, are a delight for treeclimbers. Hawks and owls roost in the upper branches.

The trail follows the canyon on a gentle northern traverse across Point Mugu State Park, the largest preserved area in the Santa Monica Mountains. This trail, combined with the Overlook Trail, gives the hiker quite a tour of the park.

During October and November, Sycamore Canyon offers the twin delights of falling autumn leaves and fluttering butterflies. (Ask park rangers where the monarchs cluster in large numbers.) Bring your swimsuit; when you finish this hike, you can take a plunge into the ocean.

Directions to trailhead: Drive upcoast on Highway 1, 32 miles from Santa Monica, to the Big Sycamore Canyon Campground in Point Mugu State Park. Outside the campground entrance there's a dirt area where you may park. Walk past the campground entrance through the campground to a locked gate. The trail begins on the other side of the gate.

The Hike: Take the trail up-canyon, following the creek. Winter rains cause the creek to rise, and sometimes keeping your feet dry while crossing is difficult. Underground water keeps much of the creekside vegetation green year around—so this is a fine hike in any season.

One half mile from the campground you'll spot the Overlook Trail, which switchbacks to the west up a ridge and then heads north toward the native tall grass prairie in La Jolla Valley. Make note of this trail for a return trip.

A second ½ mile of nearly level canyon walking brings you to another major hiking trail that branches right—the Serrano Canyon Trail. Serrano Canyon is a steep-walled rock gorge that features some seasonal waterfalls.

Another easy mile of walking beneath the sycamores brings you to a picnic table shaded by a grove of large oak trees. The oaks might be a good turnaround spot for a family with small children. The total round-trip distance would be a little over 4 miles.

Continuing up the canyon you'll pass beneath more of the giant sycamores and soon arrive at Wood Canyon Junction, the hub of six trails which lead to all corners of the park. Bear left on the signed Wood

La Jolla Canyon from Overlook Trail

Canyon Trail and in a short while you'll reach Deer Camp Junction. Drinking water and picnic tables suggest a lunch stop. Oak trees predominate over the sycamores along Wood Canyon Creek; however, the romantic prefer the sycamores, some of which have large clumps of mistletoe in the upper branches.

You can call it a day here and return the way you came. As you hike down the canyon back to the campground, the large and cranky bluejay population will continually scold you, but don't let them stop you from enjoying one of California's finest sycamore savannas.

Option: Return via Overlook Trail. Continue past the junction with the Wood Canyon Trail and Deer Camp Junction on the Wood Canyon Trail, which becomes Pumphouse Road. You'll climb over to the divide between Sycamore Canyon and La Jolla Valley. Upon reaching a junction, you'll head south on the Overlook Trail, staying on the La Jolla Canyon side of the ridge. True to its name, Overlook Trail offers good views of grassy mountainsides, Boney Peak and Big Sycamore Canyon. You'll pass an intersection with Scenic Trail, a rough path that hugs the ridge separating La Jolla and Big Sycamore Canyons. Overlook Trail descends to Big Sycamore Canyon, where you'll bear right and follow the fire road ½ mile back to the trailhead.

14

Rancho Sierra Vista Loop Trail

8 miles RT; 1000' gain

Acre by acre, the Santa Monica Mountains National Recreation Area is slowly expanding. One new park, Rancho Sierra Vista/Satiwa, on the northern boundary of Point Mugu State Park, was purchased by the National Park Service in 1980. Twenty miles of trail wind through the park, connecting with about 70 miles of trails in Point Mugu State Park. You can trek from Rancho Sierra Vista to the ocean.

This day hike, which explores, both state and national parkland, offers a variety of scenery—a Santa Monica Mountains sampler—including chaparral-covered slopes, oak woodland, a waterfall and giant woodwardia ferns.

The name of the park, Rancho Sierra Vista/Satiwa, reflects its history as a 1940s horse ranch and as the longtime tribal land of the Chumash. Parkland has been designated as the Satiwa Native American Indian Natural Area. A short walk from the parking lot is the Native American Indian Cultural Center, which has exhibits of Chumash, Gabrielino and Hopi crafts and culture; it's open Sundays from 10 to 4.

Directions to trailhead: From the Ventura Freeway (U.S.' 101) in Newbury Park, exit on Wendy Drive. Head south for 4 miles, then turn west on Potrero Road for 2 miles. Follow the signs to the park's parking lot on your left.

The Hike: From the parking lot, begin hiking on the dirt road. In a mile you reach an overlook perched above upper Sycamore Canyon. Turn left, heading east here, on the Fence Trail, which true to its name follows a barbed wire fence.

The trail reaches Old Boney Road, which you'll follow to the right as you begin ascending the north slope of the canyon. After dropping down to a creek, the road leads beneath oaks and sycamores.

When you reach the first switchback to the right, enjoy a brief diversion by following the trail leftward. You'll soon intersect a creek, which can be followed a short distance to the waterfall. Woodwardia ferns thrive in the cool moist canyon. A series of a half dozen tiny falls cascade from pool to pool.

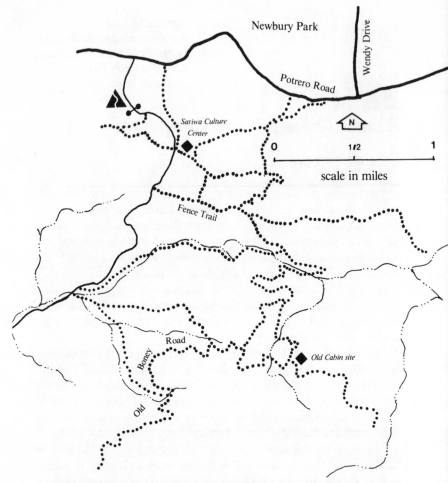

After enjoying the falls, return to Old Boney Road and continue your ascent. On a clear day, the upper reaches of the road offer views of the wide Pacific and Channel Islands. The road forks and you'll continue straight ahead.

A little farther along, you'll spot a stone chimney standing amongst some oaks. The cabin that once stood here was used by ranch hands when cattle and sheep grazed the high country. When a 1956 fire burned from the valley side of the mountains to the ocean, the cabin was destroyed. Near the cabin, a year-around spring offers drinking water. If the bugs aren't biting, this area around the cabin makes a nice lunch stop.

You'll notice a trail that leads up to Boney Mountain, but this day hike continues another mile on the road that brought you here. You'll intersect a steep one mile connector trail branching right and take it a mile back to the paved park service road, which returns you to the trailhead.

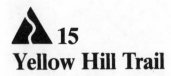

15
Yellow Hill Trail

Leo Carrillo State Beach to Sequit Ridge
6 miles RT; 1650′ gain

The state beach is named after Angeline Leo Carrillo, famous for his TV role as Pancho, the Cisco Kid's sidekick. Carrillo was also quite active in recreation and civic matters.

In recent years the state has added inland parkland to Leo Carrillo State Beach. Nicholas Flat Trail and Yellow Hill Trail connect the mountains to the sea.

Sequit Point bisects the beach, forming a bay to the south. Surfers tackle the well-shaped south swell, battling the submerged rocks and kelp beds. Beach hikers enjoy exploring the point's caves and coves. After heading inland on the trail described below, I recommend hiking along Leo Carrillo State Beach to the County Line.

Yellow Hill Trail climbs Arroyo Sequit Ridge for panoramic views of the coast and Channel Islands.

Leo Carrillo State Beach

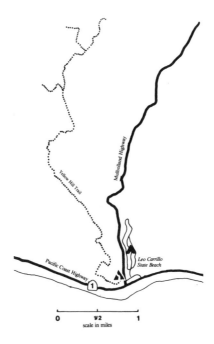

Directions to trailhead: Leo Carrillo State Beach is located just down-coast from Mulholland Highway on the Pacific Coast Highway 26 miles north of Santa Monica. Park along PCH (free) or at the State Beach (fee).

The Hike: The trail (Yellow Hill Fire Road) begins near ranger residences on the west side of Mulholland Highway. For 1/3 mile, you'll parallel the coast, then turn inland, climbing all the while. You can see several Channel Islands: Anacapa, Santa Cruz, Santa Rosa. On an especially clear day, you can sometimes see miniscule Santa Barbara Island due south.

The fire road passes through sage and chaparral to a 1600-foot peak. This is the northwest boundary of the park, where you turn around and return the same way you came.

"The Gorge" on Malibu Creek

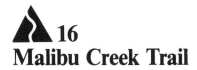

16
Malibu Creek Trail

Entrance Station to Rock Pool
3½ miles RT; 150′ gain
Entrance Station to Century Lake
4½ miles RT; 200′ gain

Before land for Malibu Creek State Park was acquired in 1974, it was divided into three parcels belonging to Bob Hope, Ronald Reagan, and the Twentieth Century Fox Ranch. Although the park is still used for moviemaking part of the year, it is primarily for day hiking, picnicking and birdwatching.

The park is a birdwatcher's paradise. Golden eagles and hawks soar above the high rocky points, while ducks and blue herons patrol the waterways.

This day hike explores the heart of the state park. It's a nearly level walk across the floor of the valley. You'll visit some of the park's features: a dramatic rock gorge, Century Lake, the park Visitors Center.

Directions to trailhead: From Pacific Coast Highway, turn right on Malibu Canyon Road and proceed 6½ miles to the park entrance, located ¼ mile south of Mulholland Drive. If you're coming from the San Fernando Valley, exit the Ventura Freeway on Las Virgenes and continue 4 miles to the park entrance. There's a state park day use fee.

The Hike: From the parking area, follow the wide fire road. Notice the cottonwood trees along the creek. The road soon forks into a high road and a low road. Take the oak-shaded high road, which makes a wide left turn as it follows the north bank of Malibu Creek. You'll intersect a fire road in a grove of cedar, and continue upstream on the Gorge Trail.

A short walk brings you to The Gorge, one of the most dramatic sights in the Santa Monicas. Malibu Creek makes a hairpin turn through 400 foot volcanic rock cliffs and cascades into aptly named Rock Pool. The "Swiss Family Robinson" TV series was filmed here.

Return along the Gorge Trail. A right turn at the bridge brings you to the Park Visitors Center in the building upstream.

Option: to Century Lake. A left turn on the fire road and a short ascent offers a fine view of Las Virgenes Valley. When you gain the crest of the hill, you'll look down on Century Lake. Near the lake are hills of porous lava and topsy-turvy sedimentary rock layers that tell of the violent geologic upheaval that formed Malibu Canyon. The man-made lake was scooped out by members of Crag's Country Club, a group of wealthy, turn-of-the-century businessmen who had a nearby lodge. The lake is slowly filling in. When moviemakers owned it, they periodically dredged it to retain its scenic qualities. Now rain deposits silt in the lake and cattails and willows advance from shoreline to shallows.

Return to the trailhead the same way or you may wish to take the leftward bearing Lookout Trail ¼ mile to the park lookout for a fine view of Malibu Creek.

Or continue hiking along the fire road, which parallels the creek. You'll pass the location of the (now removed) set for the "M*A*S*H" TV series. (The set is now on display in the Smithsonian.) The prominent Goat Buttes that tower above Malibu Creek are featured in the opening shot of each episode.

Ambitious hikers will continue on to Bulldog Motorway for a steep ascent to national parkland in the Castro Crest area.

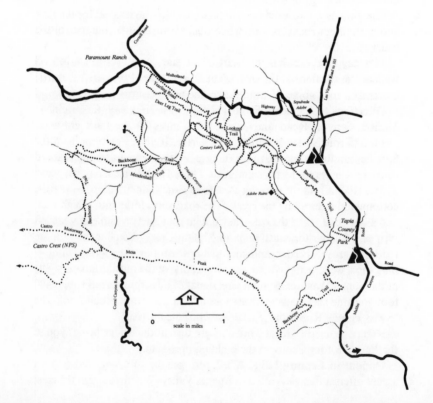

 17
Backbone Trail

**Tapia County Park to Castro Crest
7 miles one way; 2000' gain
Return via Bulldog Motorway,
Twentieth Century Road
14 miles RT; 2000' gain**

This hike utilizes a section of the Backbone Trail, which one day will cross the Santa Monica Mountains from Will Rogers State Historic Park to Point Mugu. Hikers follow well-graded fire roads, heading first west along Mesa Peak Motorway, climbing toward Castro Crest, then north and east through Malibu Creek State Park.

Fine ocean and island views are offered along the first half of the hike and a chance to explore geologically and ecologically unique Malibu Creek Canyon is yours on the second half.

Directions to trailhead: From Pacific Coast Highway turn north on Malibu Canyon Road and proceed 5 miles to Tapia Park, located a little less than a mile south of Malibu Creek State Park. From the Ventura Freeway, exit on Las Virgenes Road and proceed 5 miles to Tapia Park. The hike begins at the Tapia County Park parking lot.

The Hike: Mesa Peak Motorway ascends steeply at first, gaining 1500' in 2½ miles. With the elevation gain comes sweeping panoramic views of Point Dume, Santa Monica Bay, and Palos Verdes Peninsula. On clear days, Catalina, San Clemente, Anacapa and Santa Cruz Islands float upon the horizon.

The trail veers left toward Mesa Peak (1844') and continues climbing in a northwesterly direction through an area rich in fossilized shells. Hillside roadcuts betray the Santa Monica Mountains' oceanic heritage. As you hike the spine of the range, a good view to the north is yours: the volcanic rocks of Goat Butte tower above Malibu Creek gorge; the path of Triunfo Canyon can be traced.

The road passes through an area of interesting sandstone formations, intersecting paved Corral Canyon Road, which is termed Castro Motorway from this point. Continue west on Castro Motorway for one mile, reaching the intersection with Bulldog Motorway.

The Backbone Trail continues west toward the forest of antennas atop Castro Peak (2824′) and hopefully, some day, to Point Mugu.

Option: Return Via Bulldog Motorway For a nice loop trip back through the state park, bear right on Bulldog Motorway. Descend steeply under transmission lines, veering east and dropping into Triunfo Canyon. In 3½ miles, the hiker reaches Twentieth Century Road. Turn right and soon pass what was once the location of the exterior sets used by the "M*A*S*H" TV series.

The road passes Century Lake, crosses a ridge, then drops down to Malibu Creek and comes to a fork in the road. Take either the left (high road) or continue straight ahead and over the bridge on the low road; the roads meet again downstream, so you may select either one. One-half mile after the roads rejoin, the route reaches the main gate of the state park.

18

Eagle Rock Loop Trail

Eagle Rock/Eagle Springs Loop
6.5 miles RT; 800′ gain
Topanga parking lot via Eagle Rock,
Fire Road 30, and Rogers Road to
Will Rogers SHP
10.4 miles one way; 1800′ loss

The name Topanga is from the Shoshonean Indian dialect. These Indians and their ancestors occupied the canyon on and off from several thousand years B.C. until the Spanish evicted them and forced them to settle at the San Fernando Mission.

Until the 1880s, there was little permanent habitation in the canyon. Early settlers tended vineyards, orchards and cattle ranches. In the 1920s, the canyon became a popular weekend destination for Los Angeles residents. Summer cabins were built along Topanga Creek and in subdivisions in the surrounding hills. For $1 roundtrip fare, tourists could board a Packard Auto Stage in Santa Monica and be driven up Pacific Coast Highway and Topanga Canyon Road to the Topanga Post Office and other, more scenic, spots.

This hike departs from quiet and imperturbable Topanga Canyon, surrounded by L.A. sprawl but retaining its rural character. The trail is good fire road, part of the Backbone Trail route. A longer one-way option takes you along brushy ridges to Will Rogers State Park.

Directions to trailhead: From Topanga Canyon Boulevard, turn east on Entrada Road; that's to the right if you're coming from Pacific Coast Highway. Follow Entrada Road by turning left at every opportunity until you arrive at Topanga State Park. The trailhead is at the end of the parking lot. There is a park day use fee.

To Will Rogers SHP trailhead: From Sunset Boulevard in Pacific Palisades, turn north at the park entrance. The road leads up to Rogers' estate, now a state historic park. Near Will Rogers' home, a signed trail climbs to Inspiration Point. Rogers Trail intersects 1/10 mile past Inspiration Point junction.

The Hike: From the parking lot, follow the distinct trail eastward to a signed junction, where you'll begin hiking on Eagle Springs Road. You'll pass through an oak woodland and through chaparral country. You'll slowly and steadily gain about 800 feet in elevation on the way to Eagle Rock. When you reach a junction, bear left on the north loop of Eagle Springs Road to Eagle Rock. A short detour will bring you to the top of the rock, its caves, and an impressive view of Santa Ynez Canyon.

To complete the loop, bear sharply right (southwest) at the next junction, following the fire road as its winds down to Eagle Spring. Past the spring, you return to Eagle Spring Road and retrace your steps back to the trailhead.

The 3-mile-long Musch Ranch Trail, which passes from hot chaparral to shady oak woodland, crosses a bridge and passes the park pond, offers a nice look at the state park and is another fine way to return to the trailhead.

Option: To Will Rogers State Historic Park. Follow the loop trail directions to the northeast end of Eagle Rock/Eagle Spring Loop, where you bear right on Fire Road 30. In ½ mile you reach the intersection with Rogers Road. Turn left and follow the dirt road (really a trail) for 3½ miles, where the road ends and meets Rogers Trail. Here a level area and solitary oak suggest a lunch stop. On clear days enjoy the spectacular views in every direction: to the left is Rustic Canyon and the crest of the mountains near Mulholland Drive. To the right, Rivas Canyon descends toward the sea.

Stay on Rogers Trail, which marches up and down several steep hills, for about two more miles, until it enters Will Rogers State Historic Park near Inspiration Point.

Will Rogers Home, Will Rogers State Historic Park

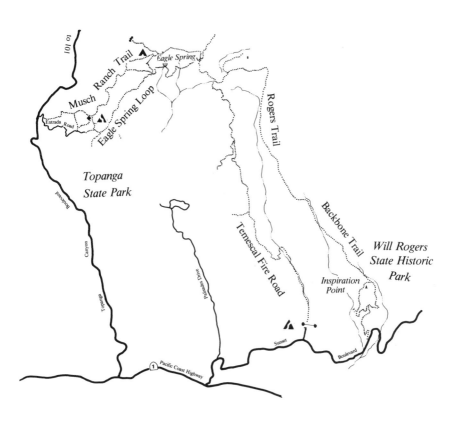

to 101

Musch Ranch Trail

Eagle Spring

Eagle Spring Loop

Rogers Trail

Entrada Road

Topanga State Park

Topanga Canyon Boulevard

Palisades Drive

Temescal Fire Road

Backbone Trail

Will Rogers State Historic Park

Inspiration Point

Sunset Boulevard

① Pacific Coast Highway

19

Temescal Canyon Trail

Canyon Floor to Ridge Overlook
5½ miles RT; 700' gain
Canyon Floor to Rogers Road
12½ miles RT; 1600' gain

As you sweat it out crossing the exposed ridge above Temescal Canyon, you might be amused to learn that "temescal" is what the Chumash Indians called their village sweathouse. The Chumash took as many as two ceremonial sweat baths a day, in what anthropologists speculate might have been a religious ritual. A fire burned in the center of the sweathouse. When the Chumash began to perspire, they scraped the sweat off with special sweat sticks, then rushed out and leaped into a cold stream. The mission fathers complained that the Chumash took too many baths and were a little *too* clean. More work at the mission and less relaxation in the sweathouse would be more productive, the padres thought.

This steep hike gradually climbs via Temescal Fire Road to scenic overlooks among the highest summits (over 2000') in the Santa Monicas. From the overlooks, you can see Santa Ynez, Temescal and Rustic Canyons, as well as the Los Angeles Basin and the great blue Pacific.

Directions to trailhead: From Sunset Boulevard in Pacific Palisades, turn north on Temescal Canyon Road. Proceed for ½ mile and park in the open area, just before the Presbyterian Conference Grounds. Hikers must sign in and out at the gate. Respect the quiet and privacy of the grounds.

The Hike: Walk into the canyon on the paved road, passing a number of meeting halls and residences. The route, shaded by coast live oak, next follows a washed out road along Temescal Creek.

The trail climbs through the narrow gorge of the canyon and, 1½ miles from the trailhead, crosses over to the west (left) side of the canyon. You might want to stop and cool off at a small waterfall. At the canyon crossing stands an old burned bridge, which fell victim to the 1978 Mandeville Fire that blackened the upper reaches of Temescal Canyon.

Scramble up the steep slope to the other side of the canyon and begin switchbacking up the mountainside. The fire road levels out atop a northwest-trending ridge. The view to the southwest down at the housing developments isn't too inspiring, but the view of the rough unaltered northern part of Temescal Canyon is. Proceed along the ridge; you'll see some rock outcroppings. A short side trip off the fire road will bring you to Skull Rock, where you can climb inside the wind-formed (aeolian) caves to cool off or picnic.

Return the same way or continue on the fire road.

Option: First Ridge to Rogers Road. If you want to stretch your legs and get better and better views of the Santa Monicas, continue on Temescal Fire Road. Joining the fire road from the left are Split Rock Road and a mile farther north, Trailer Canyon Road. A microwave tower, atop what locals have dubbed "Radio Peak," stands halfway between the two points.

One and a half miles of mostly level walking beyond the Trailer Canyon intersection brings you to Rogers Road. Near the intersection is Temescal Peak (2126'), highest peak in Topanga State Park. If you wish, scramble up a short and steep firebreak to the top for a fine view.

Rogers Road, a segment of the Backbone Trail, leads six miles rightward to Will Rogers State Historic Park and leftward to intersections with both loops of the Eagle Springs Trail, which in turn lead to Topanga State Park headquarters (see hike #18).

The above extensions suggest a car shuttle or a very long day of hiking. Otherwise, return the same way via Temescal Canyon Fire Road to the trailhead.

Elysian Park

Chapter 5

WILD SIDE OF L.A.

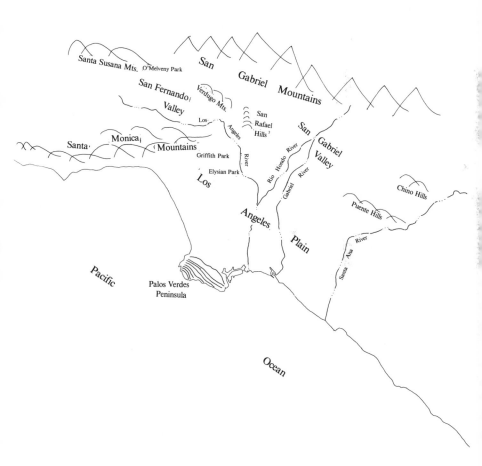

Santa Susana Mts. O'Melveny Park

San Gabriel Mountains

San Fernando Valley

Verdugo Mts.

San Rafael Hills

Santa Monica Mountains

Los Angeles River

Griffith Park

Elysian Park

San Gabriel Valley

Rio Hondo River

Gabriel River

Los

Angeles

Plain

Chino Hills

Puente Hills

Santa Ana River

Pacific

Palos Verdes Peninsula

Ocean

The Wild Side of L.A.

IT WAS A PARADISE once, Lotus Land: Los Angeles, California. The worst insult cynic H.L. Mencken could muster was that "the whole place stank of orange blossoms." Then came the immigrants, by the thousands. They came for retirement, for health, for oil, for aerospace, for movies, for a new life and new start. Most found enough of what they were looking for to settle in L.A. or one of its hundred suburbs.

The immigrants brought their autos and furniture and dreams and they brought a whole new landscape to the Los Angeles Basin. Few people realize that virtually every animal, vegetable and mineral in the region is imported: flowers, plants, shrubs, trees, water and energy. The trees most visitors believe are indigenous, such as eucalyptus and acacia, pepper and most palms, are imported from the wilds of Australia and South America. Even the Basin's grasses, rats, sparrows and weeds are not native.

It seems a hundred novels have opened with: "The smog hung heavy over the L.A. Basin." Los Angeles residents curse the bowl-shaped topography encircling them and hold the Basin personally responsible for their stinging eyes and scratchy throats. This, of course, is misplaced criticism, like holding the shape of the bottle responsible for the quality of the wine. It's worth taking a closer look (on a clear day) at this bowl many Southern Californians call home because this natural province shapes who we are and how we act. The Basin isn't always an eye irritant, and in fact its geography can be quite pleasing to the eye.

Geographically, the L.A. Basin extends south from the base of the San Gabriel Mountains to the sea and southwest from the Santa Monica Mountains to the Santa Ana Mountains. Faults border on two sides: the Palos Verdes Fault on the southwest and the Foothill Fault on the north. The Basin is divided by the Puente Hills, near Whittier. South of these hills is a coastal plain spreading toward the ocean. North is the San Gabriel Valley, surrounded by more hills and mountains—a basin within a Basin.

A short time ago, 20 million years or so, the landscape was pockmarked by furious volcanoes exploding fire, ash, and lava into the skies. One can only speculate how "smoggy" it was then! (These volcanic rocks can be seen near two trails in this guide: #39 along the Palos Verdes Hills and # 22 in Griffith Park.) After Mother Nature laid a fiery foundation of bedrock over the area, the land went through a time of uplift

View from Hastain Trail, Franklin Canyon

and subsidence. During Miocene, Pliocene and Pleistocene times (2 to 20 millions years ago) the ocean deposited thick sedimentary beds, which covered the igneous and metamorphic rocks.

A sea of tract houses now covers the ocean's former floor. It appears at first glance to be a relentless, monotonously flat landscape. But the lack of varied topography is an illusion. It's fun to speculate what the basin would look like if all the sedimentary fill left behind by ancient seas were scoured out, scooped up and dumped elsewhere. If all the sediment were removed, bedrock mountains over 30,000 feet high would be unveiled. The San Gabriels would be higher than the Himalayas! At 37,000 feet, Mount Wilson would dwarf Mount Everest! So the next time life in the Big Basin gets you down and the San Gabriel and Santa Monica Mountains are lost in a smoky haze, comfort yourself by remembering that beneath your feet is a majestic mountain range.

If you take a walk on the wild side of the L.A. Basin, you'll realize how much Los Angeles needs open space. New York City has some eighteen percent of its land area in parks; San Francisco has fourteen percent (not counting the Golden Gate Recreation Area), but Los Angeles has only four percent. Still, there's some surprisingly rugged open space within the L.A. city limits and it's all the more precious because of its scarcity. It's space you never imagined when stuck in rush hour traffic on the Santa Ana Freeway. On a clear day, when the sprawled skyline of L.A. is not lost in the ozone, a hiker can see much of the Basin from these selected trails.

Season: All year
Recommended map: park brochure,
    Angeles National Forest
Topo: Mint Canyon
    San Fernando

20
Placerita Canyon Trail

Nature Center to Walker Ranch Picnic Area
    4 miles RT; 300′ gain
Nature Center to Los Pinetos Ridge
    8 miles RT; 1600′ gain
Return via Manzanita Mountain
    10 miles RT

In 1842, seven years before the 49ers rushed to Sutter's Mill, California's first gold rush occurred in Placerita Canyon. Legend has it that herdsmen Francisco Lopez awoke from his siesta beneath a large shady oak tree. While asleep he dreamed of gold and wealth. When he awoke, he settled into the more mundane routine of fixing his evening meal. He dug up some onions to spice his supper and there, clinging to the roots, were small gold nuggets. Miners from all over California, the San Fernando Placers as they became known, poured into Placerita Canyon. The prospecting was good, though not exceptional, for several years. The spot where Lopez made his discovery is now called the Oak of the Golden Dream. A plaque marks his find.

The canyon has a gentleness that is rare in the steep, severely faulted San Gabriel Mountains. This hike through Placerita Canyon County Park takes you along the oak and sycamore shaded canyon floor by a creek, then climbs through chaparral and oak woodland to Los Pinetos Ridge for a view of the metropolis you've left behind. An optional return route via Manzanita Mountain and the Hillside Trail really gives you a grand tour of the park.

Be sure to visit the Nature Center, open 9 to 5, every day.

Directions to trailhead: From Interstate Highway 5 go east on Highway 14 (Antelope Valley Freeway) to Newhall. Exit on Placerita Canyon Road and turn right (east) two miles to Placerita Canyon County Park. Park in the large lot near the Nature Center.

The Hike: Walk up-canyon, following the stream and enjoying the shade of oaks and sycamores. A 1979 fire scorched brush within a hundred feet of the Nature Center, but remarkably spared the oak wood-

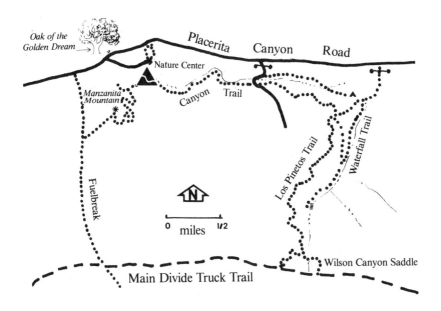

Oak of the Golden Dream →

Nature Center

Placerita Canyon Road

Manzanita Mountain

Canyon Trail

Fuelbreak

Los Pinetos Trail

Waterfall Trail

N

0 miles 1/2

Main Divide Truck Trail

Wilson Canyon Saddle

land on the canyon bottom. Nature regenerates quickly in a chaparral community; many hikers looking up at the canyon walls don't realize that a severe fire took place. Some of the chamise on the slopes may be a hundred years old and veterans of dozens of fires. A short 2 miles of walking brings you to the Walker Ranch section of the park where you'll find a picnic ground with tables, water and restrooms.

Placerita Canyon has been the outdoor set for many a western movie and 1950s TV series, including "The Cisco Kid" and "Hopalong Cassiday." Movie companies often used the cabin built in 1920 by Frank Walker. Walker, his wife Hortense, and their 12 children had a rough time earning a living in what was then a wilderness. The family raised cows and pigs, gathered and sold leaf mold (fertilizer), panned for gold, and hosted movie companies. When you return to the park nature center, be sure to take the short Heritage Trail to Walker's Cabin.

Return the same way or perhaps hike back to the Nature Center on the trail that follows the right (north) bank of the creek.

Option: To Los Pinetos Ridge. Skirt the edge of the campground and pick up the trail going up the right (south) slope. The trail climbs for 2 miles over the chaparral covered slopes of Los Pinetos Canyon to Los Pinetos Spring, tucked in an oak and spruce glen. From the spring, ascend via the fire road or a steep trail to its right ½ mile to a saddle on the main divide and an intersection with a fire road. Climb to any one of the nearby high points and enjoy the view. You can look northward over

historic Placerita Canyon and Sand Canyon and southward over the San Fernando Valley sparkling below. Here on Los Pinetos Ridge, the nineteenth century meets the twenty-first century and neither gives an inch.

Option: Return via Manzanita Mountain. Continue west on the fire road, Santa Clara Divide Road, until you reach a rough trail—sometimes referred to as a fuel break. Follow this trail northward until you reach a short ridgetop route that takes you to Manzanita Mountain. Follow the cicruitous trail, which connects with the Hillside Trail and leads back to the Nature Center.

21
O'Melveny Park Trail

Bee Canyon to Mission Point
4½ miles RT; 1400' gain

Billowing grass and seasonal wildflowers paint a pastoral landscape on the slopes of L.A.'s second largest park. O'Melveny Park, located at the north end of the San Fernando Valley, is the principal recreation area in the Santa Susana Mountains. The park's peaks offer the hiker commanding clear day views of the Los Angeles basin.

O'Melveny Park takes its name from the well-known family of Los Angeles lawyers who once owned a "gentleman's ranch" here. Attorney John O'Melveny bought the land in 1941 and called it CJ Ranch. Cattle roamed the hills, a citrus orchard was planted, and family members enjoyed spending weekends roaming the Santa Susana Mountains. The family ranch house, barn, and orchard still stand near the park entrance.

Although areas near the ranch were oil rich, exploration on the ranch was unsuccessful. The O'Melvenys deeded half their ranch to Los Angeles and the city purchased the rest. The 720-acre park, which opened to the public in 1981, includes a large developed picnic area and rugged wildland laced with 10 miles of trail.

In spring, a host of wildflowers—poppies, morning glory, Indian paintbrush and Mariposa lily—splash the hillsides. Fall wildflowers include the white trumpet-shaped jimson weed, scarlet California fuchia and yellow goldenbrush. Wildlife in O'Melveny Park includes deer, golden eagle, bobcat, rabbit, raccoon, and coyote. All this flora and fauna next to super-suburban San Fernando Valley!

This hike follows a fire road to Mission Point and explores the wild part of O'Melveny Park. Bring a city map. As you climb high into the Santa Susana Mountains, you can pick out numerous natural and manmade points of interest. Views of the Southland from 2,771-foot Mission Point are often quite good.

Directions to trailhead: Exit the San Diego Freeway (I-405) on Rinaldi and turn west. Turn right on Balboa Boulevard and in 3/4 mile turn left on Jolette. Follow Jolette a mile to Sesnon Boulevard. (A right turn on Sesnon will take you to the developed part of O'Melveny Park.) Turn left on Sesnon, then right on Neon Way. Park at the end of Neon Way. The fire road leading to Mission Point starts here.

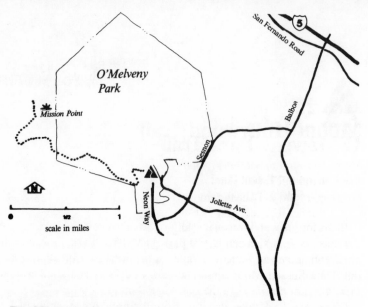

The Hike: The fire road leads you past a seasonal brook and begins rising high above the nearby residential area. It is moderate to strenuous climbing in the first mile. Evidence of the 1971 earthquake that damaged the nearby Golden State Freeway and Van Norman Dam is present in the form of fissures and slides. Seismically, the Santa Susana mountain range is one of California's most active areas.

As you make your ascent, you'll notice quite a difference in vegetation between north and south slopes. The canyon's dry north slopes are blanketed with sage and other coastal scrub. To the south, the hills are coverd with grasses punctuated with an occasional live oak or California walnut.

As you near the top, you'll pass a small stand of Aleppo pine, which is a tree native to Mediterranean countries. This pine is successful in Southern California's Mediterranean climate too.

Close to the top, a couple of washed-out dirt roads and bulldozer lines converge. (All roads lead toward Mission Point, but the "main road" is easier walking.) Navigate toward four sturdy oaks, which offer a nice picnic or rest stop.

Just past the oaks, a dirt road branches left and leads to wind-blown Mission Point. A 1932 U.S. Geological Survey marker is atop the point. Two seasonal cow ponds are located on the southwest slope. Below Mission Point to the northwest are oil fields and natural gas underground storage areas.

Enjoy the view of the Santa Susana Mountains—including nearby Oat Mountain, highest peak in the range. The San Gabriel Mountains, Santa Monica Mountains, Santa Clarita Valley, and downtown Los Angeles are also part of the 360-degree panorama. Return the way you came.

22
Mount Hollywood Trail

Merry-go-round to Mt. Hollywood
6 miles RT; 800′ gain
Merry-go-round to Planetarium
9 miles RT; 800′ gain

There are really two Griffith Parks. One is the familiar urban park with its landscaped shrubbery, rolling manicured lawns, observatory and zoo. The other is a wild park; this area forms the eastern terminus of the Santa Monica Mountains and offers the hiker a taste of the range's cliffs and crags.

You would expect *everyone* to climb the ridges on a clear day, but that's not the case; most visitors are content to remain with their barbecues and softball games in the flatlands below. Two-thirds of 4,107-acre Griffith Park, one of the largest municipal parks in the world, is mountain country. Fifty-three miles of trail give hikers access to the call of the mourning dove, the joys of our native chaparral and sycamore communities and a host of exotic plants imported from faraway lands. The route to Mt. Hollywood, highest peak in the park, offers delightful clear-day views of the Big Basin.

This is a nice outing in winter, when the rich green crown of the toyon bush is aglow with a mass of red berries. At a time when most members of the chaparral community have donned their gray apparel, the toyon—also known variously as Christmas berry or California holly—is the most festive of flora. It's believed that masses of this California native shrub growing on the hills above Holly-wood gave the community its name. The Christmas berry bushes alongside the trail to Mount Hollywood frame fine city views.

Directions to trailhead: Griffith Park, with its central location, is accessible by numerous freeways and surface streets. The trailhead to Mount Hollywood is best reached from the Los Feliz Boulevard entrance, turning onto Griffith Park Drive. Follow the signs to the merry-go-round and park in the lot off Griffith Park Drive. The trail begins across the Drive from the parking lot.

You can pick up a trail map at the Ranger Station in the park center, located on Griffith Park Drive. The park is open daily from 6 A.M. to 10 P.M..

Dante's View

The Hike: Three trails embark from the road opposite the parking lot. The lowermost trail leaves for Five Ponts, the hike's first destination, the middle path is the Fern Canyon Nature Trail, a pleasant and educational experience, but the uppermost trail, marked "Bridle Trail," is our departure point today for Mt. Hollywood. This trail almost immediately forks, and you'll veer left. The trail climbs high above lush Fern Canyon and offers fine views into the San Fernando Valley. Soon you'll arrive at Five Points, a place where five trails converge.

From Five Points, take the trail to your right (southwest). You'll cross Vista Del Valle Drive, continuing your ascent as the sparkling observatory comes into view. The trail grows more rugged as it nears Dante's View.

How did Dante's View get its name? Some hikers, climbing to Dante's during a Smog Alert, look out over a smokey metropolis, and conclude that the viewpoint must have been named for the fourteenth-century

Florentine Dante Alighieri and his vision of *The Inferno*. The more romantic, no doubt inspired by a clearer day, hypothesize that some jilted young man wandered about these hills to this promontory in a search similar to Dante's quest for his fair, lost Beatrice. Actually, Dante's View was named for twentieth-century artist-writer Dante Orgolini. Orgolini, an immigrant of Italian descent was a mural painter during the Depression. In his later years, after suffering the heartbreak of a divorce, he put his artistic energies into planting a two-acre retreat of pine, palm and pepper trees high on the south-facing slope of Mount Hollywood. A water fountain and picnic tables welcome the hiker.

From Dante's, continue the short distance to the top of Mount Hollywood. By now you've figured out that Mount Hollywood is *not* the mountain crowned by the historic Hollywood sign, where disappointed screen actresses leap to their deaths. You can, however, see the sign quite well as you near the summit of Mount Hollywood (elevation 1,625'). Wonderful sunsets can be observed from the peak and on clear days the entire basin is spread out before you from the San Gabriel Mountains to the Pacific Ocean. Sometimes Mounts San Gorgonio, Baldy and San Jacinto can be seen.

Option: Mt. Hollywood to Planetarium. This stretch is the most popular hike in the park and you have several routes to choose from. One way is to retrace your steps to Dante's View and continue along this path to the Observatory parking lot. Several other trails branch off from this one and also lead to the Observatory. One of them on the east slope descends steeply to the Bird Sanctuary. After visiting the birds, you may hike ½ mile up Vermont Canyon Road to the Observatory.

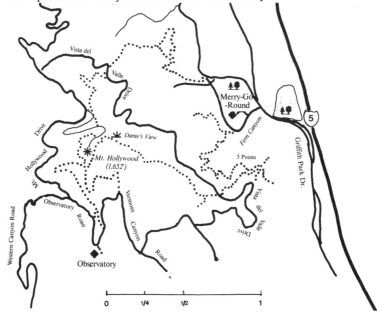

A 23

Hastain Loop Trail

Season: All year
Recommended map: park brochure
Topo: Beverly Hills

From Franklin Canyon Visitors Center
2½ miles RT; 400′ gain

It's appeared in your living room a hundred times, but you probably don't know its name.

The many faces of Franklin Canyon can be seen almost daily on television. Moviemakers have found the canyon to be a convincing substitute for a wide variety of locales ranging from High Sierra forest to jungle lagoon. "Bonanza," "Andy of Mayberry," and countless TV shows have used the canyon as a stage. Nowadays, the canyon is more popular than ever with filmmakers.

Despite frequent invasions of Hollywood stars and technicians, Franklin Canyon on most days offers hikers, bird watchers, and nature lovers, a tranquil retreat. The canyon is protected by Franklin Canyon Ranch, a national parkland preserve perched atop the hills above Beverly Hills.

Franklin Canyon and its visitors benefit enormously from interpretive efforts provided by WODOC, the William O. Douglas Outdoors Classroom, named for the Supreme Court justice and environmentalist whose eloquence on behalf of American's wildlands will long be remembered. WODOC offers a hike/nature experience for almost everyone. Docents each year conduct thousands of school children through the canyon. Leading through the canyon are special trails for senior citizens, the handicapped, and the blind. Aerobic walks, bird walks, and map and compass walks are offered.

The upper part of the canyon centers around Upper Franklin Reservoir, which was constructed in 1910, then improved and expanded in the 1930s. After the 1971 earthquake, the earthen dam was declared unsafe, so the reservoir is no longer part of Los Angeles' far-reaching waterworks system. Today the reservoir—now more lyrically referred to as Franklin Lake—is home to bass, catfish, ducks and coots. The 9-acre lake is a valuable stopover for migratory birds. More than 90 different species of birds have been sighted in the canyon.

Hastain Trail explores the lower part of Franklin Canyon. It ascends the eastern ridge of the canyon and offers fine views of both the San Fernando Valley and the westside of Los Angeles.

Directions to trailhead: *From the westside of Los Angeles:* reach the intersection of Beverly Drive and Coldwater Canyon Drive and follow Beverly Drive north for 1.2 miles. Turn right onto Franklin Canyon

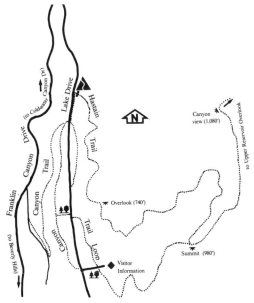

Drive and continue .8 miles to Lake Drive. Make a sharp right for 0.7 of a mile to Franklin Canyon Ranch House, WODOC headquarters. Park along Lake Drive.

From the San Fernando Valley: Exit the Ventura Freeway on Coldwater Canyon Drive and continue up to Mulholland Drive. Turn right and then immediately left onto Franklin Canyon Drive. After a mile, the pavement ends. Continue .8 of a mile on dirt road past Upper Franklin Reservoir to a junction and bear left onto Lake Drive. Parking is available on Lake Drive.

You can pick up a trail map at the Visitor Center/WODOC headquarters. For more information on WODOC programs call: (213) 858-3834.

The Hike: From the Visitor Center, you may walk up Lake Drive to the start of Hastain Trail or cross Lake Drive to the Canyon Trail, which winds beneath live oaks and sycamores and through a chaparral community on the west slope of the canyon. A rightward fork of Canyon Trail returns you to Lake Drive, which you'll follow a short distance to a fire road (Hastain Trail).

Hastain Trail ascends sage, bay laurel and chamise-covered slopes. Notice the outcroppings of Santa Monica slate, oldest rock in the Santa Monica Mountains. The slate is geological evidence that the mountains were once beneath the ocean.

A bit more than a mile's walk brings the hiker to an overlook, where there'a good view of Beverly Hills and the Wilshire corridor. (The fire road continues climbing to good views of Upper Franklin Canyon and the San Fernando Valley.) Turn right onto the distinct trail that descends to the nature center/WODOC headquarters. Walk back up Lake Road to your car.

▲ 24
Elysian Park Trail

Douglas St. to North Broadway
5 miles one way; 200′ loss.

Elysian Park, close to downtown L.A., is a 575 acre retreat from urban angst. Its hilly acreage is an undeveloped remnant of the original 17,172-acre Spanish land grant from which Pueblo de Los Angeles grew. Although it's near the central city, the park is surprisingly uncrowded. It has a remote feeling and access is a bit confusing. Elysian Park appears to be everywhere and nowhere at the same time. You can see the park from the Golden State (I-5) and Pasadena Freeways (110) and when arriving at Dodger Stadium, so it appears to be everywhere. But it seems like the middle of nowhere when you try to explore it on foot.

More than ten miles of hiking trails lead through some surprisingly wild terrain. Although the park has been cut by many roads, it's possible to follow trails that will immerse you in greenery and leave the roar of traffic far behind. This particular hike takes you through shady glens, over grass carpets and past rare palms. You can picnic under imported rubber trees or native oaks and enjoy the views of the Big Basin offered by the park's promontories.

Directions to trailhead: The park can be entered from either end of this hike, but for route-finding purposes, it's best to enter on Douglas Street. From Sunset Boulevard, east of Glendale Boulevard, turn north on Douglas Street. There's street parking near the trailhead. The unmarked trail begins to your left near an apartment building.

The North Broadway trailhead is located one block north of Cassanova St. off Elysian Park Drive. Buses run so often toward both trailheads that an urban mountaineer rarely has to wait more than a few minutes.

The Hike: From Douglas Street, follow the unmarked, unsigned trail on your left past an apartment building. The first ½ mile skirts some hillside houses and crosses a couple of roads. Soon the trail loses its tentative look, widens, and begins to climb. Fine views of the park, Dodger Stadium and downtown appear over your right shoulder.

The cacophony of urban life is gradually overwhelmed by bird music. Mockingbirds, jays, red-tailed hawks, bush tits, Audubon's warblers, red-shafted flickers and house finches make their nests in Elysian Park.

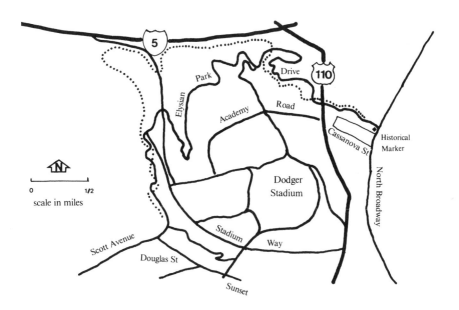

The great wealth of trees here attracts many birds. In 1940 the California Audubon Society dedicated Elysian Park as a bird sanctuary.

Periodically, you'll emerge from the greenery and look down at the metropolis in miniature: freightyards, Glendale and the Golden State Freeway. But you're much closer to the sky than the freeway and it's easy to imagine you're in a private plane over the heart of the city.

The trail descends a grassy slope through a zany mixture of trees that you would only find in Southern California—eucalyptus, pine and palm! It then cuts through a pleasant picnic area to Stadium Drive. The trail resumes on the other side of the Drive and contours around a brushy slope. The wide path narrows for about a hundred yards and plunges through a blackberry thicket. The berries are a summer treat if you're willing to brave the brambles and poison oak. Emerging the thicket you soon cross Elysian Park Drive and stroll through a pungent eucalyptus grove. You pass a reservoir and eventually emerge on Park Row Drive. Go left and follow the road ¾ mile to the North Broadway entrance of the park, where there's a historic marker. Here on August 2, 1769, Don Gaspar de Portolá and Padre Juan Crespi, leading the first overland exploration of California, pitched camp on the site of the future city.

25

Season: All year
Topo: Baldwin Park,
El Monte

Puente Hills Skyline Trail

7th Ave to Overlook
    5 miles RT; 800′ gain
7th Ave to Rio Hondo College
    5 miles one way; 800′ gain
7th Ave to Otterbein Park
    12 miles one way; 1000′ gain

The Puente Hills divide the Los Angeles Basin into a northern one-third and a southern two-thirds. North is the San Gabriel Valley, an alluvium filled basin. South of the hills is a coastal plain, a flatland tilted gently toward the Pacific. The Whittier Fault, which pushes the hills around a bit, extends along the south base of the range and ends west of Whittier Narrows.

Puente Hills Skyline Trail, under the jurisdiction of the Los Angeles County Parks Department, is a 28-mile riding and hiking trail that rambles through the canyons and over the mustard-covered crests of the hills. The trail extends from Whittier Narrows Regional Park to Angeles National Forest via Otterbein and Bonelli Park.

This day hike offers both short and lengthy samples of the Skyline Trail. All the options offer fine clear day views of the metropolis from scenic overlooks.

Bring plenty of water; none is available along the described sections of Skyline Trail.

Directions to trailhead: Exit the Pomona Freeway (60) on 7th Ave. and drive four blocks south to its end at Orange Avenue. Park near the traffic barrier. (To reach Otterbein County Park, end point for one of this day hike's options, exit the Pomona Freeway on Azusa Avenue. Proceed south and turn left on Colima, then right into the park.)

The Hike: Walk up 7th Avenue, which is a bulldozed dirt road beyond the traffic barrier. Pass some private horse corrals and ascend briefly on a paved road to a San Gabriel Water Company facility. Here a dirt trail picks up and you begin ascending a mile through a small forest of thistle and mustard. You reach a long plateau and are treated to views of the San Gabriel Valley. Atop the plateau, you intersect the Puente Hills Skyline Trail.

Bear right on the Puente Hills Skyline Trail, following a fence along the plateau's perimeter. The land belongs to Rose Hills Memorial Park,

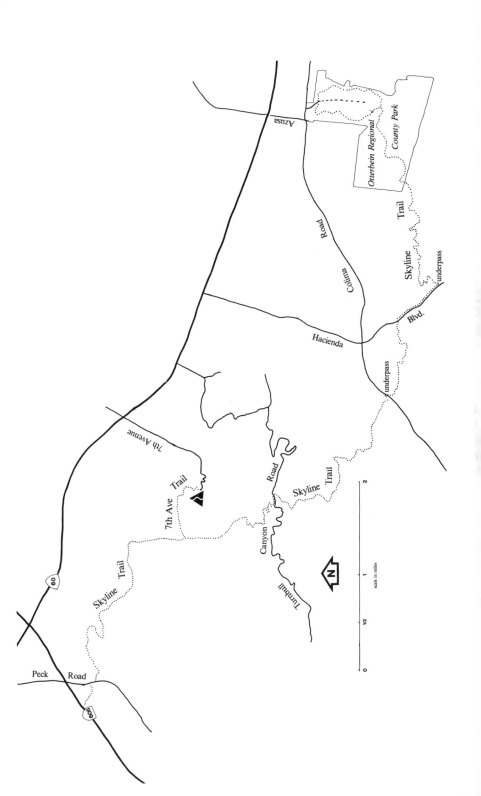

but the county has easements for its trail system. The cemetery is just a bone's throw away on the other side of the hill.

The wild mustard atop the plateau is prolific. In *Ramona*, Helen Hunt Jackson rhapsodized about the miles of gold mesh that once blanketed Southern California, calling it a "golden snowstorm."

After hiking the length of the mustard smothered plateau, you'll reach an unmarked junction. Bear left here and ascend the hill. Up top, there are some picnic tables. From the overlook, where a NIKE facility once stood, you can see Whittier to the south, San Gabriel Valley to the north. It's an urban view—sometimes you can even see dump trucks chugging up to Puente Hills Landfill. On clear winter days, you'll spot the Pacific and Catalina on one side and snow-capped Mount Baldy and the San Gabriel Mountains on the other.

Return the same way or continue on to Rio Hondo College.

Option: To Rio Hondo College. From the overlook, the trail stays briefly with a crumbling road, passes another picnic area, then veers off from the road at an unsigned junction. You look down at the gardens of Rose Hills Memorial Park. Noisome civilization grows more evident as you descend toward Workman Mill Road. The trail leads to North Drive at Rio Hondo College.

Option: To Otterbein Park. At the first junction, bear left on the Skyline Trail. A thicket of prickly pear cactus lines the trail. A right turn at an unmarked junction keeps you on the trail, which descends through sage and monkeyflowers into Turnbull Canyon. After a short ascent the trail reaches and crosses Turnbull Canyon Road. More climbing brings you to an overlook for fine views of downtown Los Angeles, the west side of the city, and the Pacific.

The trail angles toward the suburb of Hacienda Heights, and actually passes right behind some homes (whose pools look inviting on a hot day), before dropping down to Colima Road. Follow the pedestrian/equestrian underpass underneath Colima and ascend past soon-to-be-developed "Equestrian Estates." The trail then descends to Hacienda Boulevard, where the hiker makes use of another pedestrian/equestrian underpass.

The Skyline Trail is anything but for the next ½ mile as it turns southeast and follows a culvert alongside Hacienda Boulevard. This trail ends at Leucadia Road, where the hiker joins a fire road and begins ascending above La Habra Heights. Stay right on the fire road at a junction and pass a locked gate. The trail ascends through a eucalyptus grove and passes another of the many microwave towers in the Puente Hills. Civilization, in the form of Puente Hills Mall and the Pomona Freeway, appears close-in to the north. The trail descends a last mile to the wide lawns and picnic areas of Otterbein Park.

26
Hills-for-People Trail

Ranch Road to McDermont Spring
4 miles RT: 400' gain.
Ranch Road to Carbon Canyon Regional Park
7½ miles one way; 800' loss from McDermont Spring.

Chino Hills State Park, located in Orange, San Bernardino and Riverside Counties, preserves some much needed "breathing room" in this fast-growing area. Nearly three million people live within sight of the Chino Hills and over nine million people live within a 40-mile radius of the park!

The park is the state's most expensive ever, with over $47 million spent by the time it opened for full time use in 1986. Right now, Chino Hills is a park-in-the-making. Few signs or facilities have been installed. Development plans call for 35 miles of hiking trails and 62 miles of riding trails.

The 10,000-acre park is located near the northern end what geologists call the Peninsular Ranges Geomorphic Province. The Chino Hills are part of the group of hills that include the Puente Hills (See Hike #25) to the northwest. These hills form a roughly triangular area of approximately 35 square miles of valleys, canyons, hills, and steep slopes.

Extensive grasslands blanket the slopes. The hills are covered with wild oats, rye, black mustard and wild radish. On south-facing slopes is the soft-leaved shrub community, dominated by aromatic herbs, including California sagebrush, white sage, purple sage and black sage.

High temperatures, often combined with heavy smog, suggest that a summer visit can be something of an ordeal. The park is much more pleasurable in the cooler months, and especially delightful in spring.

Hills-for-People Trail was named for the conservation group that was instrumental in establishing Chino Hills State Park. The trail follows a creek to the head of Telegraph Canyon. The creek is lined with oak, sycamore and the somewhat rare California black walnut.

Currently the park trail system for the most part is a complicated system of old dirt ranch roads, so hikers are advised to stop at the ranger station for a good look at the large topographic map that locates trails.

Directions to trailhead: Despite its location so close to the metropolis, Chino Hills State Park can be a bit tricky to find. The park is located east of Highway 71 between the Riverside Freeway (91) and the Pomona Freeway (60). Traveling south on 71 and 60, visitors should turn right on Los Serranos Road and then make a quick left onto Pomona-Rincon Road. (Visitors heading north on 71 from 91 will spot, before reaching Los Serranos Road, a left turn lane leading directly to Pomona-Rincon Road.) A half mile of travel along Pomona-Rincon Road brings you to a brickyard with a mailbox marked "15838 Rolling M Ranch." Take the dirt road next to the brickyard for 2 miles to the park entrance. Continue on the main park road and follow signs to the park office and ranger station. The road forks just before the ranger station. To the right is the ranger station and trailer housing the temporary Visitors Center. Bear left ½-mile on the dirt road to a vehicle barrier and trailhead parking. The signed trailhead is located a short distance past the vehicle barrier on the right of the road.

The park is open daily 9 A.M. to 5 P.M.

The Hike: Hills-for-People Trail descends to a small creek and follows the creek up canyon. Shading the trail—and shielding the hiker from a view of the many electrical transmission lines that cross the park—are oaks, sycamores and walnuts. Of particular interest is the walnut, a small tree, 15-30 feet tall. Often the tree has several dark brown trunks, which gives it a brushy appearance. This native tree's sturdy rootstock has aided commercial walnut production in the state.

The trail, which can be quite slippery and muddy after a rain, passes a small (seasonal) waterfall. The slopes just above the creekbed are carpeted with lush grasses and miners lettuce.

Along the trail is found evidence of the park's ranching heritage, including lengths of barbed wire fence and old cattle troughs. Sometimes

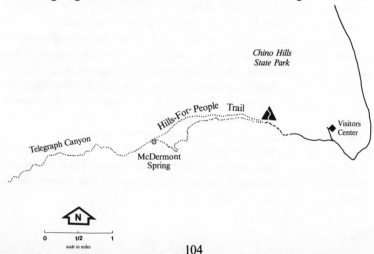

Chino Hills
State Park

Hills-For-People Trail

Visitors
Center

Telegraph Canyon

McDermont
Spring

N

0   1/2   1
scale in miles

a trespassing cow will wander down the trail from a nearby ranch. For more than a century this land was used exclusively for cattle ranching.

Near its end, the trail ascends out of the creekbed to the head of Telegraph Canyon and intersects a dirt road. McDermont Spring is just down the road. One unique aspect of the state park is the livestock ponds, which were constructed during the area's ranching era. Some of these ponds still exist, and hold water year-round during most years. McDermont Spring—along with Windmill and Panorama ponds— provide water for wildlife, and habitat for aquatic plant life.

Return the same way or loop back to the trailhead on the dirt road.

Option: To Carbon Canyon Regional Park. Telegraph Canyon Trail (a dirt park road closed to public vehicular traffic) stays close to the canyon bottom and its creek. It's a gentle descent under the shade of oak and walnut trees. The walnuts are particularly numerous along the first mile of travel and the hiker not inclined to hike the length of Telegraph Canyon might consider exploring this stretch before returning to the trailhead.

The route passes an old windmill and farther down the canyon, remains of a shepherd's camp. Near the bottom of the canyon the walnuts thin out. A lemon grove, owned by the state park but leased to a farmer, is at a point where the dirt road intersects Carbon Canyon Road. Walk along the broad shoulder of the latter road ½-mile to Carbon Canyon Regional Park.

Limber pine atop Mt. Baden-Powell

Chapter 6

SAN GABRIEL MOUNTAINS

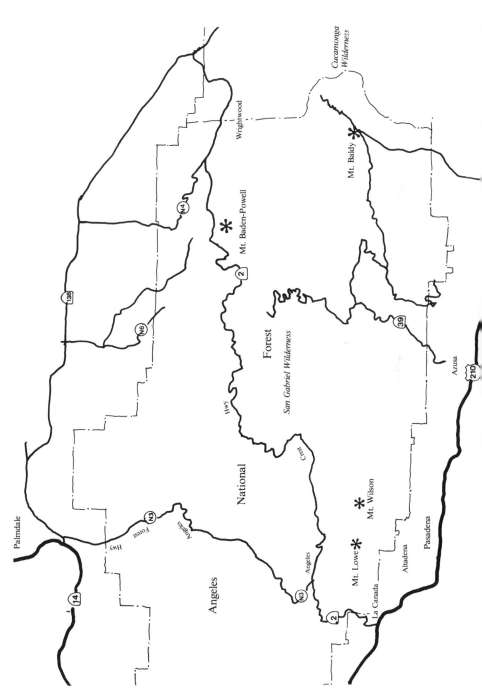

San Gabriel Mountains

THE SAN GABRIEL MOUNTAINS bless L.A. by keeping out desert winds and curse it by keeping in the smog. Most of the range is included in the 700,000 acres of the Angeles National Forest, the most heavily used national forest in the U.S. The San Gabriels twist atop the San Andreas Fault. Geologists claim these mountians are the most fractured and shattered in California. The range consists of crystaline, metamorphic and granitic blocks, sixty miles long and twenty miles wide extending from Soledad Pass to Cajon Pass. The Los Padres mountain ranges are to the west and the San Bernardino range is to the east. The San Gabriels vary extensively in temperature. Along the northern rim at the edge of the Antelope Valley, the mountains seem an extension of the Mojave Desert. However, some alpine areas with peaks near 10,000 feet know snow from one winter to the next.

John Muir found it tough going in the San Gabriels: "The slopes are exceptionally steep and insecure to the foot and they are covered with horny bushes from five to ten feet high." Muir was referring to the dominant plant community of the San Gabriels—the chaparral—that elfin forest of burrs and brambles which covers much of the sun drenched lower slopes of the mountains. Higher elevations bring easier traveling and a wealth of taller trees: mountain laurel, oaks, pines, cedar. The arroyos are another special feature of the San Gabriels. These boulder strewn washes seem dry and lifeless in the bottomland; however, as the hiker follows their course upward, he'll soon find the arroyo's banks are verdant and graceful with a tangle of ferns, lilies and wildflowers.

As early as the 1880s, it became obvious to Southern Californians the mountains should be protected from the destruction of indiscriminate logging and other ventures. In 1892, the San Gabriel Timberland Reserve was proclaimed by President Harrison. It was the first forest reserve in California and the second in the U.S. The first was Yellowstone.

One of the first trail construction projects in the San Gabriels began in 1864 when Benjamin Wilson revamped an old Indian path to his timbering venture on the mountain that now bears his name. Later, other Indian trails were improved. William Sturtevant, who came to California from Colorado in the early 1880s and became a premier packhorseman and trail guide, linked and improved several Indian trails and made it possible to cross the mountains from west to east. Until Sturtevant figured out a route, most people did not know that a network of Indian trails reached from the desert to the L.A. basin. More trails were built around the turn of the century when Southern California's "Great Hiking Era" began. With Rough Rider Teddy Roosevelt urging Americans to lead "the strenuous life," Southlanders challenged the nearby San Gabriels. Mountain farmers and ranchers, fighting against the odds of fire, flood and distance to market began capitalizing on the prevailing interest in the great outdoors. As more and more hikers headed into the backcountry, the settlers began to offer food and accommodations. Soon every major canyon on the south side of the mountains had its resort or trail camp and many had several. Most resorts were not big business with the exception of the Mount Wilson and Echo Mountain complexes which featured luxury hotels and observatories. The majority were run by rugged entrepreneurs who offered rustic accommodations, hearty meals, and good fellowship. Visitors thronged to the resorts on weekends and holidays. Many stayed all summer.

The Depression brought about a golden age of public campground construction. These camps, tied to an ever increasing network of highways, eventually doomed the private resorts and trail camps. Angeles Crest Highway, built between 1929 and 1956 by a motley assortment of depression laborers, prison road gangs and assorted construction crews, linked many of the best high mountain picnic and camping areas.

Today, only a few stone foundations and scattered resort ruins remind the hiker of the "Great Hiking and Resort Era." Though the modern mountaineer will not be greeted with tea, lemonade, or something stronger, or a hearty welcome from a trail camp proprietor, the mountains still beckon. That bygone hiking era left us a superb network of trails, over 500 miles of paths linking all major peaks, camps and streams. Rising above the smog and din of the Big Basin, the San Gabriels still delight. When we manage to pry the fingers of our more mechanized citizens off their steering wheels and send them tramping through the San Gabriels, a second great hiking era may begin.

27

Gabrielino National Recreation Trail

Switzer Picnic Area to Switzer Falls
    4 miles RT; 600′ loss.
Switzer Picnic Area to Bear Canyon
    8 miles RT; 1000′ gain.
Switzer Picnic Area to Oakwilde
    9 miles RT; 1400′ loss.

The Arroyo Seco is undoubtedly the best known canyon in Southern California. It's the site of the Rose Bowl and has the dubious distinction of hosting California's first freeway, the Pasadena. But the ten miles of civilized urban canyon bear little resemblance to the ten miles of rugged mountain arroyo which begins near the north slope of Mount Wilson. A quiet stream lined with colonnades of alder, live oak and mountain lilac clinging to the narrow sides of the gorge, cascades over boulders of big gray granite—these are some of the joys of the wild arroyo that will greet you.

Perry Switzer, a carpenter who regained his health in the invigorating San Gabriels, built a trail up the Arroyo Seco and decided to build a trail resort. He put up some rough log cabins, despite arguments that "no one would want to pay for a bed up among the grizzlies, mountain lions and bobcats." He earned the nickname "Commodore" because of his skill in navigating his burro squadron as they forded the Arroyo Seco. His hospitality made Switzer's the most popular trail camp in the San Gabriels.

The resort passed into the hands of Lloyd Austin, who added a tennis court, chapel, and dance floor. A sign across from the resort greeted visitors: LEAVE YOUR CARS AND ANIMALS THIS SIDE OF THE STREAM. Switzer-land was popular with hikers well into the 1930s, until the Angeles Crest Highway rendered the peaceful camp "obsolete."

During the "Great Hiking Era," a hiker could venture up the Arroyo Seco and within an hour lose all signs of civilization. Amazingly, you still can today. This hike takes you past the site of Switzer's retreat and visits

Switzer's Chapel (1924-1959)

Switzer Falls. Further exploration of the Arroyo Seco country is possible by taking one of the optional trails to Oakwilde and Bear Canyon.

Directions to trailhead: Take Angeles Crest Highway (2) north from La Canada for 10 miles. A half mile past the junction of Angeles Crest and Angeles Forest Highways, turn right at entrance to Switzer Picnic Area and continue ¼ mile to parking area. Trail begins across the bridge.

The Hike: Cross the bridge and follow the trail into the canyon. The pathway meanders with the stream under oak, alder and spruce. You'll cross and re-cross the stream several times and do some easy boulder-hopping. Plan to get wet. In some places, stream crossing is quite difficult in spring. In a mile, you'll reach Commodore Switzer Trail Camp. Perched on a bench just above the falls, it's an inviting place with tables for a picnic. The creek trail below the camp dead-ends above the falls.

From the camp, cross the stream and follow the trail on the west slope. You'll soon get a nice view of the falls. A signed junction soon appears. To the right (southwest) is the main trail down to Oakwilde and Pasadena. Bear left here and hike down into the gorge of the Arroyo Seco below the falls. When you reach the creek, turn upstream ¼ mile to the falls. Don't try to climb the falls; it's very dangerous.

Return the same way.

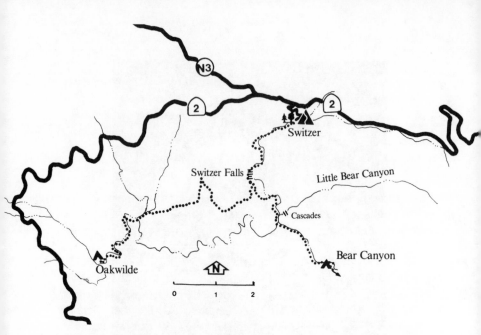

Option: To Bear Canyon Trail Camp. Continue down the Arroyo gorge on a mediocre trail ¾ mile to its junction with Bear Canyon. Follow the trail east up Bear Canyon, crossing and re-crossing the creek. Along the way are many nice swimming pools. In spring the water is cold from snowmelt and little sun reaches the canyon floor. The trail, shaded by big cone spruce, closely parallels the creek. When you look at an Angeles Forest map, you'll discover that Bear Canyon is surrounded on all sides by highways, dams, and development. The canyon has no right to be so quiet, so pristine. But it is. As you boulderhop from bank to bank, the only sound you'll hear is that of water cascading over granite into clear pools. Give thanks that there is at least one spot in the front range of the San Gabriels that is untouched wilderness and continue to Bear Canyon Trail Camp, 2 miles up the canyon.

Option: To Oakwilde. From the signed junction above Commodore Switzer Trail Camp, continue right on the Gabrielino National Recreation Trail. The trail leaves the main Arroyo Seco canyon, crosses a chaparral ridge, then drops down into Long Canyon. It then descends to Arroyo Seco creek bottom and follows the creek an easy mile to Oakwilde Trail Camp. In this canyon yuccas and a variety of wildflowers bloom in season.

Oak Wylde, as it was caled during the "Great Hiking Era," was a jump-off place for trips further up the Arroyo Seco. Pack burro trains connected Oak Wylde with the stage station in Pasadena. The trail camp is located among the crumbling stone foundation of a resort. Alder and oak shade a pleasant campground and picnic area.

Return the same way.

Season: All year
Recommended map: Angeles
National Forest
Topo: Pasadena, Mt. Wilson

 28

Mount Lowe Railway Trail

Sunset Ridge to Inspiration Point
7 miles RT; 1100′ gain.
Sidetrip: Echo Mt.
2 miles RT.

Fireplace in Alpine Tavern

Professor Thaddeus Lowe, civil war balloonist, man of fame and fortune, was the quintessential California dreamer. His dream was to build a railway into, and resort complex atop, the San Gabriel Mountains high above Pasadena. In the 1890s, his dream became a reality. During the height of its popularity, millions took Professor Lowe's "Railway to the Clouds" to fine hotels and spectacular views of Southern California.

From Pasadena, visitors rode a trolley up Rubio Canyon, where there was a pavillion and hotel. After taking refreshments, they boarded the "airships" of the great cable incline, which carried them 3,000 feet (gaining 1,300 feet) straight up to the Echo Mountain Resort Area. "Breathtaking" and "hair-raising" were the most common descriptions of this thrilling ride. Atop Echo Mountain was the White City, with a hotel, observatory, and a magnificent searchlight purchased from the Chicago World's Fair. When the searchlight swept the mountaintop, the white buildings of the resort were visible from all over Los Angeles. From Echo Mountain, tourists could board a trolley and ride another few miles to Mount Lowe Tavern at the end of the line.

This historic hike follows the old railway bed, visits the ruins of the White City and Mount Lowe Tavern, and concludes with some fine views of Los Angeles from Inspiration Point. The old railway bed with its gentle 7% grade makes easy walking.

Along the trail, the Forest Service has established ten historic markers keyed to a pamphlet explaining Mount Lowe's colorful past. You can pick up the free 24-page pamphlet, "Self-Guided Hiking Tour of Historic Mount Lowe," from Angeles National Forest Service headquarters in Arcadia. You can also receive a copy of the pamphlet by mail. Direct your request to: Public Affairs, Angeles National Forest, 701 N. Santa Anita Avenue, Arcadia, CA 91006.

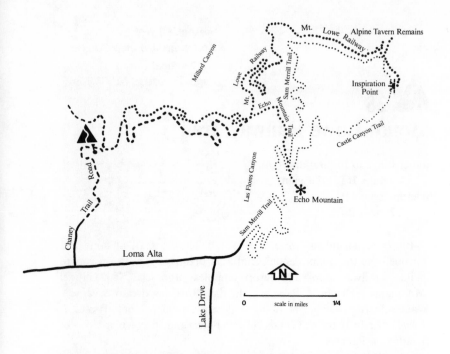

Directions to trailhead: Exit the Foothill Freeway, Highway 210, at Lake Avenue and follow it north to its end. Turn left on Loma Alta Drive. Go 1 mile to Chaney Trail Road and turn right. At a "Y" take the right fork to the Sunset Ridge parking area. The trailhead is located at the locked gate, which bars vehicles from Sunset Ridge Fire Road.

The Hike: The trail begins just past the locked gate. Follow the paved Sunset Ridge Fire Road. (You may follow the fire road 2 miles to the junction with the Echo Mountain Trail, but a more attractive alternative is described below).

Follow the road 1/4 mile to the signed Sunset Ridge Trail on your left. Join this trail, which for the most part parallels the fire road, and leads into peaceful Millard Canyon. Near the canyon bottom, the trail forks at a signed junction. Bear right and ascend back up to Sunset Ridge Fire Road. Follow the fire road about 75 yards and on your right you'll spot the signed junction with Echo Mountain Trail.

Sidetrip: To Echo Mountain Bear right on Echo Mountain Trail, which leads 1/2 mile over the old railway bed to Echo Mountain. Echo Mountain takes its name from an echo that bounces around the semicircle of mountain walls. I've never managed to get very good feedback; perhaps even echoes fade with time.

Ruins of the great cable railway

On Echo Mountain are the foundations of Echo Mountain House and the chalet. The most prominent ruin is the large iron bull wheel that pulled the cars up the steep incline from Rubio Canyon. A fire swept Echo Mountain in 1900, leveling all of the White City except the observatory. Picnic tables suggest a lunch stop amongst the ruins. Leave behind the ruins of the White City, return to Sunset Ridge Fire Road and bear right.

The paved road soon becomes dirt and an interpretive sign at "Cape of Good Hope" lets you know you've joined the Mt. Lowe Railway tour. Continue along the railway bed, passing the tourist attractions that impressed an earlier generation of travelers: Granite Gate, Horseshoe Curve, and the site of the Great Circular Bridge. Near the top, you'll come to the site of Mount Lowe Tavern, which burned in 1936. Almost all signs of the tavern are gone, but this peaceful spot under oaks and big cone spruce still extends its hospitality. On the old tavern site is Mount Lowe Trail Camp, which welcomes day hikers with its shade, water, restrooms and picnic tables.

Before heading down, follow the fire road east and then south for 1/2 mile to Inspiration Point. Where the fire road makes a hairpin left to Mount Wilson, go right. At Inspiration Point you can gaze through several telescope-like sighting tubes aimed at Santa Monica, Hollywood and the Rose Bowl. After you've found a sight that inspires you, return the same way.

29

Mt. Wilson Toll Road

Altadena to Henninger Flats
6 miles RT; 1400′ elevation gain

Consider the conifers.

A wind-bowed limber pine clinging to a rocky summit. A sweet-smelling grove of incense cedar. The deep shade and primeval gloom of a big cone spruce forest.

Where do these trees come from?

I know, I know. "... only God can make a tree."

Keep your Joyce Kilmer. Hold the metaphysical questions. Our inquiry here is limited to what happens in the aftermath of a fire or flood, when great numbers of trees lie dead or dying. Fortunately, for California's cone-bearing tree population—and tree lovers—there is a place where trees, more than 120,000 a year, are grown to replace those lost to the capriciousness of nature and the carelessness of man. The place is Henninger Flats, home of the Los Angeles County Experimental Nursery.

Perched halfway between Altadena and Mount Wilson, Henninger Flats is the site of southern California's finest tree plantation. The holiday season, a time when many of us are trimming the Christmas conifer (often a Douglas fir), is an ideal time to trek up to Henninger Flats. On the flats you'll be able to view trees in all shapes and sizes, from seedlings to mature stands. A museum with reforestation exhibits, a nature trail, and the Los Angeles County foresters on duty will help you understand where trees come from.

The Flats have a colorful history. After careers as a gold miner, Indian fighter, and first Sheriff of Santa Clara County, Captain William Henninger came to Los Angeles to retire in the early 1880s. While doing a little prospecting, Henninger discovered the little mesa that one day would bear his name. He constructed a trail over which he could lead his burros.

Atop the flats he built a cabin, planted fruit trees, raised hay and corn. His solitude ended in 1890 when the Mount Wilson Toll Road was constructed for the purpose of carrying the great telescope up to the new observatory. Captain Henninger's Flats soon became a water and rest stop for the hikers, riders and fishermen who trooped into the mountains.

After Henninger's death in 1895, the flats were used by the U.S. Forest Service as a tree nursery. Foresters emphasized the nurturing of fire- and drought-resistant varieties of conifers. Many thousands of seedlings were transplanted to fire and flood-ravaged slopes all over the Southland. Since 1928 Los Angeles County foresters have continued the good work at Henninger Flats.

A moderate outing of just under six miles roundtrip, on good fire road, the trail up to Henninger Flats is suitable for the whole family. The Flats offer a large picnic area and fine clear day city views.

Directions to trailhead: From the Foothill Freeway (I-210) in Pasadena, exit on Lake Avenue. Turn north on Lake and continue to Altadena Drive. Make a right on Altadena, continue about ten blocks, and look closely to your left. Turn left on Pinecrest Drive and wind a few blocks through a residential area to the trailhead. (If you speed by Pinecrest, don't despair; make a left off of Altadena onto Crescent Drive, which quickly leads you to Pinecrest.) The trailhead is found in the 2200 block of Pinecrest. You'll spot a locked gate across the fire road that leads down into Eaton Canyon.

The Hike: Proceed down the fire road to the bottom of Eaton Canyon. After crossing a bridge, the road begins a series of switchbacks up chaparral covered slopes. Occasional painted pipes (i.e., 1 up, 2 down) mark your progress.

The Pasadena and Mt. Wilson Toll Road Company in 1891 fashioned a trail to the summit of Mt. Wilson. Fees were 50 cents per rider, 25 cents per hiker. A 12-foot wide road followed two decades later. Long time Southland residents might recall a somewhat hair-raising Sunday drive up the steep grade. During the 1920s, the road was the scene of an annual auto race, similar to the Pikes Peak hillclimb. In 1936 the Angeles Crest Highway opened and rendered the toll road obsolete. For the last half century the Mt. Wilson Toll Road has been closed to public traffic and has been maintained as a fire road.

Henninger Flats welcomes the hiker with water, shade, and two campgrounds where you may enjoy a lunch stop. Growing on the flats are some of the more common cone-bearing trees of California mountains including knobcone, Coulter, sugar, digger and Jeffrey pines, as well as such exotics as Japanese black pine and Himalayan white pine.

Holiday and weekend visitor center hours are 8 A.M. to 10 P.M.

After your tree tour, return the same way.

Ultra-energetic hikers will continue up the old toll road to Mount Wilson; the journey from Altadena to the summit is 9 miles one way with an elevation gain of 4,500 feet.

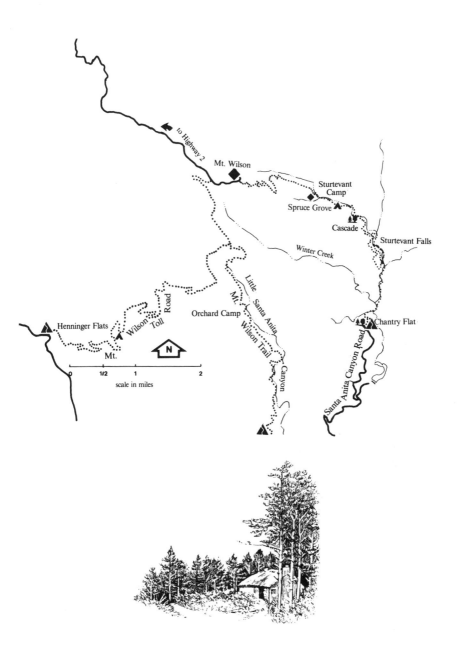

The San Gabriels would be as high as the Himalayas and Hollywood a seaside Nepal if the mountains were not being worn down as fast as they grow.

—JEROME WYCKOFF

30

Gabrielino Trail

Chantry Flat to Sturtevant Falls
3 ½ miles RT; 500′ gain
Chantry Flat to Spruce Grove Camp
8 miles RT; 1400′ gain
Chantry Flat to Mt. Wilson
8 miles one way; 4000′ gain

Cascades, a waterfall and giant woodwardia ferns are a few of the many delights of historic Big Santa Anita Canyon. The bucolic canyon has been popular with Southern California hikers for nearly a hundred years.

William Sturtevant, known to his friends as "Sturde," pioneered many miles of San Gabriel Mountain trails. He traveled from Colorado to California in the early 1880s with forty burros. A packer *par excellence* he soon found his services to be in great demand in the San Gabriels.

Sturtevant hewed out a trail over the ridge from Winter Creek to the top of the canyon and in 1898 opened Sturtevant Camp. The rustic resort consisted of a dining hall, tents, and a store and was a popular trail resort well into the 1930s.

In Santa Anita Canyon today some eighty-odd cabins are serviced by a burro train from Chantry Flats, named after another early packer, Charlie Chantry. One of the more colorful sights in the local mountains— and a look backward into a bygone era—is a glimpse at the pack animals plodding up the trail to Sturtevant Camp, now a Methodist Church retreat.

Sturtevant's trail is now a section of the 28-mile-long Gabrielino National Recreation Trail, named after the local Native American tribe. The trail to Sturtevant Falls is very popular on weekends-but not as popular as it was on Fourth of July weekend 1919 when 5,000 people tramped into the canyon and signed the trail register! The ambitious hiker may continue past the falls to Spruce Grove Camp and even as far as the top of Mount Wilson.

Sturtevant Falls

Directions to trailhead: From the Foothill Freeway (I-210) in Arcadia, exit on Santa Anita and proceed 6 miles north to Chantry Flat. Park in the large lot. The signed trailhead is located across the road from the parking lot.

The Hike: Descend on the paved fire road, part of the Gabrielino Trail, into Big Santa Anita Canyon. At the bottom of the canyon you'll cross a footbridge near the confluence of Big Santa Anita and Winter Creeks. Here a small sign commemorates Roberts Camp, a resort camp founded in 1912. Owner Otto Lynn Roberts and other canyon boosters really "sold" the charms of the canyon to Southern Californians in need of a quiet weekend. As you follow the path up canyon along the oak and alder-shaded creek, you'll soon determine that the canyon "sells" itself.

The only blemish on the pristine scene is a series of check dams constructed of giant cement "Lincoln logs" by the Los Angeles County Flood Control District and the Forest Service in the early 1960s. In their

121

zeal to tame Big Santa Anita Creek, engineers apparently forgot that fast-moving water is *supposed to* erode canyon bottoms; floods are what originally sculpted this beautiful canyon. Today, thanks to the check dams, the creek flows in well organized fashion, lingering in tranquil pools, then spilling over the dams in fifteen foot cascades. Over the last quarter century, moss, ferns, alders and other creekside flora have softened the appearance of the dams and they now fit much better into the lovely surroundings.

The trail passes some private cabins and reaches a three-way trail junction. To reach Sturtevant Falls, continue straight ahead. You'll cross Big Santa Anita Creek, then re-cross where the creek veers leftward. Pick your way along the boulder-strewn creek bank a final hundred yards to the falls. The falls drops in a silver stream fifty feet to a natural rock bowl. (Caution: Climbing the wet rocks near the falls can be extremely hazardous to your health. Stay off.)

Return the same way and enjoy a picnic back up at the Forest Service picnic area at Chantry Flat or return to the trail junction and hike onward and upward to Spruce Grove Trail Camp.

Option: To Spruce Grove Camp. Two signed trails lead toward Spruce Grove. The leftward one zig-zags high up the canyon wall while the other passes above the falls. The left trail is easier hiking while the right trail heads through the heart of the canyon and is prettier. Either trail is good walking and they rejoin in a mile.

After the trails rejoin, you'll continue along the spruce-shaded path to Cascade Picnic Area. You can call it a day here or ascend another mile to Spruce Grove Trail Camp. Both locales have plenty of tables and shade.

Option: To Mt. Wilson. Still feeling frisky? Hikers in top condition may wish to charge up the trail to Mount Wilson. Continue on the trail up canyon a short distance, cross the creek and you'll find a trail junction. A left brings you to historic Sturtevant Camp, now owned by the Methodist Church. The trail to Mount Wilson soon departs Big Santa Anita Canyon and travels many a switchback through thick forest to Mt. Wilson Skyline Park. The strenuous hike from Chantry Flat to Mt. Wilson is an 8 mile (one way) journey, with a 4,000 foot gain in elevation.

31

Mount Wilson Trail

Sierra Madre to Orchard Camp
9 miles RT; 2000' gain.
Sierra Madre to Mount Wilson
15 miles RT; 4500' gain.

The Mount Wilson Trail up Little Santa Anita Canyon is the oldest white man's trail into the San Gabriels. It was built in 1864 by Benjamin Wilson, who overhauled a Gabrielino Indian path in order to log the stands of incense cedar and sugar pine on the mountain that now bears his name. The first telescope was carried up this trail to Mount Wilson in 1904. During the "Great Hiking Era," thousands of hikers rode the Red Cars to Sierra Madre, disembarked, and hiked up this path to the popular trail resort at Orchard Camp. Forty thousand hikers and horseback riders passed over the trail in 1911, its peak year.

After the passing of the "Great Hiking Era," the trail was all but abandoned until the late 1950s when rebuilding efforts began. The good folks of Sierra Madre, aided by Boy Scout troops, rebuilt the trail all the way up canyon to its junction with the old Mount Wilson Toll Road. Sierra Madre citizens also prevented county flood control engineers from bulldozing and check-damming Little Santa Anita Canyon. The aroused citizenry established Sierra Madre Historical Wilderness Area to preserve the canyon. This area is patterned after federal Wilderness Areas; that is, the land is to be preserved forever without development or mechanized use.

This hike will take you up Little Santa Anita Canyon, visit Orchard Camp and climb to the top of Mount Wilson. There are many routes up Mount Wilson; this is one of the nicest.

Directions to trailhead: From the Foothill Freeway (210) in Arcadia take Baldwin Avenue north. Turn right on Miramonte Avenue. Park on Miramonte Avenue near the junction of Mount Wilson Trail Road, which is on your left. The trail begins 150 yards up this road and is marked by a large wooden sign. After passing some homes, the trail shortly intersects the main trail.

The Hike: After trudging 1½ miles up Santa Anita Canyon you reach a junction with a sidetrail, which leads to the nearby canyon bottom. Here you càn lean against an old oak, cool your heels in the rushing water, relax and watch the river flow.

Continue back on the ridge trail as it climbs higher and higher above the canyon floor onto sunny, exposed slopes. A hot 3 miles of walking brings you to Decker Spring and another ½ mile to Orchard Camp, a shady glen dotted with oak and spruce trees. When Wilson was building his trail, a construction camp called halfway house was built here. Later homesteaders tried their hand planting apple and cherry trees—hence the name Orchard Camp. During the "Great Hiking Era," a succession of entrepreneurs utilized Orchard Camp as a trail resort and welcomed thousands of hikers. Hikers traveled through this canyon in the 1920s reported seeing "The Nature Man of Mount Wilson," a tall, bronzed hermit who looked like he stepped out of the pages of the Old Testament. The nature man carried a stone axe and worked on the trail for his keep. Some say he's still around, protecting the canyon—though he no longer springs out of the brush and greets every hiker who passes.

Orchard Camp is a nice place to picnic. You might want to call it a day here and return the same way. Otherwise, fill your canteen and plunge on.

Option: Orchard Camp to Mount Wilson. The trail continues through thick chaparral up Santa Anita Canyon to its head. It contours on the shelf-like trail, heads east on a firebreak and crosses over a steep manzanita-covered ridge. At the intersection with Winter Creek Trail, turn left (west) and ascend steeply to Mount Wilson Toll Road, 2 miles from Orchard Camp. Turn right on the Toll Road and follow it 1 mile as it ascends through well-spaced spruce to Mount Wilson Road, just out-side Skyline Park.

32

Devil's Canyon Trail

Season: All year
Recommended map: Angeles
National Forest
Topo: Chilao Flat,
Waterman Mountain

Chilao to Devil's Canyon Trail Camp
7 miles RT; 1500' loss.
Chilao to Devil's Canyon Waterfall
11 miles RT; 2300' loss.

Los Angeles residents, while inching along on some crowded interchange, may be comforted by knowing that no other metropolis in America has a Wilderness Area so close. When you hike through the primeval canyons of the San Gabriel Wilderness Area, you won't believe you're only eighteen as-the-crow-flies miles from downtown L.A. The 36,137-acre wilderness is rough and rugged country, the bulk of which is contained in two canyons, Devil's and Bear. Chaparral coats the sunny canyon slopes and pine and fir reach from the ridges to the sky. In spring, this is color country: the laurels glow yellow with flowers, the willows fluff up, the ceanothus blossoms blue and white.

The Wilderness Area is surrounded on three sides by roads: on the north and west by Highway 2, on the east by Highway 39. Picnickers and campers crowd its edges, skiers peer down at it from nearby ridges. But despite its accessibility, most people only *look* at this wilderness. The view down from the brink of Devil's Canyon, the sharp descent, and the thought of the walk back up, scare off casual walkers.

Devil's Canyon Trail, from Chilao to the trail camp, is the most pleasant path in the Wilderness. It takes you through the middle third of the canyon, past willow-shaded pools and dancing cascades, to spots that make the Big City seem hundreds of miles away.

Directions to trailhead: From La Canada, drive 27 miles up the Angeles Crest Highway (Highway·2), ¼ mile past the entrance to the Upper Chilao Campground. There's a parking lot on the left (west) side of the highway. Leave your car here. The signed trailhead, which is usually below the snowline, is across the highway from the parking lot.

The Hike: Remind yourself, as you leave the trailhead and begin descending steeply into the canyon, that the tough part of this trip will come last. Pace yourself accordingly. The trail steps back and forth from pine and spruce on the shady slopes to thick chaparral on sunny slopes. After two miles, the trail meets a pleasant little creek and descends with

125

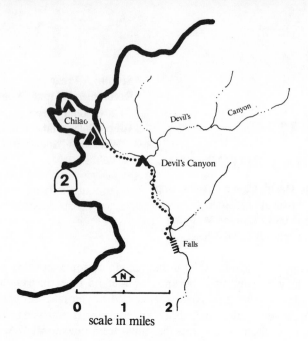

scale in miles

its bubbling waterway down into the canyon. At trail's end is Devil's Canyon Trail Camp, a primitive streamside retreat, where the only sounds you hear are the murmur of the stream and the rustling of alder leaves.

You can bushwhack and boulder-hop a mile upstream before the brush gets uncomfortably thick. From the trail camp, you can return the way you came or do some further exploring downstream.

Option: To falls. Below the trail camp, a path follows Devil's Creek for a spell, but soon ends. You pick your way across rock islands in the creek. The walls of Devil's Canyon close in on you and you find yourself in trackless boulderhopping backcountry; pleasant, but slow going. You continually cross the creek, decipher routes around deep pools and descend gingerly down misty boulders.

Blackened alder leaves cover the surface of still eddys, where pan-sized trout may lurk. The canyon narrows, its steep rock walls pinching Devil's Creek into a series of cascades. As the canyon narrows further and drops steeper, the cascades grow more spectacular and waterfalls occur. The first falls come from side creeks and ¼ mile downstream you arrive at the first mainstream falls, which plunge 20 feet to a bubbling pool.

Expert mountaineers sometimes continue downstream from the falls, but it's a precarious route and is recommended only for the very skilled. Your return to Devil's Canyon Trail Camp may be faster than your descent, because it's easier to pick routes and climb up rocks than down them. The climb from the trail camp to the canyon rim will, of course, be slower.

33
East Fork Trail

Season: All year
Caution should be used during
   winter and spring due to
   high water.
Recommended map: Angeles
   National Forest
Topo: Glendora, Crystal Lake
   Mount San Antonio
Wilderness Permit required

**Ranger Station to The Narrows
9 miles RT; 1000′ gain
Ranger Station to Iron Fork
11½ miles RT; 1400′ gain
Ranger Station to Fish Fork
13½ miles RT; 1600′ gain**

This day hike takes you through the monumental middle section of the East Fork. Sometimes you'll see a weekend gold miner find a flash in his pan, but the real treasure of this section of the San Gabriel River lies in its beauty, its alders and tumbling waters. It's wet going—you'll be doing a lot of wading as well as walking, but you'll be well rewarded for all your boulder-hopping and stream crossings. The dizzy chasm of the Narrows is awesome, the steepest river gorge in the San Gabriels.

Directions to trailhead: From Interstate Highway 10 (San Bernardino Freeway), exit to Azusa Ave. (Highway 39) and head north. If you're coming on the 210 Freeway, exit on San Gabriel Canyon Road (Highway 39) and head north. Ten miles up Highway 39, turn right (east) on East Fork Road and continue eight more miles to the East Fork Ranger Station. Park in the dirt area just below a locked gate.

The Hike: Hike north of the crumbling roadbed that contours around the slopes on the east side of the river. In ½ mile, the trail descends to the canyon floor. Your trail, what there is of it, begins crossing and recrossing the (hopefully) shallow waters of the river. You'll pass the cracked asphalt remains of the old East Fork Road that once led to the Narrows. It was chewed to pieces in the great flood of 1938. Two miles and several river crossings from the trailhead, you'll pass near Swan Rock, a mighty wall west of the river with the faint gray outline of a gargantuan swan.

As the canyon floor widens and twists northward, you'll climb up the right side of the canyon floor and continue up river on the remains of the East Fork Road, high above the rushing water. After ascending north a ways, you'll reach the "Bridge to Nowhere," a highway bridge, still intact, but going nowhere. No road meets the bridge at either end; it was carried

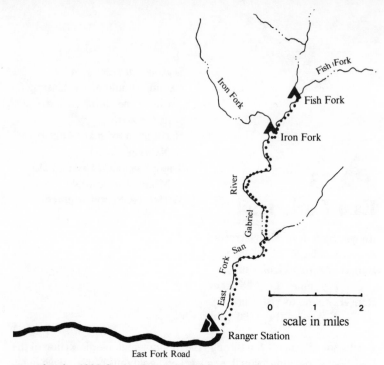

Fish Fork

Iron Fork

Iron Fork

Fish Fork

River

San Gabriel

East Fork

0   1   2
scale in miles

Ranger Station

East Fork Road

away by the 1938 flood. Cross the bridge and when you reach the other side bear right on a slim trail that soon drops you down into the Narrows. A quarter mile from the bridge, near the turbulent river is Narrows Trail Camp, a fine place to picnic and view the handsome gorge.

Option: To Iron Fork, Fish Fork. If the water isn't too high, the best way to reach both forks is to imagine yourself a spawning salmon and plunge upriver. It's ¾ of a mile to Iron Fork. You, like the river, will squeeze your way between towering granite walls. At the junction of Iron Fork with the main river, miner George Trogden had a home and angler's headquarters, where rugged miners and intrepid fishermen gathered to swap tall tales.

Fish Fork is a mile beyond Iron Fork and again, it's best to continue your amphibious journey directly up the river. The waters of Fish Fork cascade down from Mount Baldy's shoulders. It's been a popular fishing spot for generations of anglers.

GEORGE TROGDEN'S METHOD OF EATING TROUT
Hold the head of the fish between the thumb and forefinger of one hand and the tail between the forefinger and thumb of the other, and bite liberally into the body of the fish as you would an ear of corn; then, the last sweet morsel consumed, toss away the naked bones as you would the corncob and reach out for another fish.   —as reported by CHARLES FRANCIS SAUNDERS,
The Southern Sierras of California, 1923.

128

34

Mount Baden-Powell Trail

Vincent Gap to summit
8 miles RT; 2800′ gain.

This trail and peak honor Lord Baden-Powell, a British Army officer who founded the Boy Scout movement in 1907. The well-engineered trail, grooved into the side of the mountain by the CCC in the mid-thirties, switchbacks up the northeast ridge to the peak. The peak was once known as North Baldy, before Southern California Boy Scouts lobbied the Forest Service for a name change. Mount Baden-Powell is the terminus of the scouts' 53-mile Silver Moccasin Trail, a rugged week-long backpack through the San Gabriels. Scouts who complete the long trail earn the Silver Moccasin Award.

The trail follows a moderate, steady grade to the top of the mountain, where there's a monument honoring Lord Baden-Powell. On the summit, you'll meet those venerable, ancient survivors, the limber pines, and be treated to superb views across the Mojave Desert and down into the Iron Fork of the San Gabriel River.

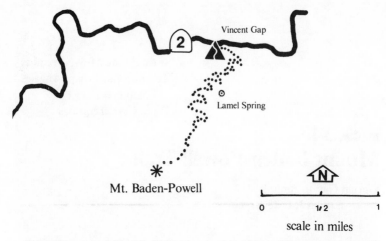

Vincent Gap

Lamel Spring

Mt. Baden-Powell

N

0   1⁄2   1

scale in miles

Directions to trailhead: Take the Angeles Crest Highway (2) for 53 miles from La Canada to the Vincent Gap Parking Area. The signed trailhead is at the northwest edge of the parking area. If you're coming from the east, take Interstate 15 to the Wrightwood exit, three miles south of Cajon Pass. Proceed eight miles west on Highway 138 to its intersection with Highway 2. Turn left on Highway 2 and follow it for 14 miles to the trailhead.

The Hike: The trail immediately begins ascending from Vincent Gulch Divide, a gap which separates the upper tributaries of the San Gabriel River to the south from Big Rock Creek to the northwest. You begin switchbacking southwest through the Jeffrey pine and fir. There are over 3 dozen of these switchbacks, though there are so many beautiful distractions it's hard to get an accurate count. In 1½ miles, a side trail (unmarked) leads 100 yards to Lamel Spring, an inviting resting place and the only dependable water on the trail.

Rangers take core samples to determine age of limber pine.

With the elevation, the switchbacks grow shorter and steeper and the vegetation changes from fir to lodgepole pine. Soon, even the altitude-loving lodgepoles give way to the heartiest of pines, the limber pine. One half mile from the summit, around 9,000 feet, the first of these squat, thick-trunked limber pines comes into view. Shortly, you'll intersect a side trail to the limber pine forest.

Sidetrip: To Limber Pine Forest: A tiny sign points right (southwest) to the limber pine stand, ⅛ mile. These wind-loving, sub-alpine dwellers are one of the few living things that can cope with the rarefied atmosphere. *Pinus flexilis,* botanists call the species, for its long, droopy, flexible branches. They bow and scrape and twist and turn like hyperextended dancers and appear to gather all their nourishment from the wind.

Back on the main trail, a few more switchbacks bring you atop the ridge, where Mount Baldy can be glimpsed. You walk along the barren crest and intersect the Pacific Crest Trail. The Pacific Crest Trail swoops off to Little Jimmy Spring. You continue past the limber pines to the summit. There is a concrete monument paying homage to Lord Baden-Powell, and a summit register for you to sign. Enjoy the superb view out across the Mojave to the southern Sierra and east to Baldy, San Gorgonio and San Jacinto.

Return the way you came.

Season: May-October
(depending on snowfall)
Recommended map: Angeles
National Forest
Topos: Mount San Antonio,
Telegraph Peak

 35

Devil's Backbone Trail

Baldy Notch to Mt. Baldy summit
7 miles RT; 2200' gain

Three saintly mountains—San Gorgonio, San Jacinto and San Antonio—tower over the City of the Angels. Lowest of the three, but by far the best known is Mt. San Antonio, more commonly known as Mt. Baldy. The 10,064-foot peak, highest in the San Gabriel Mountains, is visible from much of the Southland. Its summit gleams white in winter and early spring, grey in summer and fall. Old Baldy is so big and bare that it seems to be snow-covered even when it is not.

Legend has it, the padres of Mission San Gabriel, circa 1790, named the massive stone bulwark after Saint Anthony of Padua, Italy. The thirteenth century Franciscan friar was evidently a favorite of California missionaries; a number of geographical features both in Monterey County and around Southern California honor San Antonio. In the 1870s, San Antonio Canyon and the nearby high country swarmed with gold seekers, who dubbed the massive peak a more earthly "Old Baldy."

During the quarter century from 1890 to 1915, often referred to as the Golden Era of Hiking in Southern California, many San Gabriel Mountain resorts opened to meet the demand of hikers. Surely one of the most unique resorts in the San Gabriels was the Baldy Summit Inn, perched just below the summit of the great mountain. Gale-force winds battered the above-timberline camp, which consisted of two stone buildings and a cluster of tents. William Dewey, owner/tour guide, and Mrs. Dewey, chef, welcomed guests to their resort during the summers of 1910-11-12. Advertised rates were $1 a meal, $1 a bed. The camp burned in 1913 and never reopened.

Three trails lead to the summit of Mt. Baldy. The most difficult route is the Bear Flat, or Old Baldy Trail, which gains 5,500' as it climbs the south ridge of Baldy to the top. Another strenuous route climbs Baldy from the backside via Pine and Dawson Mountains. A more moderate, but certainly not easy, ascent follows the Devil's Backbone Trail from Baldy Notch to the summit. This is a very popular trail and the one most hikers associate with Mt. Baldy. A clear day view from the top offers a panorama of desert and ocean, the sprawling Southland and the southern High Sierras.

Baldy is a bit austere from afar, but up close the white granite shoulders of the mountain are softened by a forest of pine and fir. Dress warmly for this trip and keep an eye out for rapidly changing weather conditions.

Directions to trailhead: From the San Bernardino Freeway (I-10), exit on Mountain Avenue. Head north on Mountain, which joins Mt. Baldy Road in San Antonio Canyon and winds 12 miles to road's end just beyond Manker Campground. Park in the ski lift parking area.

Purchase a ticket ($6 roundtrip) and ride the ski lift up to Baldy Notch. The lift is operated weekends and holidays all year.

An alternative is to walk up a fire road to Baldy Notch. This option adds three miles each way and a 1,300′ gain to the walk. The fire road switchbacks up the west side of the steep San Antonio Canyon, offers a good view of San Antonio Falls, then climbs northward to the top.

The Hike: From Baldy Notch, a wide gravel path leads to a commanding view of the desert. You then join a chair lift access road/fire road, and ascend a broad slope forested in Jeffrey pine and incense cedar. The road ends in about 1¼ miles at the top of a ski lift, where a hiker's sign-in register beckons.

From the top of the ski lift, a trail leads out onto a sharp ridge known as the Devil's Backbone. To the north, you can look down into the deep gorge of Lytle Creek and to the south into San Antonio Canyon. You'll then pass around the south side of Mt. Harwood, "Little Baldy," and up through scattered stands of lodgepole pine.

The trail reaches a tempestuous saddle. (Hold onto your hat!) From the saddle, a steep rock-strewn pathway zig-zags past a few wind-bowed limber pine to the summit.

Boulders are scattered atop Baldy's crown. A couple of rock windbreaks offer some shelter. Enjoy the view of San Gabriel and San Bernardino mountain peaks, the Mojave and the metropolis, and return the same way.

Mt. Baldy

To Pine Mountain

Bear Flat

To

Mt. Harwood

To Stockton Flat

San Antonio
Falls

Angeles

National Forest

Ski Lift

Baldy Notch

Thunder Mountain

Telegraph Peak

Mt. Baldy Road

Manaker Flat

Cucamonga   Wilderness

Icehouse Canyon
Resort

Icehouse

Canyon

Timber Mountain

0   1   2

Saddle

*San Bernardino
National Forest*

Ontario Peak

Cucamonga Peak

Season: May-October
Recommended map: Angeles
National Forest
Topo maps: Mt. Baldy,
Cucamonga Peaks
Wilderness Permit required

 36

Icehouse Canyon Trail

Icehouse Canyon to Icehouse Saddle
8 miles RT; 2600' gain

Icehouse Canyon Trail, leading from Icehouse Canyon to several 8,000-foot peaks, is an ideal introduction to the high country delights of the Cucamonga Wilderness. The precipitous subalpine slopes of the wilderness, thickly forested with sugar pine, ponderosa pine and incense cedar, offer fresh mountain air and a network of good footpaths. The 4,400-acre wilderness, set aside by Congress in 1984, includes the "3 T's"—Timber Mountain, Telegraph Peak, Thunder Mountain, as well as 8,859-foot Cucamonga Peak, easternmost sentinel of the San Gabriel Mountains.

A wilderness permit is required for entry. Located at the far eastern end of the San Gabriel Mountains, the Cucamonga Wilderness sprawls across the boundaries of both the San Bernardino and Angeles National Forests and a wilderness permit can be secured from either agency. Mt. Baldy Ranger Station, located in Mt. Baldy Vilage, is open Friday, Saturday and Sunday, 8 a.m. to 4:30 p.m. (714) 982-2829.

Icehouse Canyon is the hiker's only easy entryway to the Cucamonga high country. The saddle and nearby peaks offer fine views to the hiker. Sierra Club peak-baggers like this trail because several peaks are within "bagging distance" of Icehouse Saddle, an important trail junction.

Icehouse Canyon was for many years known as Cedar Canyon because, as the story goes, the great cedar beams for Mission San Gabriel were logged here. The name Icehouse originated in the 1860s when ice was cut in the lower canyon and shipped to San Gabriel Valley residents.

Directions to trailhead: From the San Bernardino Freeway (I-10) in Upland, exit on Mountain Ave. Head north on Mountain, which joins Mt. Baldy Road in San Antonio Canyon and winds its way to Mt. Baldy Village. Go 1½ miles past the village to Icehouse Canyon Resort. Park in the dirt lot. The trail starts just to the right of the resort.

The Hike: The trail leads east along the floor of the canyon. The path stays close to the oak and spruce shaded creek and passes some cabins.

135

Brick chimneys and stone foundations are all that remain of other cabins, swept away during the great flood of '38. After 1½ miles the trail forks. You may take the "high route," the Chapman Trail, one mile to Cedar Flats and then three miles up to Icehouse Saddle or continue straight ahead on the shorter and steeper Ice House Canyon Trail directly up the canyon.

The Chapman Trail, constructed in 1980, was named for the family that built the Icehouse Canyon resort and numerous cabins in the 1920s. The well-constructed trail heads up Cedar Canyon to Cedar Glen. The cedars were severely scorched by the 1980 Thunder Mountain Fire, but the canyon flora is slowly recovering. The trail climbs out of Cedar Canyon then contours on a steady grade back over to Icehouse Canyon.

Another Chapman—no relation to the family whose name is found on the trail—figured in the history of Icehouse Canyon. Yankee Joseph Chapman arrived in Monterey in 1818, was accused of insurgency by the Spanish governor of California, and soon shipped to Los Angeles as a prisoner. Los Angeles, then a remote outpost, lacked lumber and when authorities learned that the New Englander was a master woodsman, they put him in charge of timber operations in the San Gabriel Mountains. The Spaniards and their Indian helpers thought that Chapman's ability to chop a tree down—and make it fall whichever way he wanted—was nothing less than magical. Some of the more superstitious called him "Diablo Chapman."

The cedar beams, hewed square up in the mountains, were dragged out of the canyon by oxen. Chapman's logging operations here and in other parts of Southern California earned him amnesty from the governor. Some historians believe Chapman to be the third Anglo resident of California and the first to reside in Los Angeles.

If you decided to continue on the Icehouse Canyon Trail, you'll pass a few more cabins. The trail climbs up the north slope of the canyon, before dropping down again and crossing the creek. The trail switchbacks steeply through pine and spruce. The tall trees frame a nice picture of Old Baldy. The Chapman Trail and the Icehouse Canyon Trail intersect and a single trail ascends a steep ¾ of a mile to the top of Icehouse Saddle.

You can enjoy the view and return the same way, or pick one of the fine trails that lead from Icehouse Saddle and add to your day hike. You can continue eastward and drop down the Middle Fork Trail to Lytle Creek. A right (southeast) turn puts you on a trail that climbs two miles to Cucamonga Peak. A sharp right southwest leads 2½ miles to Kelly's Camp and Ontario Peak. And a left on the 3-T's Trail takes you past Timber Mountain, Telegraph Peak and Thunder Mountain, then drops to Baldy Notch.

Mount Baldy from upper Icehouse Canyon

Chapter 7

SOUTHERN CALIFORNIA COAST

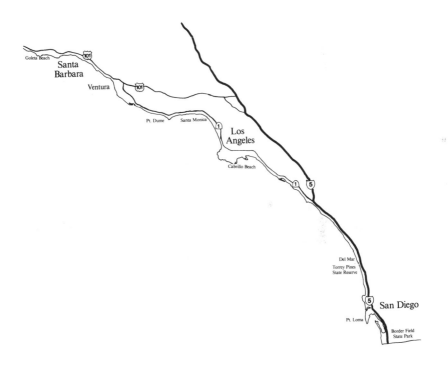

Southern California Coast

THE MOON RULES a province of living things on the margin of the restless Pacific. The moon is twenty-seven million times smaller than the sun, yet exerts twice the sun's power over the tides. A multitude of tidal creatures from crabs to grunion, observe a lunar day. These shoreline animals swim, feed, and mate in harmony with Southern California's twice-daily ebb and flow of the tide.

This lunar rhythm is illustrated by the behavior of a creature familiar to Southern California beachgoers, the sandhopper, or beach flea. At the peak of each high tide, when waves sweep the hopper's habitat, it emerges from the sand to swim and feed in the surf. A few hours later, as the tide recedes, the hopper burrows in the sand and awaits the tide's return. You may jump to the conclusion that the hopper is merely responding to getting wet or staying dry, but that isn't the case. Temperature and pressure changes delivered by waves are what motivate the sandhopper. Scientists at Scripps Institute of Oceanography found that sandhoppers kept in a jar of sea water swam actively during times corresponding to high tides and remained sedentary at the bottom of the jar during the low tides. Other experiments have left scientists with the conviction that some creatures have internal biological clocks that trigger their movements.

Another coastal creature observing a lunar day is the grunion. Grunion spawn only in Southern California between Point Conception and Baja. Actual spawning occurs only for a few hours on three or four nights following each full or new moon between March and August. Through evolutionary successes in feeding and mating, crabs, gulls, grunion, sandhoppers and a million more shoreline dwellers have adapted to a lunar cycle. Biologists are trying to find out what makes these creatures tick, trying to discover these biological clocks and how they work. So far, the clocks remain ghosts, perhaps the result of enzyme action or cell chemistry.

If the lunar time were only a matter of academic interest or affected only the lives of a few sandhoppers or grunion, it would be easy to ignore. But the moon's power governs the quality of our lives and the quality of our beaches far more than we imagine. Understanding the moon's gravitational pull on the water and the rhythm of the tides is important to all of us who love our southern coast. More than eighty percent of Southern Californians live within thirty miles of the coast. We love our beaches; in fact, we may be loving them to death. Tidal processes are something we've chosen to ignore in our rush to develop the coast and as a result we're losing our beaches, despite our best efforts.

Consider how beaches are made. The moon pulls Pacific tides against cliffs and grinds rock into sand. Without cliff erosion, there would be no beaches. However, when building occurs on the beach, this erosion can't take place. Beaches are dynamic ecosystems, forever expanding and contracting, yet they are treated by developers as steady-state systems. Dunes, marshes and sandstone cliffs are surveyed and beach lot boundaries laid out in straight lines. The shoreline is then blacktopped and condominium-ized. Motels, marinas, and parking lots spring up at water's edge. Once beachfront investments are made, property rights predominate over natural tidal rhythms. Attempts to stabilize the beach are initiated—dunes are leveled, inlets and channels are dredged, groins, sea walls and jetties—often more expensive than the property they are designed to protect—are erected. The beach, which once maintained itself, can do so no longer. Beaches disappear in some places and, with them, beachfront property. Man then tries to "save the beach," answering Nature's warning with more groins and more jetties, involving himself in a costly and ultimately futile cycle. Some day we'll learn an important lesson: the best way to save the beach is to leave it alone!

For the day hiker, our southern coast offers not only those white sand beaches depicted on postcards, but a wide variety of shoreline features—the palms of La Jolla and Santa Monica, the cliffs of Torrey Pines and Palos Verdes. Above Santa Barbara the Santa Ynez Mountains march toward the Pacific and at Point Magu the Santa Monica Mountains do likewise.

The trailess beach is ever-changing. Tidepool exploring, viewing the unique organisms that have adapted to the twice-daily change in tides, is one of the highlights of a beach walk. Another is beachcombing—picking through the flotsam and jetsam for treasures cast ashore. After a winter storm the keen-eyed beachcomber may find a unique piece of driftwood, a pretty shell, a Japanese fishing ball, or treasure from an ancient wrecked ship.

What would our feeding, sleeping and mating habits be today if we lived in harmony with the tide's ebb and flow? Would it change our wristwatches, calendars and TV-watching habits? Would we have a little more respect for the sanctity of our beaches if our bodies, like those of sandhoppers, were found to contain biological clocks keeping time with the moon? The restless ocean holds answers to questions we have not yet learned to ask.

 37

Goleta Beach Trail

Goleta Beach County Park to Coal Oil Point
7 miles RT
Goleta Beach County Park to Ellwood Oil Field
12 miles RT

Around 7:00 on the evening of February 23, 1942, while most Southern Californians were listening to President Roosevelt's fireside chat on the radio, strange explosions were heard near Goleta. In the first (and only) attack on U.S. soil since the War of 1812, a Japanese submarine surfaced off the rich oil field on Ellwood Beach, twelve miles north of Santa Barbara, and lobbed sixteen shells into the tidewater field.

"Their markmanship was poor," asserted Lawrence Wheeler, proprietor of a roadside inn near the oil fields. Most observers agreed with Wheeler, who added there was no panic among his dinner patrons. "We immediately blacked out the place," he said. "One shell landed about a quarter mile from here and the concussion shook the building, but nobody was scared much."

The unmolested, unhurried Japanese gunners were presumably aiming at the oil installations and the coast highway bridge over the Southern Pacific tracks. Tokyo claimed the raid "a great military success" though the incredibly bad marksmen managed to inflict only $500 worth of damage. The submarine disappeared into the night, leaving behind air raid sirens, a jumpy population and lower Santa Barbara real estate values.

This day hike along Goleta Beach to Ellwood Oil Field is interesting for more than historical reasons. On the way to the Oil Field/Battle Field, you'll pass tidepools, shifting sand dunes, and the Devereux Slough. The slough is a unique intertidal ecosystem and is protected for teaching and research purposes by Coal Oil Point Reserve.

Directions to trailhead: From Highway 101 in Goleta, head south on Ward Memorial Drive (Route 217) for two miles to Goleta Beach County Park. Park in the large beach lot.

The Hike: Walk north (west really; remember, you're in confusing Santa Barbara County where the coast stretches east to west). In ¼-mile you'll reach a stretch of land called the Main Campus Reserve Area, where you'll find the Goleta Slough. The same month the Japanese

142

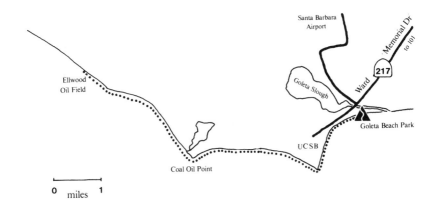

bombed Ellwood Beach, Santa Barbara voters approved a bond issue to buy land around the Goleta Slough and a modern airport was constructed on the site of the old cow pasture airfield. The slough, host to native and migratory waterfowl, is a remnant of a wetland that was once much more extensive.

Continue up the beach past the handsome sandstone cliffs. Occasionally a high tide may force you to detour on the cliff through the university campus to avoid getting wet. A mile and a half from the county park, you'll round Goleta Point and head due west. You'll pass a nice tidepool area; judging from the number of students, it is well studied. Two more miles of beachcombing brings you to Coal Oil Point. You'll want to explore the nature reserve here. (Please observe all posted warnings; this is a very fragile area.)

The dunes are the first component of the reserve encountered on the seaward side. Sandy hillocks are stabilized with grasses and rushes. Salty sand provides little nourishment yet the hardy seaside flora manages to survive, settling as close to the water as the restless Pacific will permit. The dunes keep the plants from blowing away and the plants return the favor for the dunes.

Footprints of lizards and mice and miniscule tracks of beetles can be seen tacking this way and that over the sand. The dune's surface records the lightest pressure of the smallest feet. Sometimes one set of animal tracks intersects another in a pattern suggesting the demise of one animal and dinner for another.

Pick up the trail over the dunes on the east side of the reserve. The fennel-lined trail passes under cypress tress and climbs a bluff above the slough to a road on the reserve's perimeter. It's a good place to get "the big picture" of the slough, a unique ecosystem. Something like an estuary, a slough has a mixture of fresh and salt water, but an estuary has a more stable mixture. The water gets quite salty at Devereaux Slough, with little fresh water flushing.

The slough is a birdwatcher's paradise. You'll often see curious folks, binoculars glued to eyeballs, rhapsodizing over snowy egrets and great blue herons, black bellied plovers and western sandpipers. Avid birdwatchers flock to the slough for birdathons—marathon birdsighting competitions.

In addition to scores of native and migratory species, birds affectionately known by their watchers as "vagrants"—lost birds who have no business in the area—often visit the slough. If you're the type who carries a copy of *Petersen's Guide* in your daypack, you'll spend the rest of the day here and there's no point in urging you to hike on. For the rest of you, it's on to Ellwood.

Option: To Ellwood Oil Field. Return to the beach and continue walking up the coast. Sometimes horses gallop over the dunes, suggesting Peter O'Toole and Omar Sharif's meeting in *Lawrence of Arabia*. . . except there's oil on this beach, as you'll readily notice when you look at your feet. In two miles you'll pass under an old barnacle-covered oil drilling platform and enter Ellwood Oil Field. Here the Japanese fired shots heard 'round the world. . .and missed.

38
Zuma-Dume Trail

Zuma Beach to Pt. Dume
  2 miles RT
Zuma Beach to Paradise Cove;
  4 miles RT

Zuma Beach is L.A. County's largest sand beach and one of the finest white sand strands in California. Zuma lies on the open crest beyond Santa Monica Bay and thus receives heavy breakers crashing in from the north. From sunrise to sunset, board and body surfers try to catch a big one. Every month the color of the ocean and the Santa Monica Mountains seem to take on different shades of green depending on season and sunlight, providing the Zuma Beach hiker with yet another attraction.

Zuma's wealth of sand is inherited from material dumped into the Pacific by Trancas and Zuma Creeks. Pt. Dume helps also by acting like a gigantic groin, capturing sand along its up-current side. Offshore, the slope of the sea bottom may influence wave refraction and thus dump even more sand on the beach.

This hike travels along the western part of Zuma Beach, climbs over the geologically fascinating Pt. Dume Headlands for sweeping views of the coast, and descends to Paradise Cove, site of a private beach and fishing pier.

Directions to trailhead: Zuma Beach County Park is located at the 30000 block of Pacific Coast Highway, Malibu. There is a parking-admission fee. Although the east beach is usually crowded in the summer months, the west beach is not. Find a parking space near the west end and begin your hike.

The Hike: Walk down-coast along sandy Zuma Beach. This stretch of Zuma is known as Westward Beach. The water here is clearer and colder than Santa Monica Bay to the east of Pt. Dume. A little inland from the beach is Point Dume Whale Watch, reached by a stairway from Westward Beach Road. In winter the possibility of seeing a migrating gray whale swimming south toward Baja is good. The migration route brings them quite close to shore.

On the western side of Point Dume is Pirate's Cove, two hundred yards of beach tucked away between two rocky outcroppings. It's been the scene of much dispute between nude beach advocates, residents, and the county sheriff. The state is currently developing Pirates Cove and other acreage along the Pt. Dume Headlands as an ecological reserve.

Option: To Paradise Cove. Take the sandy goat trail, which leads up the sandstone cliffs to the top of Pt. Dume. Wander atop the point and observe the white sea cliffs of Santa Monica arcing inland. As you stand atop the rocky triangle projecting into the sea, observe the dense black Zuma volcanics and the much softer white sedimentary beds of the sea cliffs extending both east and west. The volcanics have resisted the crashing sea far better than the sedimentary rock and have protected the land behind from further erosion, thus forming the triangle shape of the point.

Keep toward the edge of the bluffs, following more goat trails until you spot the one that descends the east side to the beach. A bit of beach walking brings you to Paradise Cove, sheltered from the north and northwest by Point Dume and the south by extensive kelp beds. Diving is good too. Paradise Cove, sometimes called Dume Cove, is a romantic spot and the scene of much TV and motion picture filming.

Return the same way.

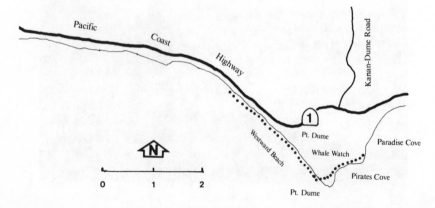

Season: All Year
Topo: Redondo Beach
Consult tide table;
hike at low tide

 39

Palos Verdes Peninsula Trail

Malaga Cove to Rocky Point
5 miles RT
Malaga Cove to Point Vincente Lighthouse
10 miles RT

Geographically, the Palos Verdes bluffs and beaches resemble the Channel Islands. Long ago, before the Ice Age began, the peninsula was an island, separated from the rest of the Los Angeles basin by the sea. However, toward the end of the last glacial period, the eighteen-mile-long peninsula was connected to the mainland by masses of sediment discharged from the mountains to the north. The peninsula is famous for its rocky cliffs, which rise from 50 to 300 feet above the ocean and for its thirteen wave-cut terraces. These terraces, or platforms, resulted from a combination of uplift and sea-level fluctuations caused by the formation and melting of glaciers. Today the waves, as they have for so many thousands of years, are actively eroding the shoreline, cutting yet another terrace into the land.

While enjoying this hike, you'll pass many beautiful coves, where whaling ships once anchored and delivered their cargo of whale oil. Large iron kettles, used to boil the whale blubber, have been found in sea cliff caves. Indians, Spanish rancheros and Yankee smugglers have added to the peninsula's romantic history. Modern times have brought white-stuccoed, red-tiled mansions to the peninsula bluffs, but the beach remains almost pristine. Offshore, divers explore the rocky bottoms for abalone and shellfish. On shore, hikers enjoy the wave-scalloped bluffs and splendid tidepools.

Wear sturdy shoes on this hike. Hiking this beach is like walking over a surface of broken bowling balls. The route is rocky and progress slow, but that gives you more time to look down at the tidepools and up at the magnificent bluffs.

Directions to trailhead: The narrow, rocky Palos Verdes beaches can be reached by a number of unofficial access points along Paseo Del Mar. To reach the Malaga Cove trailhead, take Pacific Coast Highway 1 to Palos Verdes Boulevard. Bear right on Palos Verdes Drive. As you near Malaga Cove Plaza, turn right at the first stop sign (Via Corta). Make a

Point Vincente Lighthouse

right on Via Arroyo, then another right into the parking lot behind the Malaga Cove School. The trailhead is on the ocean side of the parking area, where a wide path descends the bluffs to Malaga Cove. There's another access point from Paseo Del Mar on the bluffs above the Flatrock Point tidepools. A footpath leaves from Paseo Del Mar, 1/10 mile past Via Horcada, where the street curves east to join Palos Verdes Drive West.

The Hike: From the Malaga Cove School parking lot, descend the wide path to the beach. A sign indicates you're entering a seashore reserve and asks you to treat tidepool residents with respect. To the north are sandy beaches for sedentary sun worshippers. We active rockhoppers clamber to the south. At several places along this hike you'll notice that

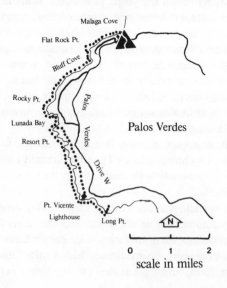

148

the great terraces are cut by steep-walled canyons. The first of these canyon incisions can be observed at Malaga Cove, where Malaga Canyon slices through the north slopes of the Palos Verdes hills, then cuts west to empty at the cove.

The coastline curves out to sea in a southwesterly direction and popular Flatrock Point comes into view. The jade-colored waters swirl around this anvil-shaped point, creating the best tidepool area along this section of coast. Above the point, the cliffs soar to 300 feet. Cloaked in morning fog, the rocky seascape here is reminiscent of Big Sur.

Rounding Flatrock Point, you pick your way among the rocks, seaweed and the flotsam and jetsam of civilization to Bluff Cove, where sparkling combers explode against the rocks and douse the unwary with their tangy spray. A glance over your right shoulder brings a view of Santa Monica Bay, the Santa Monica Mountains in gray silhouette and on the far horizon, the Channel Islands.

A mile beyond Bluff Cove, Rocky (also called Palos Verdes) Point juts out like a ship's prow. Caught fast on the rocks at the base of the point is the rusting exoskeleton of the Greek freighter Dominator, a victim of the treacherous reef surrounding the peninsula.

Option: To Point Vincente Lighthouse. Around Rocky Point is Lunada Bay, a good place to observe the terrace surfaces. From here you'll walk under almost perpendicular cliffs that follow horseshoe-shaped Lunada Bay. Shortly you'll round Resort Point, where fishermen try their luck. As the coastline curves south, Catalina can often be seen glowing on the horizon. Along this stretch of shoreline, numerous stacks, remnants of former cliffs not yet dissolved by the surf, can be seen.

The stretch of coast before the lighthouse has been vigorously scalloped by thousands of years of relentless surf. You'll have to boulderhop the last mile to Point Vincente. The lighthouse has worked its beacon over the dark waters since 1926. Lighthouses seem to fall into two categories; those that welcome and those that warn. Point Vincente obviously belongs to the latter category.

Passage is sometimes impossible around the lighthouse point at high tide. If the way is passable, another ½-mile of walking brings you to an official access (or departure) point at Long Point.

Return the way you came, walk up to the Bluffs at Long Point, or take the optional route below.

Option: Bluff Trail to Point Vincente. From Resort Point to Point Vincente. There are a number of "goat trails" that allow the beachwalker to scramble up to the top of the bluffs. There are no residences on this section of the bluffs, only a jungle of fennel and a trail to Point Vincente. The trail, offering far-reaching views of the peninsula and Pacific, winds through the licorice-smelling headlands to the lighthouse.

40

Cabrillo Beach Trail

Cabrillo Beach to White's Point
   3 miles RT

All but forgotten today, the rocky cave just downcoast from White's Point once flourished as a Roaring '20s health spa and resort. All that remains today are some sea-battered cement ruins and lush overgrown gardens.

White's Point was originally settled at the turn of the century by immigrant Japanese fishermen, who harvested the bountiful abalone from the waters off Palos Verdes Peninsula. Tons of abalone were shipped to the Far East and consumed locally at Los Angeles' Little Tokyo. In a few years the abalone was depleted, but an even greater resource was discovered at White's Point—sulphur springs.

In 1915, construction of a spa began. Eventually a large hotel was built at water's edge, palm gardens and a golf course decorated the cliffs above. The sulphur baths were especially popular with the Japanese population of Southern California.

The spa boomed in the '20s, but the 1933 earthquake closed the springs. The cove became part of Fort McArthur during World War II, the Japanese-American settlers were incarcerated in internment camps, and the resort was soon overwhelmed by crumbling cliffs and the powerful sea.

This hike begins at Cabrillo Beach, the only real sand beach for miles to the north and south, passes Cabrillo Marine Museum, and ends up at historic White's Point. For the most part this day hike stays atop the San Pedro and Palos Verdes Bluffs, but there's ample opportunity along this easy family walk to descend to the sea. Your hiking and tidepool-viewing pleasure will be increased immeasurably if you walk during low tide. Consult the tide table in the *Times*.

Cabrillo Marine Museum is well worth a visit. It has marine displays, aquariums with live fish, and good shell collections. One exhibit interprets the history of White's Point. The museum sponsors tidepool walks, grunion watches, and is a coordinating point for whale watching cruises.

Directions to trailhead: Take the Harbor Freeway south to San Pedro and exit on Gaffey Street. Follow Gaffey seaward to 22nd Street and turn left. Turn right on Pacific Avenue and then left on 36th Street. You may park either near the museum or at Cabrillo Beach. Parking is $3 for the day.

Royal Palms State Beach

The Hike: Walk up sandy Cabrillo Beach, which has a monopoly on running grunion, since the sand-seeking fish have few other spawning options along Palos Verdes Peninsula. You'll soon pass the San Pedro breakwater and Cabrillo fishing pier. John Olguin, long time Cabrillo Marine Museum Director, says that one of his favorite walks is atop the breakwater. "Great on a brisk winter day. Superb view of Los Angeles Harbor and this time of year you might even spot a whale on the horizon."

Just upcoast from Cabrillo Beach is the rocky shoreline of Pt. Fermin Marine Life Refuge. Limpets, crabs and lobsters are a few of the many creatures found in the bountiful tidepools. After rock-hopping among the tidepools, you must follow a dirt path or the paved road up to the top of the coastal bluffs; it is all but impossible to hike around Point Fermin

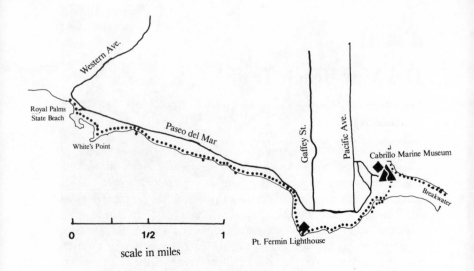

Royal Palms State Beach

White's Point

Western Ave.

Paseo del Mar

Gaffey St.

Pacific Ave.

Cabrillo Marine Museum

Breakwater

Pt. Fermin Lighthouse

0   1/2   1

scale in miles

via the shoreline route. Walk uphill along Bluff Place to a parking lot at the terminus of Pacific Avenue and join a blufftop trail. This path takes you past remains of "Sunken City," a 1930s housing tract built on bluffs that soon collapsed. Palm trees and huge chunks of asphalt are all that remain of the sunken city.

Soon you'll arive at Point Fermin Park and its handsome Victorian style lighthouse, built in 1874 from materials shipped around Cape Horn. It remained in service until shortly after the Japanese attack on Pearl Harbor, when it became an observation post.

Two coastal accessways lead down the park's bluffs to the shoreline. The shoreline route is rocky—a little like walking over broken bowling balls. As you near White's Point, you'll see a palm garden with fire pits. Royal Palms Hotel was once situated here until overcome by the sea. Storm-twisted palms and overgrown gardens are a reminder of flush times gone by. Royal Palms is a State Beach now, popular with surfers.

Ahead at White's Point are some curious cement remains of the resort. Beyond the point stretch the rugged cliffs and cobblestone shores of Palos Verdes Peninsula. Return the same way or if you have the time, hike on. The difficult terrain will ensure that few follow in your footsteps.

▲41

Del Mar Beach Trail

Train Station to Torrey Pines State Reserve
6 miles RT;

Along Del Mar Beach, the power of the surf is awesome and cliff collapse unpredictable. At this beach, permeable layers of rock tilt toward the sea and lie atop other more impermeable rock layers. Water percolates down through the permeable rocks, settles on the impermeable rock and "greases the skids"—an ideal condition for collapsing cliffs. On New Year's Day in 1941, a freight train suddenly found itself in mid-air. Erosion had undermined the tracks. A full passenger train had been delayed and the freight train's crew of three were the only casualties.

This hike takes you along the beach, visits the superb Flatrock tidepool area, and detours up the bluffs to Torrey Pines State Reserve. At the Reserve, you'll see those relics from the Ice Age, Torrey pines, which grow only along the Del Mar bluffs and on Santa Barbara Island; no other place in the world.

Directions to trailhead: *By Train:* Board the southbound San Diegan in Los Angeles' Union Station, Fullerton, Santa Ana, or another point along the line and get off in Del Mar. Call Amtrak for fares and schedules. Reservations are usually not necessary. Try to take the first train south to give yourself plenty of time to enjoy this hike.

By Car: Go south on Interstate Highway 5 and exit right on Via de la Valle. Continue west to Highway 21, then turn left (south) along the ocean past the racetrack and fairgrounds to reach the business center. Turn right on 15th Street in Del Mar to reach the train station.

The Hike: From the station, cross the tracks to the beach and begin hiking south. You should consult a tide table to learn the best time for tidepooling and to avoid being stranded by high, high tides.

Walk south along the shore. With the high cliffs on your left and the pounding breakers on your right, you'll feel you're entering another world. Follow the sometimes wide, sometimes narrow beach over sparkling sand and soft green limestone rock. Holes in the limestone give evidence of marine life that once made its home there.

After three miles of beachcombing, you'll see a distinct rock outcropping, named appropriately enough, "Flatrock." Legend has it that this gouged-out rock, also known as Bathtub Rock, was the luckless site of a Scottish miner's search for coal. Common tidepool residents,

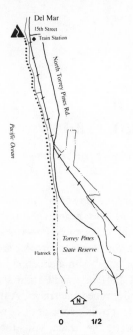

housed in the rocks and base of the bluff, include barnacles, mussels, crabs, and sea anenomes.

Just north of Flatrock, a trail ascends the bluffs to the State Reserve. The first hundred yards of the unsigned trail are tentative and precarious, but it's easy walking once it begins climbing the sandstone bluffs. The Reserve is home of the Torrey pine, which occupies the bold headlands atop the cliffs. Clinging to the crumbling yellow sandstone, these rare and graceful trees seem to thrive on the foggy atmosphere and precarious footing.

A warning: The Reserve is filled with yellow Coriopsis, lupine, Indian paintbrush, Torrey pines and much beauty. It is also filled with prohibitions: No flower picking, no picnicking, no walking off the trail. The Reserve is patrolled by rangers who will scold you if you don't respect the rules. Unpack your picnic lunch down at Flatrock or along the beach; it's the only place where picnicking is allowed.

Return the way you came.

Options: Guy Fleming Loop Trail, Parry Grove Loop Trail. If you enjoy interpretive nature trails, the Reserve has some nice ones, complete with self guiding leaflets. The Guy Fleming 6/10-mile loop trail points out the Torrey pines and takes you to South Overlook where you might glimpse a migrating California gray whale. The Parry Grove 4/10-mile loop trail will show you the many kinds of plants in the reserve: toyon, yucca, manzanita and other coastal shrubs. At the north end of the Reserve, you can visit Los Penasquitos Lagoon, a salt water marsh patrolled by native and migratory waterfowl.

42
Bayside Trail

**Old Point Loma Lighthouse to Cabrillo National Monument Boundary
2 miles RT;**

Cabrillo National Monument on the tip of Point Loma marks the point where Portuguese navigator Juan Rodriguez Cabrillo became the first European to set foot on California soil. He landed near Ballast Point in 1542 and claimed San Diego Bay for Spain. Cabrillo liked this "closed and very good port" and said so in his report to the king.

Point Loma Lighthouse, built by the federal government, first shined its beacon in 1855. Because fog often obscured the light, the station was abandoned in 1891 and a new one built on lower ground at the tip of Point Loma. The 1891 lighthouse is still in operation today, but manned by the Coast Guard. The 1855 lighthouse has been wonderfully restored to the way it looked when Captain Israel and his family lived there in the 1880s.

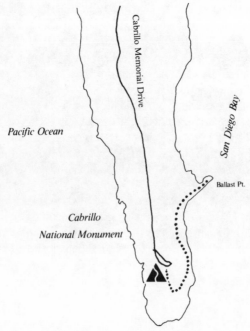

Point Loma Lighthouse

The Bayside Trail begins at the old lighthouse and winds past yucca and prickly pear, sage and buckwheat. The Monument protects one of the last patches of native flora, a hint at how San Diego Bay must have looked when Cabrillo's two small ships anchored here.

Directions to trailhead: Cabrillo National Monument is open daily from 9:00 a.m. to 5:15 p.m. (8:30 a.m. to 7:45 p.m. June 25 to September 4). Take Harbor Drive west to State Highway 209. Turn left and follow the signs to the park.

The Hike: Before embarking on this hike you may want to obtain a trail guide at the Visitors Center. The guide describes the coastal sage and chaparral communities and local history.

The first part of the Bayside Trail winding down from the lighthouse, is a paved road. At a barrier, you'll bear left on a gravel road, once a military patrol road. During World War II, the Navy secreted bunkers and searchlights along the coastal bluffs. Now, in spring, the slopes are covered with Black-eyed Susans, Indian paintbrush, sea dahlias and monkey flowers.

The Bayside Trail provides fine views of the San Diego Harbor shipping lanes. When Navy ships pass, park rangers broadcast descriptions of the vessels. Also along the trail is one of California's most popular panoramic views: miles of seashore, 6,000-foot mountains to the east and Mexico to the south.

The trail dead-ends at the park boundary.

Return the same way.

43

Border Field Trail

Border Field State Park to Tijuana River
3 miles RT
Border Field State Park to Imperial Beach
6 miles RT

This beach trail begins at the very southwest corner of America, at the monument marking the border between Mexico and California. When California became a territory at the end of the Mexican-American War of 1848, an international border became a necessity. American and Mexican survey crews determined the boundary and the monument of Italian marble was placed to mark the original survey site in 1851. Today the monument stands in the shadow of the Tijuana Bull Ring and still delineates the border between the United States and Estados Unidos Mexicanos.

During World War II the Navy used Border Field as an air field. Combat pilots received gunnery training, learning to hit steam-driven targets that raced over the dunes on rails called Rabbit Tracks. Despite multifarious real estate schemers, the Navy retained control of Border Field until the land was given to the state in the early 1970s.

Before you walk down the bluffs to the beach, take in the panoramic view: the Otay Mountains and San Miguel Mountains to the east, Mexico's Coronado Islands out to sea, and to the north—the Tijuana River floodplain, the Silver Strand, Coronado.

Much of the Tijuana River Estuary, one of the few unspoiled salt marshes left in Southern California, is within Border Field's boundaries. This hike explores the dune and estuary ecosystems of the state park and takes you to wide sandy Imperial Beach.

Directions to trailhead: Border Field State Park is located in the extreme southwestern corner of California, with Mexico and the Pacific Ocean as its southern and western boundaries. Exit Interstate 5 on Hollister. Proceed to a "T" intersection and bear west (right) 2 miles to the state park. The park closes at sunset.

The Hike: Follow the short bluff trail down to the beach, which is under strict twenty-four hour surveillance by the U.S. Border Patrol. The beach is usually deserted, quite a contrast to crowded Tijuana Beach a few hundred yards south. As you walk north on Border Field State Park's mile and a half beach, you'll pass sand dunes anchored by salt

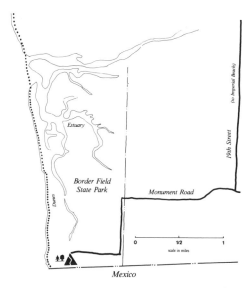

Border Field State Park

Estuary

Dunes

Monument Road

19th Street

(to Imperial Beach)

0   1/2   1
scale in miles

Mexico

grass, pickleweed and sand verbena. On the other side of the dunes is the Tijuana River Estuary, an essential breeding ground, feeding and nesting spot for over 170 species of native and migratory birds. At Border Field, the salt marsh is relatively unspoiled, unlike many wetlands encountered farther north, which have been drained, filled, or used as dumps.

Take time to explore the marsh. You may spot hawks, pelicans, terns and ducks, as well as many other nesting and shore birds. Fishing is good for perch, corbina, and halibut, both in the surf along Border Field Beach and in the estuary.

A mile and a half from the border you'll reach the mouth of the Tijuana River. Only after heavy storms is the Tijuana River the wide swath pictured on some maps. Most of the time it's easily fordable at low tide.

Continue north along wide, sandy Imperial Beach, past some houses and low bluffs. Don Santiago Arguello once owned all the land from the tip of San Diego Bay to the Mexican border in the days before California became part of the United States. Imperial Beach was named by the South San Diego Investment Company, in order to lure Imperial Valley residents to build summer cottages on the beach. Waterfront lots could be purchased for $25 down, $25 monthly and developers promised the balmy climate would "cure rheumatic proclivities, catarrhal trouble, lesions of the lungs," and a wide assortment of other ailments.

In more recent times, what was once a narrow beach protected by a seawall, has been widened considerably by sand dredged from San Diego Bay. There's good swimming and surfing along Imperial Beach and the waves can get huge. Our route reaches Imperial Pier, built in 1912 and the oldest in the county.

If you're feeling especially frisky you may hike on to Silver Strand. Otherwise, return the same way.

159

Anacapa Island

Chapter 8

ISLANDS

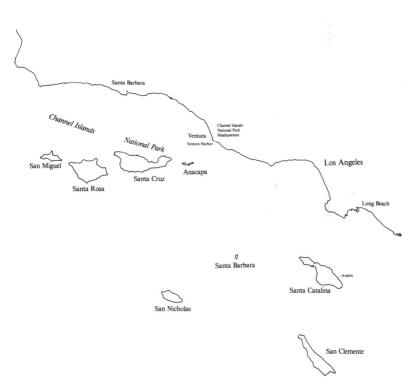

Islands

WELCOME TO Channel Islands National Park. A visit here, the park service brochure pledges, "is always an adventure." It quickly adds more discouraging words: "The seas are unforgiving; getting onto the islands is an uncertainty and the islands themselves are primitive and ecologically fragile."

According to the Park Service, hikers should remember to STAY AWAY FROM CLIFFS, which are always collapsing into the Pacific, and to KEEP ON TRAILS to avoid cacti and potholes. Also to RESPECT THE SEA ANIMALS, including the fish "which can inflict nasty punctures and bites," and the sea lions which "can seriously injure" persons getting too near.

Congress, in establishing the national park in 1980, did not intend it as a vacation spot for the comfort-loving, but rather as a preserve for what some have called the "American Galapagos." Top priority was given to the protection of sea lions and seals, endemic plants like the Santa Cruz pine, rich archaeological digs, and what may be the final resting place of Portuguese navigator Juan Rodriguez Cabrillo, who explored the California coast for the Spanish crown in the sixteenth century.

The only disappointed visitors are casual tourists who, while motoring along Highway 101, see the sign: Channel Islands National Park. They exit the freeway, only to find that the "national park" in Ventura Harbor is simply a reception building. The park is out there in the Pacific, 14 to 60 miles away, a series of blue-tinged mountains floating on the horizon.

The Channel Islands parallel the Southern California coast, which at this point is running in a more or less east-west direction. In 1980, five of the eight Channel Islands—Anacapa, San Miguel, Santa Barbara, Santa Cruz and Santa Rosa—became America's fortieth national park. The U.S. Navy practices maneuvers on San Nicolas and San Clemente. Farther south, Santa Catalina, until a decade ago owned by the Wrigley (chewing gum) family, is a developed isle with hotels, bars, restaurants and a casino where big bands like Harry James played in the '30s and '40s. However, even well-visited Catalina has great stretches of open space in the interior and offers fine hiking.

When islands can be seen offshóre, particularly from a place like Los Angeles, they almost seem to imply reproach, as if by toiling in the din of the metropolis you are missing the siren call of adventure on the near horizon. The Channel Islands beckon, not with South Seas or Caribbean sensuousness, but with dramatic mountaintops and jagged shorelines of awesome cliffs and deep caves.

San Miguel Island

From Anacapa, only 12 miles to the mainland, you get the feeling that the Channel Islands may once have been connected to the mainland. Until recently, geologists had this same feeling, figuring that the Santa Monica Mountains, which bisect Los Angeles, marched out to sea and their peaks appeared offshore as the Channel Islands. This belief was based on the assumption that a land bridge was the only way terrestrial animals could have arrived. The discovery of fossil elephant bones on Santa Rosa and San Miguel changed their thinking. Scientists at first believed that the dwarf mammoth, a six-foot cousin to the mainland behemoth, could not swim; therefore a land bridge was necessary. In truth, elephants are excellent swimmers—their trunks are superb snorkels and air pockets in their skulls give the animals excellent buoyancy. So the land bridge theory is kaput, and it's now theorized that the islands rose out of the Pacific through volcanic action 14 million years ago, later sinking and rising many times as glaciation alternated with massive melting. The four northern islands were linked, until about twenty thousand years ago, into a super-island called Santaroasae, only to part company during the final glacial melt into the wave-sculpted islands we see today.

The islands' even sea-tempered climate has preserved plants that either were altered through evolution on the mainland or perished altogether at man's hand. What you see on the islands is Southern California of a millenium ago, patches of Paradise before The Fall.

44

San Miguel Island Trail

Cuyler Harbor to Lester Ranch
3 miles RT; 715' gain

San Miguel is the westernmost of the Channel Islands. Eight miles long, four miles wide, it rises as a plateau, 400 to 500 feet above the sea. Wind-driven sands cover many of the hills which were severely overgrazed by sheep during the island's ranching days. Once owned by the U.S. Navy which used it as a bombing site and missile tracking station, the island is now managed by the National Park Service.

Three species of cormorants, storm petrels, Cassin's auklets, and the pigeon guillemot nest on the island. San Miguel is home to six pinniped species: California sea lion, northern elephant seal, steller sea lion, harbor seal, northern fur seal and Guadalupe fur seal. The island may host the largest elephant seal population on earth. As many as 15,000 seals and sea lions can be seen basking on the rocks during mating season.

A trail runs most of the way from Cuyler Harbor to the west end of the island at Point Bennett, where the pinniped population is centered. The trail passes two round peaks, San Miguel Peak and Green Mountain, and drops in and out of steep canyons to view the lunar landscape of the caliche forest. Please check in with the resident ranger and stay on the established trails because the island's vegetation is fragile.

Directions to trailhead: Plan a long day or overnight trip to San Miguel. It's at least a five-hour boat trip from Ventura. There are no regularly scheduled trips to the island. The Cabrillo Marine Museum in San Pedro and the Santa Barbara Natural History Museum sometimes sponsor trips. Contact Island Packers Company, P.O. Box 993, Ventura; (805) 642-1393 or Channel Islands National Park Headquarters (at the Ventura Harbor), 169 Anchors Way Drive, Ventura, CA 93003; (805) 644-8157.

The Hike: Follow the beach at Cuyler Harbor to the east. The harbor was named after its original government surveyor in the 1850s. The beach around the anchorage was formed by a bight of volcanic cliffs that extend to bold and precipitous Harris Point, the most prominent landmark on the San Miguel coast.

At the east end of the beach, about ¾ of a mile from anchoring waters, a small footpath winds its way up the bluffs. It's a relatively steep trail

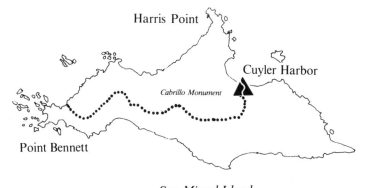

San Miguel Island

following along the edge of a stream-cut canyon. At the top of the canyon, the trail veers east and forks. The left fork takes you a short distance to the Cabrillo Monument.

Juan Rodriguez Cabrillo, Portuguese explorer, visited and wrote about San Miguel in October 1542. While on the island he fell and broke either an arm or a leg (historians are unsure about this). As a result of this injury he contracted gangrene and died on the island in January 1543 and it's believed (historians disagree about this too) he was buried here. In honor of Cabrillo, a monument was erected in 1937.

The right fork continues to the remains of a ranch house. Of the various ranchers and ranch managers to live on the island, the most well-known were the Lesters. They spent 12 years on the island and their adventures were occasionally chronicled by the local press. When the Navy evicted the Lesters from the island in 1942, Mr. Lester went to a hill overlooking Harris Point, in his view the prettiest part of the island, and shot himself. Within a month his family moved back to the mainland. Not much is left of the ranch now. The buildings burned down in the 1960s and only a rubble of brick and scattered household items remain.

For a longer 8-mile roundtrip the hiker can continue on the trail past the ranch to the top of San Miguel Peak (916′), down, and then up again to the top of Green Mountain (850′). Ask rangers to tell you about the caliche forest composed of calcified sheaths of plants that died thousands of years ago. Calcium carbonate has reacted with ancient plants' organic acid, creating a ghostly forest.

45

Anacapa Island Loop

From Visitors Center
2 miles RT

Anacapa Island, closest to the mainland, was called *Las Mesitas* (Little Tables) by Portolá in 1769. Later the Chumash Indians' name for the island, *Eneeapah* (believed to mean "deception") came into popular use and the name evolved into Anacapa. Ventura sheepmen once owned the island. There's no water on the island, so it's hard to imagine how the sheep survived. The popular belief is that night fog was so dense that the sheep's coats became soaked at night, each sheep becoming a wooly sponge by morning. So what could be more natural than one sheep drinking from the fleece of another? So the story goes...

Anacapa, just 12 miles southwest of Port Hueneme, is the most accessible Channel Island. It offers the day hiker a sampling of charms of the larger islands to the west. Anacapa also provides a refuge for schools of fish. Below the tall wind-and-wave-cut cliffs, sea lions bark at the crashing breakers. Gulls, owls, herons, and pelicans call the cliffs home.

Arch Rock, Anacapa Island.

Anacapa Island

Anacapa is really three islands chained together with reefs that rise above the surface during low tide. West Anacapa is the largest segment, featuring great caves where Indians are said to have collected water dripping from the ceiling. The middle isle hosts a wind-battered eucalyptus grove. The east isle, where the National Park Service has its visitors center, is the light of the Channel Islands; a Coast Guard lighthouse and foghorn warns ships of the dangerous channel. Anacapa's 60,000-candlepower light has been in service since 1932. The guardian light is visible for twenty-four miles in all directions and the foghorn never ceases its call.

This day hike tours east Anacapa Island. The island is barely a mile long and a quarter mile wide, so even though you tour the whole island, it's a short hike. The route follows the Park Service's figure-eight shaped nature trail, which explains some of the human history of the isle and gives you views of Cathedral Cove, a western gull rookery, and miles of blue Pacific.

Directions to trailhead: For the most up-to-date information on boat departures, contact Channel Islands National Park, 1699 Anchors Way Drive, Ventura, CA 93003; (805) 644-8157. Most commercial tour operators leave from the Ventura and Oxnard marinas. A number of "whale watching" tours are offered during winter when the gray whales migrate. Some of these tour boats land on Anacapa Island and some don't, so charter your boat with care. One company, Island Packers, runs year-round to Anacapa. Their boats leave every Saturday and Sunday. Weekday trips are scheduled during whale season and in summer. To contact them: Island Packers Company, P.O. Box 933, Ventura, CA 93001; (805) 642-1393, 642-7688.

The Hike: It's a romantic approach to East Anacapa, as you sail past Arch Rock. As you come closer, however, the island looks God-forsaken; not a tree in sight. But as you near the mooring at the east end of the isle, the honeycomb of caves and coves is intriguing and you feel

more interested. A skiff brings you to the foot of an iron stairway. You climb 150 stairs, ascending steep igneous rocks to the cliff tops.

What you find on top depends on the time of year. January through March you may enjoy the sight of 30-ton gray whales passing south on their way to calving and mating waters off Baja California. In summer, the isle's vegetation is a dormant brown. Even the giant coreopsis, the island's featured attraction, is a mass of withered leaves and flowers. However, in early spring, the coreopsis is something to behold. It is called the tree sunflower, an awkward, thick-trunked perennial, sometimes reaching ten feet in height. It sprouts large yellow blossoms. When you approach the island by boat and look up to the cliffs, it's as if someone threw a yellow tablecloth atop them.

The nature trail leaves from the visitors center where you can learn about island life, past and present. A helpful pamphlet is available which describes the trail's features. Remember to stay on the trail. The island's parched ground cover is easily damaged.

Along the trail, a campground and several inspiring cliff-edge nooks invite you to picnic. The trail loops in a figure-eight through the coreopsis and returns to the visitors center.

46

Black Jack Trail

Black Jack Junction to Little Harbor;
8 miles one way; 1500′ loss

Catalina Island's terrain is rugged and bold, characterized by abrupt ridges and V-shaped canyons. Many of the mountaintops are rounded, however, and the western end of the island is grassland and brush, dotted with cactus and seasonal wildflowers. Bison, deer, boar and rabbits roam the savannahs.

This hike is a good introduction to the island; it samples a variety of terrain on the island, inland and coastal. Transportation logistics are a bit complex, but the trail is easy to follow.

Directions to trailhead: The Santa Catalina Island Conservancy, a non-profit foundation, owns 86% of the 28-mile long, 8-mile wide island and manages it as a preserve. Permits are required for hiking and camping in the interior and are available in Avalon at the Conservancy office, 206 Metropole Avenue, (213) 510-1421, at the Department of Parks and Recreation located in the Island Plaza, 213 Catalina St., (213) 510-0688, and at the Information Center, 302 Crescent Avenue, (213) 510-0303. Permits for hiking are free.

Transportation to Catalina: Catalina Island Cruises departs daily from San Pedro to Avalon. Limited service to Two Harbors. (213) 775-6111, 330 Golden Shores Blvd., Long Beach, CA 90802.

For additional information and a trail map, contact: Los Angeles County Dept. of Parks and Recreation, Catalina Island, P.O. Box 1133, Avalon, CA 90704; (213) 510-0688.

From Avalon, you'll be traveling to the trailhead via the Catalina Island Interior Shuttle Bus, which departs from 213 Catalina Avenue (the island's "Main Street"), (213) 510-0840 (Avalon) or 510-0303 (Two Harbors). For a few dollars per person, the shuttle bus will drop passengers off at Black Jack Junction.

The Hike: At signed Black Jack Junction, there's a fire phone and good views of the precipitous west ridges. The trail, a rough fire road, ascends for one mile over brush and cactus-covered slopes. You'll pass the fenced, but open shaft of the old Black Jack Mine (lead, zinc and silver). On your left a road appears that leads up to Black Jack Mountain, at 2,006 feet the second highest peak on Catalina. Continue past this junction.

Ahead is a picnic ramada with a large sunshade and nearby a signed junction. You may descend to Black Jack Camp, which is operated by L.A. County. Here you'll find tables, shade, and water. Set in a stand of pine, the camp offers fine channel views.

Bear right on the signed Cottonwood/Black Jack Trail. A second junction soon appears. Continue straight downhill. The other trail ascends to Mt. Orizaba, the island's highest peak (2097′).

The trail descends steeply through a canyon, whose steep walls are a mixture of chaparral and grassland and are favored by a large herd of wild goats. At the bottom of the canyon pass through three gates of a private ranch. (Close all gates; don't let the horses out.) The trail reaches the main road connecting Little Harbor with Airport-in-the-Sky. You may bear left at this junction and follow the winding road 3½ miles to Little Harbor. For a more scenic route of about the same distance, turn right on the road. Hike about 200 yards to the end of the ranch fence line, then bear left, struggling cross-country briefly through spiney brush and intersect a ranch road. This dirt road follows the periphery of the fence line on the east side of the ranch to the top of a canyon. You bear left again, still along the fence line. You ascend and then descend, staying atop this sharp shadeless ridge above pretty Big Springs Canyon. When you begin descending toward the sea, you'll spot Little Harbor.

Little Harbor is the primary campground and anchorage on the Pacific side of the island. It's a good place to relax while you're waiting for the shuttle bus, or to refresh yourself for the hike through Buffalo country to Two Harbors.

Avalon Harbor, turn of century

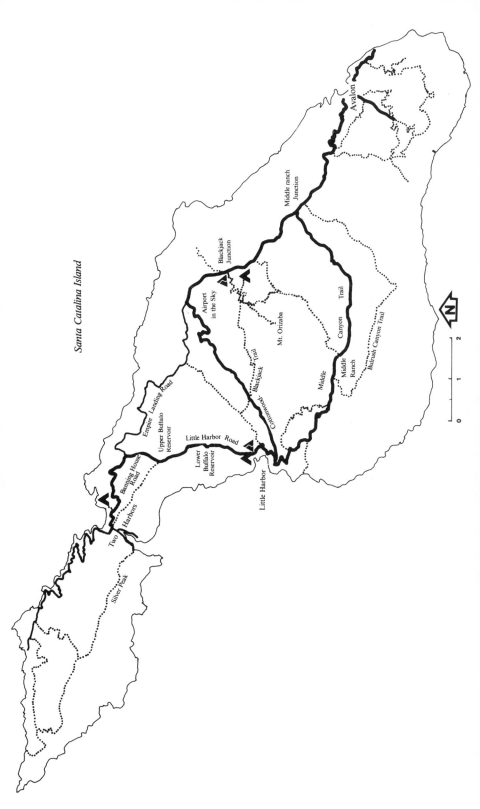

Santa Catalina Island

Avalon

Middle ranch Junction

Blackjack Junction

Airport in the Sky

Blackjack Trail

Cottonwood Trail

Mt. Orizaba

Middle Canyon Trail

Middle Ranch

Bulrush Canyon Trail

Empire Landing Road

Upper Buffalo Reservoir

Little Harbor Road

Lower Buffalo Reservoir

Little Harbor

Banning House Road

Two Harbors

Silver Peak

N

0   1   2

47

Little Harbor Trail

Little Harbor to Two Harbors
   7 miles one way

In 1602, when Vizcaino's ship sailed toward the mountains of Catalina, the explorer was certain he had reached two islands. From a distance, the mountainous land on the east end appears to be separated from a smaller portion on the west end; in fact, it's an optical illusion. The eye is tricked by a low-lying isthmus, the narrowest section of Catalina. Catalina Harbor lies on the ocean side of this isthmus, Isthmus Cove on the channel side, and together this area is called Two Harbors.

As the Wrigley family opened the isle to tourism, Two Harbors pursued a destiny far apart from Avalon. In the 1920s and 1930s it was a peaceful sanctuary for film celebrities and the Los Angeles elite who could indulge in the luxury of yachting.

This hike takes you across the island from the Pacific side to the Channel side and offers fine views and a chance to watch buffalo. Your destination is Two Harbors, popular with campers, boaters, and fishermen.

Directions to trailhead: (See Black Jack Trail for ferry and shuttle bus information.) A shuttle bus takes you across the island from Avalon to Little Harbor in the morning and will pick you up in Two Harbors for your return to Avalon. If you purchased a ferry ticket from the mainland to Avalon, and plan to leave the island from Two Harbors, please inform the ferry company; no additional charge, but the company needs to know.

The Hike: Our route departs from a former stagestop, Little Harbor, now a popular campground and anchorage. We join Little Harbor Road, ascending higher and higher into Little Springs Canyon. Buffalo graze both sides of the canyon and two reservoirs have been developed for the animals. In 1924, when Hollywood moviemakers were filming Zane Grey's classic western, "The Vanishing American," 14 head of buffalo were brought to the island for the film. Recapturing the buffalo after filming proved impossible so the beasts were left to roam. The animals adapted well to life on Catalina and quickly multiplied. Today's population is held to 400-500, the ideal number for the available pasturage.

At an unsigned junction a mile past Lower Buffalo Reservoir, bear left on Banning House Road, which will take you 3¼ miles to Two Harbors. (Little Harbor Road continues north, then west to Two Harbors if you prefer to stick to the road.) Rough Banning House Road ascends very steeply up a canyon roamed by wild boar. At the windswept head of the canyon you are rewarded with superb views of the twin harbors of Catalina Harbor and Isthmus Cove and can see both the eastern and western fringes of the island.

A steep northeasterly descent brings you to the outskirts of Two Harbors. You'll have no trouble improvising a route past ranchettes and private clubs down to the ferry building.

Chapter 9

SANTA ANA MOUNTAINS

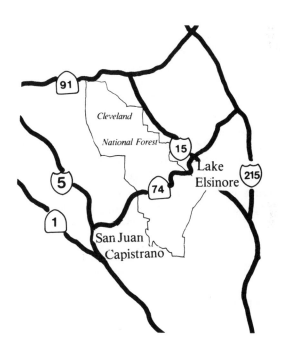

Santa Ana Mountains

THE SANTA ANA MOUNTAINS may be the most overlooked and underutilized recreation area in Southern California. Stretching the entire length of Orange County's eastern perimeter, the Santa Anas roughly parallel the coast. This coastal range is only about twenty miles inland and the western slopes are often blanketed with fog. By midmorning, the sun scatters the fog into long colorful banners that invite you to some far-off parade. The coast has a cooling influence on what is often a very hot range of mountains. Except for the dead of summer, most days offer pleasant hiking.

The Santa Anas offer no dramatic escarpment to compare with that of the San Jacintos, nor do they have the rugged tumbled look of the San Gabriels; these mountains are round, brushy, inviting. At first glance, they seem to be inundated by a monotonous sea of chaparral. But in the chaparral teems wildlife, and even the most casual hiker will be amazed at the number of rabbit and quail who hop and flutter from the dense undergrowth. The range is covered with great masses of buckthorn, greasewood, sumac and scrub oak. Alternating with the chaparral are oak woodlands, wide potreros, and boulder-strewn creeks with superb swimming holes.

The range is a granite block, which has been uplifted and depressed below sea level several times. On top of the mountains, marine sediments occur in successive formations. The Santa Anas increase in altitude from north to south, culminating in the twin peaks of Old Saddleback— Mount Modjeska (5440') and Mount Santiago (5860'). The crest of the range has been filed down and eroded by wind and weather exposing the hard granite at the surface.

The Santa Ana Mountains came under federal protection in 1893 when the Trabuco Canyon Forest Reserve was formed. The name was changed to the Trabuco National Forest in 1906, the forest later was enlarged and eventually assigned to the Cleveland National Forest in 1908. "Trabuco" is a name left behind by the 1769 Portola expedition. It means "blunderbuss" and refers to the loss of such a weapon by one of Portola's foot soldiers in these mountains. Today, 136,500 acres of the Santa Ana Mountains are included in the Trabuco District.

Many of the present hiking trails existed a hundred years ago. The San Juan and San Mateo trails are reworked Indian paths. Other trails were built by the CCC during the Depression. The Ortega Highway, which crosses the Santa Anas from San Juan Station to Lake Elsinore, opened up the mountains to camping and hiking but not to the same extent the Rim of the World Highway opened up the San Bernardinos or the Angeles Crest Highway opened up the San Gabriels.

View from Holy Jim Trail

The Santa Anas see few people because off-highway access is a real pain in the axle and many of the trailheads require traveling on dirt roads. Many Cleveland National Forest dirt roads are so washboarded that they are better suited to foot travel. In past years, motorcycles ran rampant over the trails, but the Forest Service has, of late, done a much better job of controlling trailbikers and mad jeepsters.

Highlight of the Santa Anas is the San Mateo Canyon Wilderness, set aside by Congress in 1984. The 40,000-acre preserve protects San Mateo Canyon, a relatively untouched land of 200-year-old oaks, potreros and quiet pools.

The Santa Ana Mountains can be a wonderful place to hike, particularly in the cooler months—October through May. Early morning is my favorite time here. A soft mist enshrouds the coastal range and chills the air. The wet dew glistens. As the sun slowly rises, the mist turns to haze and the brushy outlines of the ridges are silhouetted against the sky. The oak portreros glow golden, welcoming the new day.

48

Holy Jim Trail

Holy Jim Creek to Falls
2½ miles RT; 200′ gain.
Holy Jim Creek to Bear Springs
10 miles RT; 2200′ gain.
Holy Jim Creek to Santiago Peak
16 miles RT; 4000′ gain.

Holy Jim Trail, creek and canyon take their names from Cussin' Jim Smith, an early Santa Ana Mountain settler who when displeased, unleashed a string of unholy epithets. Turn of the century mapmakers were unwilling to geographically honor such a blasphemer so they changed his name to "Holy."

The trail is one of the most popular in the Santa Anas though many hikers go only as far as the falls. Holy Jim Trail is in fair-to-mediocre shape and is sometimes heavily overgrown with brush. The trail is something of a Santa Ana Mountains sampler, giving the hiker a creek, a lush canyon, a waterfall, oak woodland, and chaparral smothered slopes. All this and a view too!

Directions to trailhead: Take Interstate Highway 5 to the El Toro Road exit(S-18); go east through Mission Viejo. Turn right on Live Oak Canyon Road (S-19). One mile after passing O'Neil Park, the road crosses Trabuco Wash. Turn left into the wash and head up rocky Trabuco Road. Don't be intimidated; the road gets better, not worse, as it heads up the wash and is suitable for most passenger cars. In 5 miles you'll pass a volunteer fire department station and reach Holy Jim turnoff on your left. Park in the dirt area near the turnoff.

The Hike: Walk up Holy Jim Road, passing a number of summer homes. Beyond the last home, you'll reach a gate (locked during fire season). Holy Jim Trail (6W03) begins on the other side of the gate and heads up vine- and oak-filled lower Holy Jim Canyon. The trail stays near Holy Jim Creek for the first mile, crossing and re-crossing the bubbling waters near some stone fish dams. A mile from the gate, the trail crosses the creek one last time. At this creek crossing, an unsigned, but well used, side trail heads upstream to Holy Jim Waterfall. It's ¼ mile to the falls and well worth a visit. Push your way through the wild grape

and boulderhop up the creek bed to the cool grotto. The falls will seem even more spectacular if you engage in a little delayed gratification and save them for your return from Bear Springs.

Option: To Bear Springs. At the creek crossing, the Holy Jim Trail turns downstream for a few hundred yards. You're treated to a good view of the northern Santa Ana Mountain country. The trail soon takes you on a stiff climb up the west side of the canyon. If the trail is severely overgrown and seems fit for mice not men, it's time to put on your long pants. After some hearty switchbacking through thick brush, the trail begins a long contour along the canyon wall. As the trail nears Bear Springs, it gets less brushy and there is some flora you can look *up* to: shady oaks with an occasional big cone Douglas fir or Coulter pine. Santiago Peak comes into view. The northern Santa Anas were once known as Sierra de Santiago for this dominant peak. You can't miss Santiago Peak; it's the only mountain around with a forest of antennas atop it.

Bear Springs is located at the intersection of the Holy Jim Trail and the Main Divide Truck Trail. An enclosed concrete water tank is at the intersection, but the tank does not dispense water to thirsty hikers. You can get plenty of water from the creek, but it probably should be purified. The shady area around the springs is cool and pleasant, an ideal lunch stop.

Option: To Santiago Peak. Return the same way, or if you're feeling rambunctious, continue another 3 miles (gaining 1800 feet) on the Main Divide Truck Trail to Santiago Peak, the highest summit in the Santa Anas. On a clear day, you can see a hundred miles from the 5,687 foot peak.

Season: All year
Recommended map: Cleveland
National Forest
Topo: Sitton Peak
See map p. 183

49
Bear Canyon Trail

Ortega Highway to Pigeon Springs
5½ miles RT; 700′ gain
Ortega Highway to Sitton Peak
10½ miles RT; 1300′ gain

Bear Canyon Trail offers a pleasant introduction to the Santa Ana Mountains. The trail visits refreshing Pigeon Springs, which welcomes hot and dusty hikers to a handsome oak glen. If you hike to the springs early in the morning, before other visitors arrive, you may see a coyote, bobcat, or deer sipping the cool waters.

Bear Canyon Trail climbs through gentle brush and meadow country, visits Pigeon Springs, and arrives at Four Corners, a meeting place of several major hiking trails that tour the southern Santa Anas. One of these trails takes you to Sitton Peak for a fine view.

Directions to trailhead: Take the Ortega Highway (74) turnoff from the San Diego Freeway (Interstate 5) at San Juan Capistrano. Drive east 20 miles to the paved parking area across from Ortega Oaks store. Bear Canyon Trail starts just west of the store on Ortega Highway.

Departing from the parking lot is the 2-mile San Juan Loop Trail, another nice introduction to the Santa Ana Mountains.

You can obtain trail information and purchase a Cleveland National Forest map at El Cariso Station, located a few miles up Highway 74.

The Hike: From the signed trailhead, the broad, well-graded trail climbs slowly up brushy hillsides. The trail crosses a seasonal creek, which runs through a tiny oak woodland.

A half mile from the trailhead, you'll enter the San Mateo Canyon Wilderness, set aside by Congress in 1984. The 40,000-acre preserve protects San Mateo Canyon, the crown jewel of the Santa Ana Mountains. If hiking in the Santa Ana Mountains agrees with you, you'll want to return for further exploration of this wilderness.

After a mile, a deceptive fork appears on the left. Ignore it. The trail climbs on, skirts the periphery of a meadow and crests a hot chaparral-covered slope. Just before the trail joins the Verdugo Trail, there's a nice view down into San Juan Canyon. Turn right (south) on Verdugo Trail and proceed ¾-mile to Pigeon Springs.

"Old Saddleback," linoleum cut by Jean Goodwin.

Pigeon Springs includes a storage tank and a horse trough. Forest rangers recommend that you purify the water before drinking. The springs are located among oaks on the left of the trail. If the bugs aren't biting, this can be a nice place to picnic.

Option: Pigeon Springs to Four Corners, Sitton Peak. Hike down the Verdugo Trail another ½-mile and you'll arrive at Four Corners, a convergence of trails (fire roads). The Verdugo Trail pushes straight ahead to an intersection with the Blue Water Trail. To the left is Blue Water Fire Road leading down to Fisherman's Camp in San Mateo Canyon. To proceed on Sitton Peak, bear right on the Sitton Peak Trail.

Follow the trail as it begins to climb and contour around the peak. There are a few trees up on the ridge but little shade en route. In a mile you'll be at the high point of Sitton Peak Trail, a saddle perched over San Juan Canyon. The high point is approximately at Forest Service marker W-56. Follow the trail another mile until you reach the southeast face of the peak. Leave the trail here and wend your way past the rocky outcroppings of Sitton Peak. On a clear day, there are superb views of the twin peaks of Old Saddleback (Mount Modjeska and Mount Santiago), Mount San Gorgonio and Mount San Jacinto, Catalina and the wide Pacific.

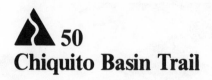

50
Chiquito Basin Trail

Ortega Hwy to Lion Canyon
11.6 miles RT; 1100' gain.

Old time mountaineers who know the rough, overgrown, and generally shoddy condition of most Santa Ana Mountains trails, joke that Chiquito Basin Trail is the first Forest Service trail project in these mountains since the invention of the automobile. The oldtimers may be pulling your gaiters, but it's true that the Chiquito Basin Trail, completed in 1974, was the first Forest Service Trail project in decades. Since it's completion, the men and women in green have done a good job of keeping it pruned and pampered, so that it remains one of the best trails in the Santa Anas.

"Chiquito" which names a basin, a spring, and the trail, is not named after a major brand of banana as you might guess, but rather was the name bestowed upon these features by a forest ranger in 1927 to honor his horse. The trail will take you past a sparkling little fall, over brushy hillsides and oak-studded slopes to shady Lion Canyon Creek.

Directions to trailhead: Take the Ortega Highway 74 turnoff from the San Diego Freeway (Interstate Highway 5) at San Juan Capistrano and drive east 19½ miles to the paved parking area across from Ortega Oaks store. The trailhead is at the east end of the parking area and is signed as the San Juan Loop Trail.

The Hike: From the signed trailhead, you'll embark on the San Juan Loop Trail in a counterclockwise direction. Bear right at the first fork. The loop trail circles the base of a small peak, following a creek much of the way. Soon the trail arrives above San Juan Falls, a pleasant place for a return visit after you've completed this hot hike. The trail then drops down into a narrow, oak-lined canyon.

A mile from the trailhead, near the junction of Bear Creek and San Juan Creek, there's a flat area and the signed intersection with the Chiquito Basin Trail. You cross San Juan Creek then follow an unnamed creek for a spell. All too soon the trail leaves this peaceful creek and begins switchbacking up the west side of the canyon. Up, up, up the dry slopes you climb on this trail lined with toyon, buckwheat and chamise. The slopes are alive with lizards and horned toads. In spring and early summer, wildflowers abound along the trail. Views are excellent when you emerge in open areas and atop ridges. Just as you despair of ever finding any shade, an oak magically appears.

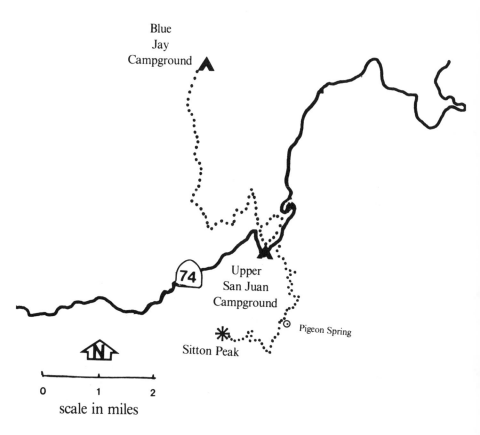

Blue Jay Campground

74

Upper San Juan Campground

Pigeon Spring

Sitton Peak

N

0 1 2

scale in miles

Five miles from the trailhead, the trail rounds a ridge and bears north toward Lion Canyon. Three quarters of a mile after rounding the ridge, you'll arrive at a meadow watered by Lion Canyon Creek. There are a number of large oak groves in Lion Canyon. Any one of them makes a splendid picnic spot.

Return the same way. When you arrive at the junction with the San Juan Loop Trail, you may want to bear right and follow this trail through a campground back to your car. Or take the left fork and retrace your steps back to inviting San Juan Falls.

Season: All year, except
times of very high water
Recommended map: Cleveland
National Forest
Topo: Sitton Peak

51
San Mateo Canyon Trail

Forest Road 7S01 to Fisherman's Camp
3 miles RT; 300' loss
Forest Road 7S01 to Lunch Rock
8 miles RT; 400' loss
Forest Road 7S01 to Clark Trail Junction
14 miles RT; 500' loss

Two hundred-year-old oaks, tangles of ferns, nettles and wild grape, and the quiet pools of San Mateo Creek make the bottom of San Mateo Canyon a wild and delightful place. This section of the Santa Ana Mountains is steep canyon country, sculpted by seasonal but vigorous streams. San Mateo Creek, a cascading waterway in winter, slows to a gurgle in summer and flows above ground only sporadically in fall.

San Mateo Canyon Wilderness, set aside by Congress in 1984, protects 40,000 acres of the Cleveland National Forest, including the headwaters and watershed of San Mateo Creek.

San Mateo Canyon takes its name from one of the padres' favorite evangelists and holy men. It's the crown jewel of the Santa Ana Mountains, a relatively untouched wilderness of oaks, potreros, and cattail lined ponds. It's a haven for turtles and rabbits. Spring brings prolific wildflower displays. The canyon drops from 3,500 feet to the coastal plain at Camp Pendleton.

This day hike plunges through the southern part of San Mateo Canyon, easily the wildest place in the Santa Ana Mountains. The San Mateo Canyon Trail and other riding and hiking trails in the wilderness have been in use since the turn of the century. Orange County Sierra Clubbers have worked on the trail, but it's often in rough shape. Creek crossings are sometimes difficult to spot.

You can journey almost as far down the canyon as you like in one day. It's 9 miles from Fisherman's Camp to the marine base, with a hundred ideal picnic spots along the way.

Directions to trailhead: Take either Highway 74 or Interstate 15 to Lake Elsinore and from there, drive southeast on I-15 to Wildomar and exit on Clinton Keith Road. Proceed 7 miles southwest to the Tenaja turnoff, forking right on Tenaja Road (7S01). You'll pass Tenaja Fire Staton and adjoining Tenaja Campground. Drive another 3 miles on 7S01 until it intersects Forest Road 7S02. Park here.

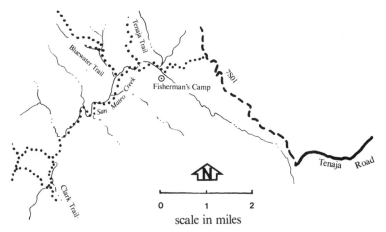

scale in miles

The Hike: Walk down the fire road, which is lined with wildflowers in spring. 1½ miles of travel brings you to Fisherman's Camp, now abandoned. Once, many "fisherman's camps" lay along San Mateo Creek. In the 1930s, anglers were attracted by superb fishing for steelhead and trout. San Mateo Canyon Trail was the favorite route to the fishing holes. Steelhead ran into the forest up San Mateo Creek as late as 1969.

Cross the creek to the oak shaded former campsite and begin hiking through ceanothus to a ridge offering a commanding view down San Mateo Canyon. The trail soon switchbacks down to the creek.

Along the creek the trail may be indistinct; simply continue down creek. About a mile after reaching the creek, you'll come to a small potrero dotted with oaks and sycamore. Here Bluewater Creek flows into San Mateo Creek and the Bluewater Trail leads off 3 miles to the Clark Trail and Oak Flat. You can picnic under the oaks near the trail junction and return, or continue down the canyon.

Option: San Mateo Canyon to Lunch Rock. Continue down the creek on the San Mateo Canyon Trail, which follows the right side of the canyon, now and then dropping to wide sandy beaches along bends in the creek. The boulders get bigger, the swimming holes and sunning spots, nicer. One flat rock, popular with Sierra Clubbers, has been nicknamed "lunch rock." A cluster of massive giant boulders form pools and cascades in the creek. It's a nice place to linger.

Option: To Clark Trail Junction. The trail takes you under ancient oaks and sycamores and along the cattail lined creek. As you near the Clark Trail, San Mateo Canyon Trail utilizes part of an old mining road. Beyond the Clark Trail junction San Mateo Canyon Trail soon peters out and the route down-canyon is trailless to Camp Pendleton, 9 miles from Fisherman's Camp. The Clark Trail, if you're game, ascends very steeply 1½ miles to Indian Potrero.

Return the same way.

185

Chapter 10

SAN BERNARDINO MOUNTAINS

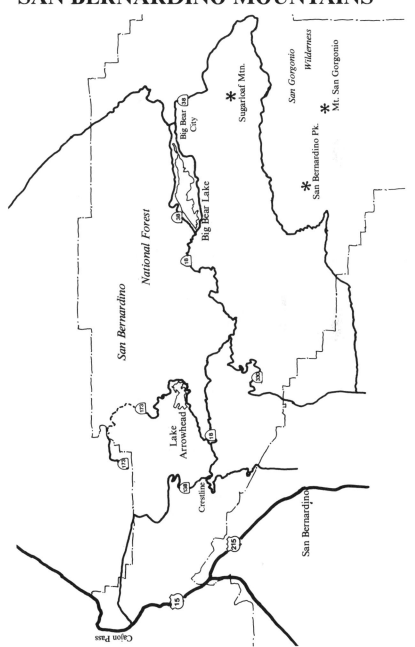

San Bernardino Mountains

WHEN THAT RESTLESS breed of American—the trapper the trader, the Army mapmaker—pushed westward, they had to reckon with arid country beyond the lower Colorado River. The Mojave Desert gave sustenance to few and mercy to none. And if crossing the desert's uncharted sands wasn't enough of a problem, another formidable obstacle barred the way west—the San Bernardino Mountains. Sheer granite cliffs, thorny chaparral, snow-bound passes. The San Bernardinos today suffer the indignities of the sewer line, and the TV antenna, and may seem a little *too* accessible; however, the high peaks still challenge the hardy.

The San Bernardino range is a vast fault block about sixty miles long and thirty miles wide, extending in a southwesterly direction across Southern California. The western portion is plateau-like with some rather broad uplands—unusual for Southern California mountains. At its western end, the mountains terminate abruptly at Cajon Pass, which separates the range from the San Gabriel Mountains. Geologists speculate that the two ranges may originally have been one. Rocks on both sides of the pass suggest the earth's convulsions wrenched the mountains fifteen to twenty-five miles apart. The earth is still shuddering in this area; the San Andreas Fault runs through the pass. It's an excellent place to observe fault features and view this Maker and Shaker of continents.

Although the two ranges look something alike at first glance, they aren't the same age. The San Gabriels are more sheer, more faulted. The San Bernardinos are younger, less fractured by earthquakes.

The southern slopes of the San Bernardinos consist of high ridges cut by many deep stream gorges. At the western end of the highest ridge is San Bernardino Peak. The ridge culminates toward the east in Mount San Gorgonio (Old Greyback, 11,502'), the highest peak in Southern California. To the south, San Gorgonio Pass separates the San Bernardinos from the San Jacinto Range. The discovery of the pass in 1853 enabled Los Angeles to be tied to the rest of the United States by railroad line.

By the mid-nineteenth century, industrious Mormons and other settlers invaded the San Bernardinos. They drove the Serrano and Cahuilla Indians into the desert. Newcomers clearcut miles of forest, dammed and channeled the wild waters into irrigation ditches, and dynamited the mountains in search of gold. But not all visitors blasted, mined, and milled. Some came to relax in the alpine air and enjoy the good life. Summer tents and homes clustered around highcountry lakes. To many people, the San Bernardinos no longer seemed so remote, so formidable.

A large portion of the San Bernardino Mountains was protected by the establishment of the San Bernardino Forest Reserve, created by President Benjamin Harrison in 1893. Subsequently, the name "Reserve" was changed to "National Forest." In 1908, the San Bernardino National Forest and Angeles National Forest were brought together and administered under the latter's name, but in 1925, President Coolidge divided them.

The San Bernardino National Forest is a huge parcel of land, bigger than the state of Rhode Island, the second largest national forest in California (first is Los Padres). It's also one of the most heavily used national forests in the nation. One year over 7,000,000 people came to the San Bernardino Mountains. It was as if everyone in the L.A. Basin visited once.

The Rim of the World Highway, leading from San Bernardino to Lake Arrowhead and Big Bear Lake, opened up the mountains to recreation on a large scale. Chiseled into rock walls, the road takes many a switchback and hairpin turn, following the crest of the range and ascending to over 7,000 feet. Even the highway's primitive forerunners with their forty-one percent grades, didn't stop thousands of guns and fishing rods from assaulting the wilderness. Big Bear and Arrowhead Lakes became one of Southern California's most popular resort areas. The rustic hotels, spas and lodges delighted Southern Californians in the same manner the Catskills and Berkshires served the needs of New Yorkers.

There are many quiet places in the 700,000-acre San Bernardino National Forest where the hiker can behold waterfalls, stunning fields of flowers, and golden eagles soaring above lofty crags. The San Gorgonio Wilderness contains all the delights of these mountains and none of its "civilization." The San Gorgonio Wild Area was created by a law in 1931 as a place free of restaurants and roads, camps and resorts. In 1965, Congress declared it a Wilderness.

Seventy-one miles of hiking trails wind through the highcountry wilderness. The 56,000-acre Wilderness is a lonely refuge from the glass and chrome world far below. On the high spine of the range, Mount San Gorgonio and other 10,000-plus foot peaks—Dobbs, Jepson, Charlton and San Bernardino—stand shoulder to shoulder. When you reach the summit on one of these peaks you'll be only ninety miles from downtown L.A. and two miles high; but the city will seem more remote than the map indicates, and you'll feel much higher.

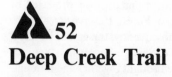

Season: All year
Topo: Lake Arrowhead
Recommended: San Bernardino
National Forest

52

Deep Creek Trail

Highway 173 to Deep Creek Hot Springs
12 miles RT: 800' gain
Mojave River Forks Dam to Deep Creek Hot Springs
8 miles RT; 800' gain

Kick off your Levis and slip into the relaxing waters of Deep Creek, site of the only hot spring in the San Bernardino Mountains. Float awhile and gaze up at the sky. Feel your urban anxieties vaporize in one of nature's hot tubs.

No one is quite·sure what makes the water hot in Deep Creek Hot Springs. Some believe the heat is left over from the earth's smoldering beginnings; others think the warmth comes from radioactive elements. Most Deep Creek devotees consider it a moot point anyway.

Deep Creek is a study in contrasts. Upstream it contains pools of great size, flanked by sheer masses of stone. The water has scoured great basins and the creek bounds down the waterworn rocks from one pool to the other. The pools are home to rainbow trout, who attract the angler. Downstream Deep Creek is but a shadow of its former self. It ends ingloriously in the desert sands; only water-polished stones indicate its path among the dunes.

This is a fine hike on a well-built stretch of Pacific Crest Trail. The trailhead, formerly at Mojave River Forks Dam, has been relocated to Highway 173. The Army Corps of Engineers has closed the dam to the public. However, most day hikers still begin this trail at the dam. Call the San Bernardino National Forest, Arrowhead Ranger District, in Rimforest, for the latest trail information.

A more popular route, because it's only a 3-mile roundtrip to Deep Creek Hot springs, is via Goat Trail. Directions to this alternate trailhead are given below.

The trash situation sometimes gets out of hand in the vicinity of the hot springs. Please pack out what you packed in. Due to frequent injuries caused by broken glass, the Forest Service now prohibits the possession of glass containers in the Deep Creek area.

The hot springs can be crowded on weekends. Bronzed children frolic at water's edge, oldsters emit gurgles of delight as they settle into the soothing heat, hikers enjoy a reward for a hike well done. Weekdays the springs are deserted. You'll "take the cure" by yourself.

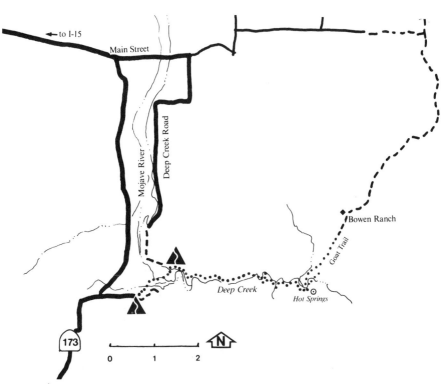

Directions to trailhead: From Interstate Highway 15, a few miles north of Cajon Pass, take the Hesperia turnoff. Go east through Hesperia on Main Street, following it as it curves south at the outskirts of town. Turn left (east) on Rock Springs Road. If the bed of the Mojave River is dry, you're in luck. Cross it and turn right (south) on Deep Creek Road. Follow this road to pavement's end. Bear left on a dirt road and drive straight up the spillway of the Mojave River Forks Flood Control Dam. Don't worry, you won't drive into a reservoir; the dam holds no water. The trail begins at the east (left) end of the parking lot.

Directions to Highway 173 trailhead: Exit Interstate 15 on Highway 138. Go right (east) 9 miles and veer left on Highway 173, following the latter highway 8 miles to pavement's end. At the point where the dirt road begins, you'll find parking and a signed trailhead for the Pacific Crest Trail.

To Goat Trail trailhead: From Rock Springs Road, turn right (east) on Roundup Way. Follow it to Bowen Ranch Road and make a right (south) turn. When the road forks, bear right to the Bowen Ranch house, where you pay a toll. The road will then lead to a parking area at the beginning of Goat Trail. Note that Goat Trail ends on the north side of Deep Creek and you will have to cross Deep Creek to get to the hot pools. Crossing Deep Creek during spring or at times of high water can be difficult.

191

The Hike: The trail heads on a straight line for Deep Creek Canyon. It follows the roadbed of an asphalt road (broken up but not removed) through sagebrush down into the lower reaches of Deep Creek near its meeting with the Mojave River. Uncontrolled motorcycle and ATV use has seriously eroded the creekbed. The noise echoing through the canyon is simply awful.

The trail proceeds on the right bank of the creek. You will have to cross the creek and pick up the trail on the other side. You can scramble around to the top of the dam and make your way over to the spillway, where good trail resumes.

Past the spillway you'll find another signed trailhead. Ascend five easy switchbacks to the north canyon wall. You stay high on the almost barren wall for 2 miles until the trail descends to Deep Creek, then crosses it on an arched bridge. Now you follow the south slope for another mile and reach oak shaded McKinley Creek. This is a good area for picnicking, cooling off, or exploring. The last mile of trail contours along the south slope, then drops down close to the creek just before the hot springs.

The hot springs, enclosed by rocks bordering the creek, range from warm to hot. Pick your spot. You may be joined by the Hesperia locals, who usually take the Goat Trail.

Leave behind the skinny-dippers and return the same way.

▲ 53

Siberia Creek Trail

Season: April-November
Recommended map: San
Bernardino National Forest
Topo: Big Bear Lake,
Keller Peak

Forest Road 2N11 to Champion Lodgepole Pine
1 mile RT; 100' loss
Forest Road 2N11 to The Gunsight
3 miles RT; 600' loss
Forest Road 2N11 to Siberia Creek Trail Camp
8 miles RT; 2500' loss

California nurtures some superlative trees. The tallest tree on earth is a coast redwood, the oldest tree a bristlecone pine. And in the San Bernardino Mountains grows the world champion lodgepole pine.

It's a pleasant stroll, suitable for the whole family, to the world champion. More ambitious hikers will enjoy tramping down Siberia Creek Trail to the appropriately-named rock formation, "The Gunsight," and on to Siberia Creek Trail Camp for a picnic.

Siberia Creek, born atop the high mountains near Big Bear Lake, is a delightful watercourse. It flows southwest through a deep coniferous forest and lush meadowlands, then cascades down a steep rocky gorge and adds its waters to Bear Creek.

From Forest Road 2N11, Siberia Creek Trail passes the Champion Lodgepole, the largest known lodgepole pine in the world. It then travels alongside Siberia Creek through a wet tableland, detours around a ridge while Siberia Creek crashes down a precipitous gorge, then rejoins the creek at Siberia Creek Trail Camp.

This is an "upside down" hike; the tough part is the trek uphill back to the trailhead. Pace yourself accordingly.

Directions to trailhead: From Highway 18 at the west end of Big Bear Lake Village, turn south on Tulip Lane. You'll pass Coldbrook Campground on the right and ½-mile from the highway, turn right on Forest Road 2N11. Follow the "Champion Lodgepole" signs five miles to the signed trailhead. Parking is alongside the road.

The Hike: The trail follows a fern-lined little brook. You'll notice some tall cornstalk-like plants—corn lillies—and a generous number of red flowers—Indian paintbrush.

A half mile's travel brings you to a signed junction. Go right 75 yards to the Champion Lodgepole, which towers above the east end of an emerald green meadow. You can't miss it. It's the only 110-foot tree around.

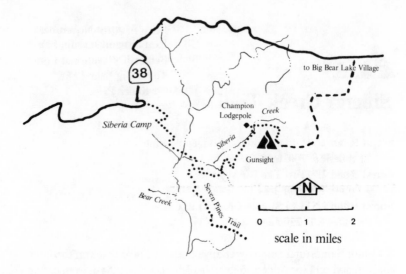

scale in miles

Lodgepole—also called tamarack—pines are usually found at higher elevations; but here at 7,500 feet, nurtured by the rich, well-watered soil, they not only thrive, but achieve mammoth proportions. The World Champion is 75 inches in diameter (usually the species measures 12 to 24 inches) and is estimated to be over 400 years old. Lodgepoles are easily identified by their yellow-green paired needles. While hiking in Southern California, these pines are probably the only ones you'll come across that have two needles per bundle. By way of comparison, you might notice that the pinon pine has one needle, the ponderosa pine three and the limber pine, five.

Option: To the Gunsight. Return to the main trail and continue through open forest, skirting the meadowland. You cross and re-cross Siberia Creek. After the second crossing, the meadowland ends and the creek crashes down the gorge. The trail avoids the gorge and swings down and around the steep slopes of Lookout Mountain. About one mile from the Champion Lodgepole, an interesting rock formation called The Gunsight appears. Squint through the Gunsight, aim your anti-civilization gun at the haze below, and squeeze off a few shots.

Option: To Siberia Creek Trail Camp. From The Gunsight, the trail descends the slopes of Lookout Mountain. A series of switchbacks brings you to a trail junction. Bear right (north) on the Seven Pines Trail and proceed ¾-mile to Siberia Creek Trail Camp. For the day hiker, this oak and alder-shaded camp makes a nice picnic spot or rest stop.

Return the same way.

Season: Apr.-Nov. Manzanita Springs;
June-Nov. San Bernardino Peak
Recommended map: San
Bernardino National Forest
Topo: San Gorgonio Mt.
Wilderness Permit required

54

San Bernardino Peak Trail

Camp Angelus to Columbine Spring Camp
9 miles RT; 2000' gain
Camp Angelus to Limber Pine Bench Camp
12 miles RT; 3200' gain
Camp Angelus to San Bernardino Peak
16 miles RT; 4700' gain

Mount San Bernardino, together with its twin peak Mount San Gorgonio, just five miles away and 900 feet higher, anchors the eastern end of the San Bernardino Mountains. Mount San Gorgonio, the peak by which all other Southern California peaks are measured, is a landmark. Mount San Bernardino too is, quite literally, a landmark. In 1852, Colonel Henry Washington and his army surveying party were directed to erect a monument atop Mount San Bernardino. The monument was to be an east-west reference point from which all future surveys of Southern California would be taken. The colonel's crew took many readings but heat waves from the San Bernardino Valley below befuddled their triangulations. The surveying party ingeniously solved this dilemma by lighting bonfires atop the peak in order to make their calculations at night.

This trail takes you from deep pine forest to exposed manzanita slopes and visits the old survey monument. The higher slopes of Mount San Bernardino are beautiful and rugged subalpine terrain. A number of trail camps along the way offer spring water and rest. You won't forget this hike for a long time.

Directions to trailhead: Drive east on Interstate Highway 10 to Redlands, leaving the freeway at the Highway 38 exit. Follow Highway 38 twenty miles east to Camp Angelus. Turn right near the ranger station at a sign that reads: "San Bernardino Peak Trail." Follow the dirt road ¼-mile to the large parking area. The signed trailhead is at the north end of the lot.

The Hike: The trail begins ascending through a mixed forest of pine, fir and oak, switchbacking up the beautifully wooded slope. You mount a ridge, walk along its crest for a brief distance, then continue climbing. You're welcomed into the glories of the San Gorgonio Wilderness by a wooden sign, 2 miles from the trailhead. A little beyond the wilderness

boundary, the grade grows less severe. As you climb above 8,000 feet, the Jeffrey pine become widely spaced. Shortly, the trail penetrates a manzanita covered slope. You pass a sidetrail leading down Manzanita Springs. Don't drink the water. The sidetrail continues on ¼-mile to Columbine Springs Trail Camp, which usually has water later in the season than Manzanita.

Option: To San Bernardino Peak. A short distance beyond Manzanita Springs Trail Junction the trail begins climbing more earnestly. The trail ascends in fits and starts over slopes covered with manzanita and homely chinquapin and in 1½ more miles reaches Limber Pine Springs Camp. Actually, all the shade in the area is provided by lodgepole pines. Another ¼-mile up the trail is Limber Pine Springs, usually a dependable source of water. The trail begins a long traverse south, switchbacking up to Camp Washington, a trailcamp with plenty of view and nothing to drink. One hundred yards from the trail is Colonel Washington's baseline monument, which looks like little more than a pile of stone rubble. The trail climbs another ½-mile, where it intersects a brief side trail that takes you to the summit of Mount San Bernardino (10,624′).

Sign the summit register, enjoy the view, and return the way you came.

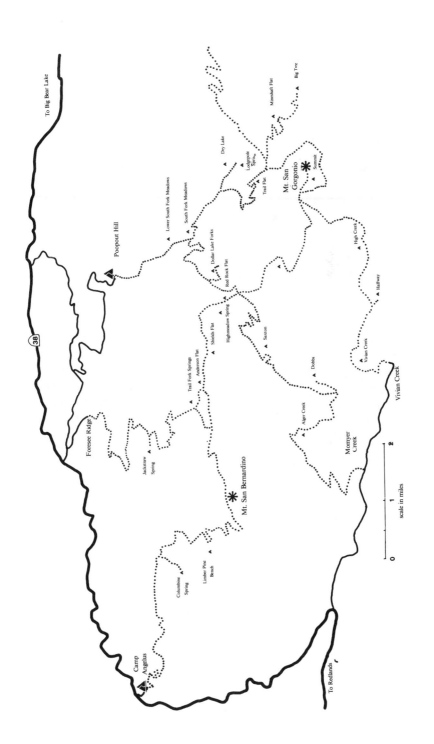

To Big Bear Lake

38

To Redlands

Camp Angelus

Foresee Ridge

Jackstraw Spring

Columbine Spring

Limber Pine Bench

Mt. San Bernardino

Poopout Hill

Trail Fork Springs

Anderson Flat

Shields Flat

Highmeadow Spring

Saxton

Alger Creek

Dobbs

Momyer Creek

Vivian Creek

Halfway

High Creek

Vivian Creek

Lower South Fork Meadows

South Fork Meadows

Dollar Lake Forks

Red Rock Flat

Dry Lake

Lodgepole Spring

Trail Flat

Mt. San Gorgonio

Summit

Minehaft Flat

Big Tree

scale in miles

0   1   2

Season: June-Oct.
Topo: Moonridge, San
  Gorgonio Mountains
Recommended map: San
Bernardino National Forest
Wilderness Permit required

 55

Mount San Gorgonio Trail

Poopout Hill to South Fork Meadows
3½ miles RT: 600′ gain.
Poopout Hill to Dollar Lake
7½ miles RT; 1400′ gain.
Poopout Hill to Mount San Gorgonio
16 miles RT; 3700′ gain.

Optional return via Dry Lake and Sky High Trail
17 miles RT;

Most of us in the Southland have looked east and marveled at Mount San Gorgonio, the highest peak in Southern California. The 11,499-foot mountain is most striking in winter when its snow-covered peak can be seen reaching far above the smog-covered metropolis. In summer, the view from the basin to the top is not so spectacular; the dull gray granite summit is hard to find among the hydrocarbons. But summer is the best time in the alpine high country, looking down at what you left behind. Every Southern California hiker should climb Mount San Gorgonio once in his life. From the top there's a 360-degree panoramic view from the Mexican border to the southern Sierra, from the Pacific to the far reaches of the Mojave!

Luiseno Indian legend has it that San Gorgonio and San Jacinto peaks were brothers and among the first born of the Earth Mother, who made all things. It would be hard to improve on Earth Mother's handiwork. Mount San Gorgonio's alpine vegetation includes carpets of buttercups and that venerable survivor of inclement weather, the limber pine. Mountain lions, mule deer and bighorn sheep roam the high slopes and golden eagles soar over the summit.

The mountain got its name from an obscure fourth-century Christian martyr. Irreverent Americans began calling the mountain "Grayback." Its bare, gravelly summit stretches laterally for quite some distance above the timberline, giving the appearance of a long, gray back. American slang agrees with Luiseno semantics. The Indians called it Pewipwe or "Gray Head."

This strenuous hike on good trail will take you on a long trek through the heart of the San Gorgonio Wilderness. You'll slosh through soggy

Dollar Lake

meadows and a riot of wildflowers, pass two small lakes, Dry and Dollar, and gain the summit of "Old Grayback" for the best view of Southern California available to a hiker. You can make a loop trip out of the hike (adding only 1 more mile) for a splendid tour de force.

Directions to trailhead: From Interstate Highway 10 in Redlands, take the Highway 38 exit. Follow the Highway 38 signs and proceed 25 miles to Jenk's Lake Road West. Follow this road for 7 miles to its end near the summit of Poopout Hill and park in the large parking area. Caution: Hikers have experienced a large number of thefts in this lot. Lock your car and secure your valuables.

The Hike: From the northeast edge of the parking area, you follow the beaten path to the top of Poopout Hill, where you can look up at the mountain you are about to climb. You then dip down the hill and begin ascending through the woods. In a mile, South Fork Creek appears on your left and you parallel it to South Fork Meadows, also known as Slushy Meadows.

South Fork Meadows is a well stocked delicatessen of flowery delights: wild rose, giant lemon lily, mountain iris, Indian paintbrush, golden yarrow. Dozens of tiny streams, which form the headwaters of the Santa Ana River, roam at will through the ferns and wispy waist-high grasses. Walking through this slushy sanctuary you feel you are treading on a giant, emerald green sponge. Beneath the ponderosa pine and white fir, you'll find the idyllic picnic spot you've always dreamed about. If you're not feeling especially energetic, you could spend a day here and be quite happy.

Option: Dollar Lake. Energetic souls will return to the trail. It skirts the west edge of the meadow, passes the junction with the trail that heads toward Dry Lake (you'll descend on this trail if you take the return option from the peak), and begins switchbacking up wooded slopes. After a mile of climbing, first through ponderosa pine and then through lodgepole pine, you'll begin a long contour around the wall of the basin that holds Dollar Lake. The trail passes a manzanita-covered slope and reaches a junction 1¾ miles from South Fork Meadows. Go left. In a few hundred yards you reach another junction and turn left again. Follow the easy ¼-mile trail down the basin wall to the lake. Dollar Lake, so named because it gleams like a silver dollar, is one of the most popular backcountry spots in the San Gorgonio Wilderness and is another ideal place to picnic or laze away a day. Return to the main trail the way you came.

Option: To Gorgonio Summit. You resume climbing for another mile to Dollar Lake Saddle (approx. 10,000') and a three-way junction. One trail goes northwest to San Bernardino Peak, a second southwest to Mill Creek Canyon. You bear left and proceed southeasterly toward San Gorgonio. One half mile beyond the junction, you pass another junction with the rocky side-trail that ascends Charlton Peak. In another ½-mile you pass Dry Lake View Camp, a waterless trail camp amidst great boulders. From here, you can look down into Dry Lake Basin, where you'll pass if you return from the peak via the Sky High Trail. Soon you'll pass junctions with the Vivian Creek Trail and the Sky High Trail. Keep to your left at both junctions. Cross a last rise and climb to the summit of San Gorgonio.

No other Southern California mountain commands such an uninterrupted panoramic view. To the north are the deep green meadowlands of the upper valley of the Santa Ana River. To the west is the murky megalopolis. To the east is the Mojave. South is San Gorgonio Pass and just across it, nearly level with your feet, is Mount San Jacinto.

After enjoying this 360 degree view from the top of the world, return the way you came or via the Sky High Trail.

Option: Return via Sky High Trail. This trail descends the east slope of San Gorgonio to Mine Shaft Saddle and Dry Lake and deposits you in South Fork Meadows where you intersect the trail back to Poopout Hill.

From the summit, retrace your steps on the main trail to its intersection with the Sky High Trail. Begin your descent from the clouds on the latter trail, circling first east, then north around the mountain's great shoulders. As you descend there are good view of the Whitewater drainage, gorges bearing snowmelt from San Gorgonio and carrying copious waters to the desert sands below. The awesome Whitewater country was in 1984 added to the San Gorgonio Wilderness. On its steep slopes the bighorn sheep have their lambing grounds and in its waters the legendary San Gorgonio trout is making its last stand.

As you round the east ridge, you'll pass the wreckage of a DC-3 squashed against the mountain. Three and a half miles from the summit you reach Mine Shaft Saddle on the divide between Dry Lake Basin and the Whitewater River.

Continue your descent and in two more miles you'll reach Dry Lake at 9,200 feet. In dry years it *is* dry by midsummer, but often the ten acre lake is filled to the brim, its waters lapping against the trail that surrounds the lake. The Sierra Club has sometimes stocked Dry Lake with rainbow trout.

From the Dry Lake basin, you switchback down through pine and fir 1¾ miles to South Fork Meadows, where you intersect the trail back to Poopout Hill.

On the trail to Mount San Gorgonio

Season: May-November
Recommended map: San
Bernardino National Forest
Topo: Moonridge

 56

Sugarloaf National Recreation Trail

Green Canyon Creek to Sugarloaf Mountain
8 miles RT; 2000' gain

Sugarloaf Mountain, highest peak in the San Bernardino Mountains outside the San Gorgonio Wilderness, is a particularly fine destination on a hot summer's day. The ridgeline leading to the summit is forested with pine, fir and cedar. A breeze cools the massive round shoulders of the mountain.

In the 1920s and 1930s, wild horses roamed the lower slopes of Sugarloaf Mountain. After World War I, the U.S. Calvary realized that modern warfare would not include the use of horses and allowed their horses to run wild. The horses wandered from Lucerne Valley to the Whitewater country across onto Sugarloaf Mountain where a site today is known as Wildhorse Meadows. At about the same time, fox coats became quite the rage and a number of fox farms got started in the Big Bear area. Alas, many of the horses—and wild burros that had found their way into the area—were trapped for fox food.

Sugarloaf National Recreation Trail begins at a point where Green Canyon Creek crosses Forest Road 2N93 and climbs, steeply in some places, to the 9,952' summit of Sugarloaf Mountain.

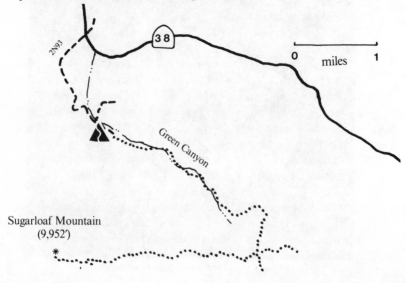

Big Bear Lake

Directions to trailhead: From Big Bear City, head east on State Route 38. The highway turns south, and about 3 miles from town, turn right on Forest Road 2N84. Take note here that the Forest Service has posted "passenger car not recommended" signs; those with low slung cars should proceed with caution—or be prepared to walk part of the 1½-mile distance to the trailhead—if the road is poor. When 2N84 veers left, proceed straight ahead on Forest Road 2N93, which climbs a mile to Green Creek crossing. On the other side of the creek, turn right (south) onto an unsigned dirt road and follow it a few hundred yards to a parking area at a locked gate.

The Hike: Ascend on the steep dirt jeep road, which stays close to Green Creek. Two miles of hiking brings you to a saddle on the ridgeline and a trail junction.

(Straight ahead the trail continues a short distance to Wildhorse Meadows Trail Camp and descends 3 miles alongside Wildhorse Creek to the Santa Ana River and a junction with Highway 38. The upper part of this trail, which passes through Jeffrey pine and fir, is quite pleasant; the lower reaches, which descend through an eroded and messy burn area, is not.)

Turn right (west) and ascend on the Sugarloaf Trail. Above 9,000 feet, the trail passes through thick stands of lodgepole pine. The trail contours around Peak 9775 (Anybody have a more lyrical name?) and dips to a saddle. Gnarled and picturesque junipers hug the ridgeline. The trail then ascends to the forested summit of Sugarloaf Peak. Eastern San Bernardino Mountain peaks and the San Gorgonio Wilderness are part of the fine view.

Return the same way.

Season: All year but best Nov.-May
Recommended map: San
Bernardino National Forest
Topo: Palm Desert 15′

57
Cactus Springs Trail

Pinyon Flat to Horsethief Creek
5 miles RT; 900′ loss
Pinyon Flat to Cactus Spring
9 miles RT; 300′ gain

The Santa Rosas are primarily a desert range and a unique blend of high and low desert environments. Desert-facing slopes of these mountains are treeless; scorched and sparse as the desert itself. Throughout the foothills and canyons, lower Sonoran vegetation—chamise, barrel cacti, ocotillo and waxy creosote predominate. In some of the canyons with water on or near the surface, oases of native California fan palms form verdant islands on the sand. With an increase in elevation, the wrinkled canyons and dry arroyos give way to mountain crests bristling with pinyon pine and juniper.

The Santa Rosa Wilderness, set aside in 1984, is located near the border of San Diego and Riverside Counties, about 120 miles from L.A., about 90 miles from San Diego. The 20,000-acre wilderness lies within the boundaries of the San Bernardino National Forest. Another part of the Santa Rosa Mountains is under state stewardship and protects habitat for the bighorn sheep; a third section was proposed as wilderness by the California Desert Protection Act of 1986, but Congress failed to act on the bill.

When visiting the Santa Rosas, early California botanist/travel writer Charles Francis Saunders was so overwhelmed by the contrast between the harshness of the lower desert slopes and relative gentleness of the higher slopes that he called it "a botanic version of the millenial day when lion and lamb shall lie down together." Saunders may have massacred a metaphor but the hiker who dodges cholla and yucca, then takes a snooze upon a soft bed of pinyon pine needles, will find it easy to tell lion from lamb, botanically speaking.

Trails are few in the Santa Rosas; most are faint traces of Cahuilla Indian pathways. The ancients climbed the mountains to hunt deer and gather pinyon pine nuts and escape the desert heat. When the snows began, they descended from the high country to the gentle, wintering areas below.

The Cactus Spring Trail, an old Indian path overhauled by the Forest Service, gives the hiker a wonderful introduction to the delights of the

Horsethief Creek crossing

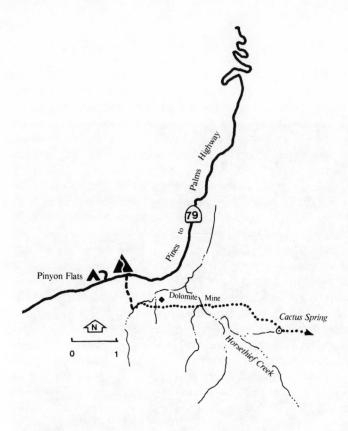

Santa Rosas. The trail first takes you to Horsethief Creek, a perennial waterway that traverses high desert country. A hundred years ago horse thieves pastured their stolen animals in this region before driving them to San Bernardino to sell. The cottonwood shaded creek invites a picnic. Continuing on the Cactus Spring Trail, you'll arrive at Cactus Spring. Along the trail is some wild country, as undisturbed as it was in 1774 when early Spanish trail blazer Juan Bautista Anza first saw it.

Two hiking tips: (1) No dependable water source exists along the Cactus Spring Trail, so bring your own. (2) Although the trail traverses a wilderness area, it also crosses private land; please respect private property.

Directions to trailhead: From Highway 111 in Palm Desert, drive 16 miles up Highway 74 to the Pinyon Flat Campground. (From Hemet, it's a 40-mile drive along Highway 74 to Pinyon Flat Campground.) Opposite the campground is Pinyon Flat Transfer Station Road, also signed "Elks Mountain Retreat." You'll follow this road about ¾-mile. Just before reaching the (trash) Transfer Station, a rough dirt road veers to the left. Follow this road 200 yards to road's end.

206

The Hike: Follow the dirt road east a short distance to Fire Road 7SO1, then head south for ¼-mile. You'll then take the first road on your left. A sign reassures you that you are indeed on the way to Cactus Spring, and you'll soon pass the abandoned Dolomite Mine, where limestone was once quarried. Approximately ¼-mile past the mine site, the dirt road peters out and the trail begins. Here you'll find a sign and a trail register.

The trail bears to the east and dips in and out of several (usually) dry gullies. A half mile past the sign-in register, a sign welcomes you to the Santa Rosa Wilderness. Cactus Spring Trail does not contour over the hills, but zigs and zags, apparently without rhyme or reason. The bewitching, but easy to follow trail finally drops down to Horsethief Creek. At the creek crossing, Horsethief Camp welcomes the weary with flowing water and shade.

Return the same way, explore up and down the handsome canyon cut by Horsethief Creek, or continue to Cactus Spring,

Option: To Cactus Spring. Crossing the creek, you climb east out of the canyon on a rough and steep trail past sentinel yuccas guarding the dry slopes. The trail stays with a wash for a spell (the route through the wash is unmarked except for occasional rock ducts), then gently ascends over pinyon pine-covered slopes. It's rolling, wild country, a good place to hide out. Alas, Cactus Spring, a few yards north of the trail is almost always dry.

207

Mount San Jacinto

Chapter 11

SAN JACINTO MOUNTAINS

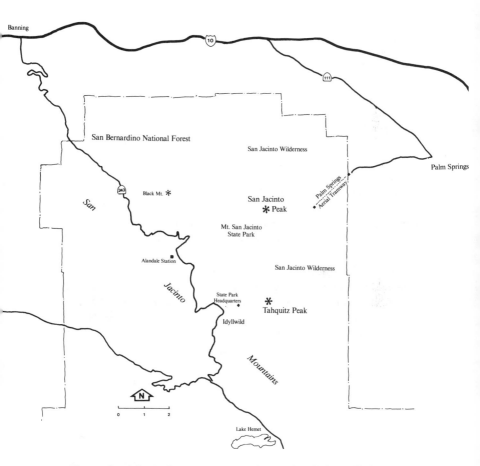

*The trails of the Indians went everywhere. They led up all the
canyons. They were hunting trails for the men and used by the
women to gather the seeds, nuts, plums and acorns, so many
things. They led from one tribe to the other. All the Indians did
their part to keep the trails clear. These trails were sacred to the
Indians.*

—CHIEF FRANCISCO PATENCIO
Palms Springs Indians

San Jacinto Mountains

MANY HIKERS in the San Jacinto Mountains can't resist comparing this range and the High Sierra. While comparisons often leave low chaparral-covered mountains on the short end, the alpine San Jacintos fare well because the range shares many geologic similarities with the Sierra Nevada. Both ranges are bold uplifted masses of granite. Both are westward tilted blocks located near powerful earthquake faults. Both veer abruptly out of the desert without a geologic fanfare of foothills preceding them.

The late Carey McWilliams called Southern California an island on the land. The San Jacintos could well be described the same. The ten thousand foot peaks of the San Jacintos and their shorter but no less majestic stony neighbors are completely separated from the rest of Southern California by low passes and desert valleys. The range is bounded by San Gorgonio Pass on the north, the San Jacinto Valley on the west, the Colorado Desert and the great Coachella Valley on the east and Anza-Borrego Desert State Park to the south. The San Jacintos seem an island in the sky because of their incredibly rapid rise from the desert floor. No other place in California do alpine and desert vegetation thrive in such close proximity. Six distinct life zones, from cactus dotted desert and palm canyons to arctic alpine summits can be encountered within five horizontal miles of travel. On the base is Lower Sonoran vegetation of creosote and ironwood. Above this is the Upper Sonoran of manzanita and scrub oak, soon giving way with rise in elevation to dense mountain forests of pine and cedar. In narrow belts around the high summits are those hearty survivors—the lodgepole pine and limber pine. Finally some stunted species, including alpine sorrel grow on the peaks and are classified in the Arctic-Alpine Zone. Each life zone has a unique set of inhabitants. Shy and reclusive bighorn sheep patrol the desert-facing high country, mule deer browse the verdant meadows, golden eagles soar over the high peaks.

During the great logging boom of 1880-1910, timber barons sent their choppers farther and farther up the slopes of the San Jacintos. Ranchers grazed thousands of sheep and cattle in the alpine meadows. Even the most shortsighted could see the destruction of the mountain watershed and with local settlers urging protection for the range, President Grover Cleveland established the San Jacinto Timberland Reserve in 1897. It was a huge chunk of land, extending from the San Gorgonio pass to the Mexican border. The San Jacinto Reserve was later combined with a portion of the Santa Ana Mountains to create the Cleveland National Forest. After several horrible fires in 1924, federal foresters decided the huge tract of land was too unwieldy for fire suppression purposes and the San Jacintos were taken from the Cleveland National Forest and attached to the nearby San Bernadino National Forest, where they remain today.

In the mid-thirties, CCC workers camped in Round and Tahquitz Valleys and built an extensive, well engineered trail system through the San Jacintos. Some years as many as 15,000 hikers travel the backcountry on these trails.

The wild areas in the San Jacinto Mountains are now administered by both state park and national forest rangers. The middle of the region, including San Jacinto Peak, is included within Mount San Jacinto Wilderness State Park. On both sides of the peak, north and south, the wilderness is administered by the San Jacinto District of the San Bernardino National Forest.

Access to the San Jacintos was difficult until Highway 243, "The Banning to Idyllwild Panoramic Highway" was built. As late as World War II, it was a muffler massacring, steep, narrow, unpaved route that forded streams. A new paved "high gear" road opened in 1948, with actress Jane Powell performing the ribbon cutting duties as the Banning High School Band played.

Boosterism in Southern California has rarely taken a backseat to beauty and one result of this attitude is the Palm Springs Aerial Tramway. To attract tourists, it became a Palm Springs Chamber of Commerce scheme to build a tramway up Mount San Jacinto. An organization called the San Jacinto Winter Park Authority was formed and tried to sell the idea to the public as an attraction for skiers. Only the most naive believed there could be any possibility of skiing down the mountain's impassable middle slopes. Conservationists thought a mechanical contrivance would despoil the wilderness and waged a fifteen-year battle with developers. The developers won. The Palm Springs Aerial Tramway opened in 1963 and now provides eighteen minute access to country once requiring a day's strenuous hiking to reach.

The range is one of those magical places that lures hikers back year after year. The seasons are more distinct here than anywhere else in Southern California. Hikers also enjoy the contrasts this range offers— the feeling of hiking in Switzerland while gazing down on the Sahara.

Season: June-Oct.
Recommended map: California
State Parks Guide, San
Bernardino National Forest
Topo: Palm Springs
Wilderness Permit required
See map p. 217

▲58

Mount San Jacinto Trail

Mountain Station to Round Valley
  4 miles RT; 600' gain
Mountain Station to San Jacinto Peak
  11 miles RT; 2300' gain

Palm Springs Aerial Tramway makes it easy for hikers to enter Mount San Jacinto State Wilderness. Starting in Chino Canyon near Palm Springs, a tram takes passengers from 2,643-foot Lower Tramway Terminal (Valley Station) to 8,516-foot Upper Tramway Terminal (Mountain Station) at the edge of the wilderness.

The day hiker accustomed to remote trailheads may find it a bit bizarre to enter Valley Station and find excited tourists sipping beers and shopping for souvenirs. The gondola rapidly leaves terra firma behind. Too rapidly, you think. It carries you over one of the most abrupt mountain faces in the world, over cliffs only a bighorn sheep can scale, over several life zones from palms to pines. The view is fantastic! When you disembark at Mountain Station, your ears will pop and you'll have quite a head start up Mt. San Jacinto.

Directions to trailhead: From Interstate 10, exit on California 111 (the road to Palm Springs). Proceed nine miles to Tramway Road, turn right, and follow the road four miles to its end at Mountain Station.

For information about tramway prices and schedules: (619) 325-1391.

State park trail information can be obtained from the Long Valley Ranger Station: (619) 327-0222.

The Hike: From Mountain Station, walk down the cement walkway through the Long Valley Picnic Area. Soon you will arrive at the state park ranger station. Obtain a wilderness permit here.

Continue west on the trail, following the signs to Round Valley. The trail parallels Long Valley Creek through a mixed forest of pine and white fir, then climbs into lodgepole pine country. Lupine, monkey flower, scarlet bugler, and Indian paintbrush are some of the wildflowers that add seasonal splashes of color.

After passing a junction with a trail leading toward Willow Creek, another 3/10 mile of hiking brings you to Round Valley. There's a trail camp and a backcountry ranger station (manned on weekends) in the valley and splendid places to picnic in the meadow or among the lodgepole pines.

An alternative to returning the same way is to retrace your steps 3/10 of a mile back to the junction with the Willow Creek Trail, take this trail a mile through the pines to another signed junction, and follow the signed trail north back to Long Valley Ranger Station. This alternative route adds only about ¼ of a mile to your day hike and allows you to make a loop.

Option: To Mount San Jacinto Peak. From Round Valley, a sign indicates you may reach the peak by either Tamarack Valley or Wellman Divide Junction. Take the trail toward Wellman Divide Junction. From the Divide, a trail leads down to Humber Park. At the divide, you'll be treated to spectacular views of Tahquitz Peak and Red Tahquitz, as well as the more distant Toro Peak and Santa Rosa Mountain. You continue toward the peak on some vigorous switchbacks. The lodgepole pines grow sparse among the crumbly granite. At another junction, ½-mile from the top, the trail continues to Little Round Valley but you take the summit trail to the peak. Soon you arrive at a stone shelter (another example of CCC handiwork) built for mountaineers who have the misfortune to be caught in winter storms. From the stone hut, you boulder-hop to the top of the peak.

There is a strong geologic similarity between the High Sierra and the San Jacintos. While standing upon the summit of Mount San Jacinto, the perceptive mountaineer may notice a subtle atmospheric similarity; both the San Jacintos and Sierra Nevada can be called "a range of light." Powerful sunlight illuminates the San Jacintos, creating sharp contrasts between light and shadow, the kind of contrast found in an Ansel Adams photograph, a six f-stop difference between the bright light shimmering on the rocky summit and the dark forest primeval below. The sun burns upon the lower slopes of Mount San Jacinto like a fire in the wind, but the upper elevations receive a more gentle incandescent light and a fraction of the heat disbursed below. Our civilization measures time by the sun, yet as you watch sunlight and shadow play tag across the slopes, you are left with a feeling of timelessness.

The view from the summit—San Gorgonio Pass, the shimmering Pacific, the Colorado Desert, distant Mexico—has struck some visitors speechless while others have been unable to control their superlatives. Helen Hunt Jackson's heroine Ramona found "a remoteness from earth which comes only on mountain heights" and John Muir found the view "the most sublime spectacle to be found anywhere on this earth!"

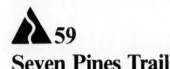

Season: May-Nov.
Recommended map: California
State Parks Guide, San
Bernardino National Forest
Topo: Palm Springs 15′

▲59
Seven Pines Trail

Dark Canyon to Deer Springs
7½ miles RT; 2600′ gain.
Dark Canyon to Little Round Valley Camp
10½ miles RT; 3600′ gain.
Dark Canyon to San Jacinto Peak
13½ miles RT; 4400′ gain.

Seven Pines Trail ascends the cascading North Fork of San Jacinto River to its headwaters at Deer Springs. The pathway travels along a granite ridgetop, then drops down forested slopes to the North Fork. Energetic hikers will join the Deer Springs Trail for an ascent of Mount San Jacinto.

Directions to trailhead: Take Highway 243 (Banning-Idyllwild Road) about 20 miles from Banning or 6 miles from Idyllwild. Just south of Alandale Forest Service Station, take the turnoff (Forest Road 4SO2) toward the Dark Canyon Campground. After a mile's travel on the dirt road, veer left at a junction. Pass through the camp and bear left at Azalea Trail junction to the trailhead.

The Hike: Seven Pines Trail ascends the ridge between Dark Canyon and the canyon cut by the North Fork. You hike out of the San Bernardino National Forest into Mount San Jacinto State Park. After a mile, the trail tops the ridge and descends eastward to the North Fork. In spring, when the river is swollen with snowmelt, the North Fork has quite a heady flow.

The trail climbs along a pine and fir covered slope, recrosses the river, and reaches a junction with Deer Springs Trail. (A right turn on the trail leads to Strawberry Junction, past Suicide Rock to Highway 243. (See Hike 60). Another possibility is to bear south on the Marion Mountain Trail which descends steeply a little over 2 miles to Marion Mountain Camp. A 3-mile car shuttle or 3-mile walk leads back to Dark Canyon Campground and the trailhead.)

Follow Deer Springs Trail left (east) ¼-mile to the former site of Deer Springs Trail Camp. The camp, overused in past years, has been abandoned by Mount San Jacinto State Park. However, its all-year water supply and pleasant locale makes it an ideal lunch or rest stop.

Option: To Little Round Valley Camp. A short walk up Deer Springs Trail from the former camp brings you to another junction. The leftward fork is Fuller Ridge Trail, which leads northwest 5 miles to Black Mountain Camp. Bear right at this junction. The trail passes through some meadowland on the way to Little Round Valley Trail Camp.

Option: To Mount San Jacinto. From Little Round Valley, the trail climbs through stands of lodgepole pine and in a little more than a mile arrives at a junction with San Jacinto Peak Trail. A left turn on this trail takes you ¼-mile past a stone shelter cabin to the top of the 10,084′ peak.

Season: May-Nov.
Recommended map: California
State Parks Guide, San
Bernardino National Forest
Topo: Palm Springs
Wilderness Permit Required

 60

Deer Springs Trail

Idyllwild to Suicide Rock
7 miles RT; 2000′ gain.

Suicide Rock is a sheer granite outcropping that provides the romantic with a tale of star-crossed lovers and rewards the hiker with splendid views of Strawberry Valley and a forest wonderland of pine and fir. Legend has it that the rock got its tragic name from an Indian princess and her lover who leaped to their deaths over the precipice rather than be separated as their chief had commanded.

Directions to the trailhead: The Deer Springs Trail begins across the highway from the Idyllwild County Park Visitor Center parking area, 1 mile west of town on the Banning-Idyllwild Highway 243. If you'd like to learn something about the history of the area, the nature museum at the county park is helpful.

The Hike: The signed Deer Springs Trail picks its way through an elfin manzanita forest, then ascends past spreading oaks and tall pines. You switchback up a ridge to Suicide Junction, 2.3 miles from the trailhead. Here you leave the Deer Springs Trail and bear east, contouring across Marion Ridge. You cross Marion Creek, whose performance is seasonal and on wet years, inspiring. A long mile from Suicide Junction you reach the back side of Suicide Rock.

From the white granite rock you'll be able to look down and see tiny Idyllwild and Strawberry Valley. On the far horizon are Tahquitz Peak and Lily Rock. Suicide Rock is a splendid place to observe the ever-changing four seasons (though you'll have a hard time climbing the rock in winter). The seasons fade in and out with clarity and distinction in the San Jacintos. Fall colors tint the black oak and azalea, winter brings a white blanket, spring is heralded by a profusion of wildflowers and the long hot summers are tempered with thunder and lightning displays. Views like this bring hikers back again and again to sample the beauty of the San Jacinto Mountains.

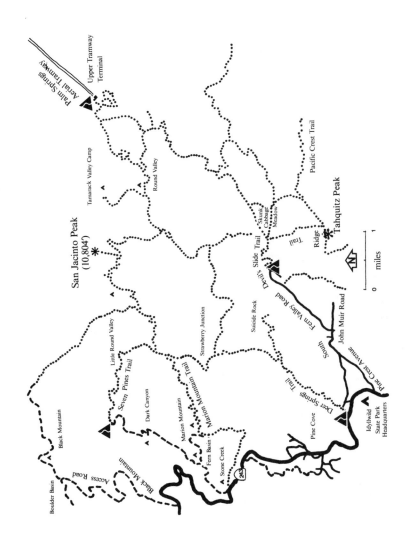

Palm Springs Aerial Tramway

Upper Tramway Terminal

Tamarack Valley Camp

Round Valley

San Jacinto Peak (10,804')

Pacific Crest Trail

Skunk Cabbage Meadow

Tahquitz Peak

Ridge

Trail

Devil's Slide Trail

Little Round Valley

Suicide Rock

Strawberry Junction

Seven Pines Trail

Fern Valley Road

South

John Muir Road

Dark Canyon

Marion Mountain

Marion Mountain Trail

Deer Springs Trail

Pine Crest Avenue

Black Mountain

Fern Basin

Stone Creek

Pine Cove

Idyllwild State Park Headquarters

Black Mountain Access Road

Boulder Basin

miles

N

0   1

61
Devil's Slide Trail

Humber Park to Skunk Cabbage Meadow
  6 miles RT; 1600′ gain.
Humber Park to Tahquitz Valley
  8 miles RT; 1700′ gain.
Humber Park to Tahquitz Peak Lookout
  8 miles RT; 2400′ gain.

Season: June-Oct.
Recommended map: California
  State Parks Guide, San
  Bernardino National Forest
Topo: Palm Springs
Wilderness Permit
  Required

Humber Park is the main jumping-off point to the San Jacinto Wilderness for hikers and rock climbers. The Devil's Slide Trail switchbacks up to Saddle Junction, where the hiker can take trails leading in four different directions—to lush flower-strewn meadows and craggy granite peaks. Today the Devil's Slide Trail is such a well-engineered, well-constructed route that its name ought to be changed. In the nineteenth century, however, the trail was an infamous bone-crusher for man and beast.

Directions to the trailhead: From downtown Idyllwild, head up Fern Valley Road. Follow the signs for Humber Park for 2 miles to the large parking area.

The Hike: Devil's Slide Trail begins below Lily (Tahquitz) Rock and the day hiker will often find himself in the company of rock climbers, jingle-jangling along with half a hardware store on their backs, out to conquer one of the six routes up Tahquitz Peak. The trail switchbacks up through a mixed forest of oak and Jeffrey pine and gives you occasional views over Strawberry Valley. In a mile, Jolley Spring, the barest of trickles by mid-summer, is passed. After switchbacking across an exposed manzanita slope, the trail enters the piney woods and shortly arrives at Saddle Junction. Here is a five-way trail intersection with signs posted high on the trees.

Option: To Skunk Cabbage Meadow. From Saddle Junction, follow the signed east fork. You'll pass through some tall pines to another junction in a short half mile. Continue toward Willow Creek, following the trail another ½ mile to Skunk Cabbage Meadow. The "cabbages" are not cabbages at all but corn lily and very poisonous. The corn lily grows thick along the waterways, all but hiding the streams from view. There's ideal picnicking in the meadow.

Return the same way or make a loop by continuing to the Willow Creek Trail back to Saddle Junction.

Hauling Lumber from Mt. San Jacinto.

Option: To Tahquitz Valley. From Saddle Junction, follow the right (east) trail, whose sign points to Tahquitz Valley. In a ½ mile another trail junction offers opportunities to hike to Skunk Cabbage Meadow, Laws, Caramba and Tahquitz Valley. Head toward the valley, hiking an easy mile through a Jeffrey pine forest to a lush meadowland. Here you'll walk hip-high among ferns and azaleas through a meadow which is splashed with cream-colored buttercups and purple lupine. As you stroll through this green bowl below Tahquitz Peak, you'll get the feeling you're hiking through a tossed salad. For the hiker who likes sylvan beauty colored in purple, yellow and emerald green pastels, this is paradise. A century ago, the cows who survived the Devil's Slide Trail found grass and contentment here.

Return to Saddle Junction the same way, loop through Chinquapin, or go down South Ridge Trail.

Option: To Tahquitz Peak. From Saddle Junction, take the south (far right) trail indicating Tahquitz Peak. A mile hike through the forest brings you to Chinquapin Flat Junction, appropriately named for the dense colonies of this spiny burred shrub found in the vicinity. Take the signed southwest trail (right) and follow the trail through chinquapin and scattered lodgepole pine toward the summit.

You may notice insect-like creatures high on the rock walls of this mountain. Southland rock climbers come to practice their craft on the superb rock walls of Tahquitz. You may hear the distinct shouts of "On belay," "climbing," or sometimes "Ohhhhhhhh shhhhhhh..." Lily Rock is the official name of the great rock, though most climbers prefer the more Indian-sounding Tahquitz.

Tahquitz Peak dominates the southern San Jacinto high country, lording over Strawberry Valley on one side, Tahquitz Valley on the other. There's a fire lookout tower on the summit manned during the long (June-November) fire season. The view is inspiring. You can look out over the San Jacintos and to the distant Santa Rosas.

Return the same way or go down South Ridge Trail, or return through Tahquitz Meadow.

Anza-Borrego State Park

Chapter 12
SOUTHERN CALIFORNIA DESERT

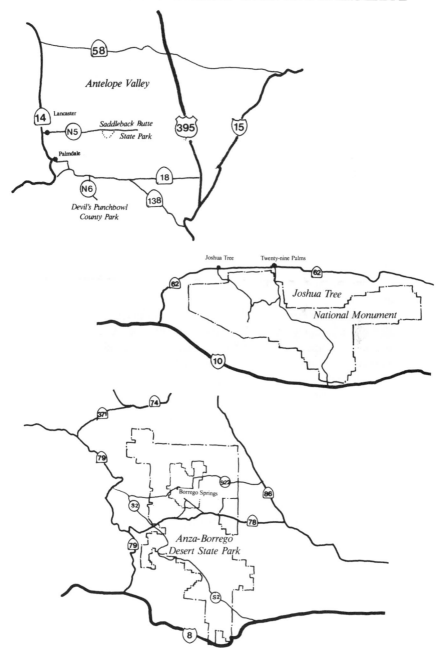

SOUTHERN CALIFORNIA DESERT

OF ALL SOUTHERN CALIFORNIA'S natural provinces, the desert is the most difficult to explore, to study, to know. Its vastness denies access and defies description, though many writers have struggled with the subject. On his expedition of 1844, explorer John C. Fremont, who usually had a good word for every California vista, found the Mojave Desert to be a repugnant wasteland. Too much sand, too much sun, too many horse skeletons, thought Fremont. "The most sterile and repulsive desert we have ever seen," he complained.

Southern Californians, those who like the desert anyway, are fortunate in having not one, but two vast deserts in close proximity to population centers: the Mojave and the Colorado. The Mojave is referred to as a high desert, for reasons of latitude and altitude. There is (relatively) more rainfall in this region and the hot season isn't as hot and severe as it is in the lower desert. The Colorado Desert is only a small part of the larger Sonoran Desert, which covers about 120,000 square miles of the American Southwest. Lower in elevation and latitude than the Mojave Desert, it is also hotter. In this guide we will day hike sections of Mojave Desert in Joshua Tree National Monument and the Antelope Valley and we'll visit a part of the Colorado Desert protected by Anza Borrego Desert State Park.

The Mojave isn't the largest or hottest desert in the west, but like the Colorado, it's ecologically one of the most diverse. At Joshua Tree National Monument, about 150 miles east of Los Angeles, the lower Colorado Desert meets the northern, higher Mojave Desert and here the flora and fauna of the former mixes with the latter. Geologically, the Mojave is diverse as well. Rockhounds find everything from Precambrian gneisses to Cenozoic volcanics. Many of the rocks, both old and new, brightly colored and drab, are tinted dark brown or black. This iron-manganese coating is known popularly as desert varnish.

During the '20s, cactus gardens became popular and entrepreneurs hauled truckloads of desert plants into L.A. for a quick sale. The Mojave was in danger of being picked clean of its cacti, yuccas and ocotillos. A wealthy socialite, Mrs. Minerva Hoyt, organized the International Desert Conservation League to halt this destructive practice. Through her lobbying efforts and Washington crusade, Joshua Tree National Monument was established in 1936.

Today, a half million acres of Colorado Desert are preserved in Anza Borrego Desert State Park and its desolation attracts rather than repels visitors. In places, the Colorado Desert appears a little *too* civilized.

Irrigation in the Imperial Valley, the All-American Canal, and a host of water reclamation projects have turned parts of the Colorado green. In Palm Springs, water and boosterism have brought "fairway living" to Southern California.

Anza Borrego country is anything but gentle, however. The state park includes virtually every feature visitors associate with a desert—washes, badlands, mesas, palm oases, and a thousand more. Birdwatchers flock to Anza Borrego. Not only is there an abundance of native species, but migratory birds along the global flyways are attracted to the park's mistletoe berries, desert springs and seeps. Anza Borrego is diverse, and it is huge: more than three times the size of Zion National Park. The park stretches almost the whole length of San Diego County's eastern border between Riverside County and Mexico. It ranges from 100 feet below sea level near the Salton Sea to 6,000 feet above sea level atop San Ysidro Mountain and offers visitors a desolation that many find pleasant.

Hiking Southern California's deserts is complicated by a lack of foot trails. Anza Borrego Desert State Park and Joshua Tree National Monument are vehicle-oriented parks; most of the popular scenic attractions can be reached by some semblance of a road. The day hiker is often forced to choose between heading cross country or putting up with jeeps and motorcycles on the dirt roads and trails. This chapter is not intended to give you a few typical desert hikes, because there is no such thing in desert terrain. Its purpose is to introduce you to our two gargantuan parks, Anza Borrego and Joshua Tree, and to encourage exploration of the wilder side of the Antelope Valley. Included are a few of the author's favorite day hikes, which follow good trails and encounter little or no motorized traffic.

Desert day hikers have some extraordinary terrain at their feet, even though it is the antithesis of all that we normally find desirable. To all the needs of a hiker—shade, water, easy-to-follow trails—the desert answers with a resounding "no."

Despite the outward harshness of the land, there are times, while wandering the wasteland, that you see the desert in a different light. As naturalist Joseph Krutch put it: "Hardship looks attractive, scarcity becomes desirable, starkness takes on unexpected beauty."

62

Saddleback Butte Trail

Campground to Saddleback Peak
4 miles RT; 1000′ gain.

Rarely visited Saddleback Butte State Park, located on the eastern fringe of Antelope Valley, offers an easily reached but out-of-the-way destination for a day hike.

This is high-desert country, a land of creosote bush and Joshua Tree. The state park, located 75 miles north of Los Angeles, takes the name of its most prominent feature—3,651 foot Saddleback Butte, a granite mountaintop that stands head and shoulders above the Antelope Valley.

The spartan country around the butte once supported thousands of pronghorn antelope—hence the name Antelope Valley—and the numerous Indian tribes who hunted them. The antelope are all gone now, victims to hunting and encroaching civilization. By interrupting the antelope's migration, Southern Pacific railroad tracks also doomed the animals; the antelope could easily cross the tracks, but instinct prevented them from doing this and they soon perished from exposure to harsh winters and the shrinkage of their habitat.

Today's park visitor may glimpse several other animals native to the Antelope Valley, including coyotes, jack rabbits, lizards and the Antelope Valley ground squirrel. Some fortunate hikers may even witness the unhurried lifestyle of a desert tortoise.

Before you hike to the top of the butte, you may wish to walk the short nature trail located near the park entrance. It's a good introduction to the Joshua Tree and other plant life found in this corner of the desert.

The trail to the boulder-strewn summit of Saddleback Peak takes a straightline course, with most of the elevation gain occurring in the last half mile. Atop the peak, the hiker is rewarded with far-reaching desert views.

Directions to trailhead: From Highway 14 (Antelope Valley Freeway) in Lancaster, take the 20th Street exit. Head north on 20th and turn east (right) on Avenue J. Drive about 18 miles, past barren land and farmland, to Saddleback Butte State Park. Follow the dirt park road to the campground, where the trail begins. Park near the trail sign. There's a state park day use fee.

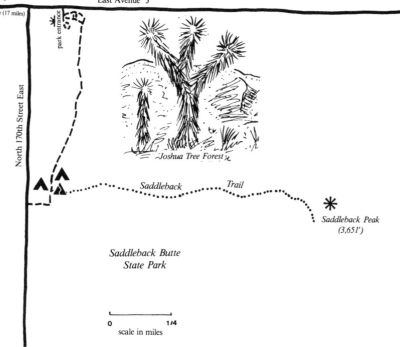

to Lancaster (17 miles)

park entrance

North 170th Street East

Joshua Tree Forest

Saddleback   Trail

✳ Saddleback Peak
(3,651')

Saddleback Butte
State Park

0   1/4
scale in miles

The Hike: The signed trail heads straight for the saddle. The soft, sandy track, marked with yellow posts (this may be the best marked trail in the state park system), leads through an impressive Joshua Tree woodland.

With the exception of pathfinder John C. Fremont, who called them "the most repulsive tree in the vegetable kingdom," most California travelers have found Joshua Trees to be quite picturesque. Mormon pioneers thought that the tree's outstretched limbs resembled Joshua pointing to the promised land.

After 1½ miles, the trail begins to switchback steeply up the rocky slope of the butte. An invigorating climb brings you to the saddle of Saddleback Butte. To reach Saddleback Peak, follow the steep leftward trail to the summit.

From the top, you can look south to the San Gabriel Mountains. You may be able to spot Mount Baldy, lording over the eastern end of the range. At the base of the mountains, keen eyes will discern the California Aqueduct, which carries water to the Southland from the Sacramento Delta. To the east is the vast Mojave Desert, to the north is Edwards Air Force Base. To the west are the cities of Lancaster and Palmdale and farther west the Tehachapis.

Return the same way.

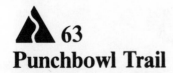 **63**

Punchbowl Trail

Season: All year, but
very hot in summer
Topo: Valyermo

South Fork Campground to Devil's Chair
6 miles RT; 1000' gain
South Fork Campground to County Park Headquarters
12 miles RT; 1000' gain

Southern California has many faults and the mightiest of these is the San Andreas. It's responsible for many a crack and crevice and much slipping and sliding in the Southland. Nowhere is the presence of the fault more obvious than in Devil's Punchbowl County Park. The dun-colored rocks have been tilted every which way and weathered by wind and rain. They are a bizarre sight to behold.

Punchbowl Trail takes you into the devil's domian, a satanically lands-caped rock garden on the desert side of the San Gabriel Mountains. The trip offers views of the Punchbowl Fault and the San Jacinto Fault— part of what seismologists call the San Andreas Rift Zone. If you're superstitious, you'll want to carry a good-luck charm in your daypack when you hike to the monstrous white mass known as the Devil's Chair.

"Bowl season" is a fine time to visit the Punchbowl. Winds scour the desert clean and from the Devil's Chair, you can get superb views of this hellish land, as well as the seemingly infinite sandscape of the Mojave.

Note that 6-mile long Punchbowl Trail may be hiked from two direc-tions. For aesthetic and logistical reasons, I prefer the route from the Forest Service's South Fork Campground to Devil's Chair.

The leg weary or families with small children may wish to proceed directly to Punchbowl County Park. A 1/3 mile nature trail, Pinyon Pathway, introduces visitors to park geology and plant life and a 1 mile loop trail offers grand views of the Punchbowl. A picnic area is perched on the rim of the Punchbowl.

Directions to trailhead: From Pearblossom Highway in Pearblossom (Highway 138) turn south onto Longview Road, then briefly left on Fort Tejon Road and right on Valyermo Road. Follow Valyermo 3 miles to Big Rock Creek Road. Two and a half miles past this junction turn right on a signed dirt road to South Fork Campground and proceed 1 mile to the special day use/hiker's parking lot below the campground. The road is suitable for passenger cars, but on occasion, Big Rock Creek may be too high for a low slung car to ford; you might have to walk an extra mile to the trailhead. The signed trail departs from the parking area.

Devil's Chair

To reach Devil's Punchbowl County Park: turn south on County Road N6 from Highway 138 in Pearblossom and follow it to Devil's Punchbowl County Park. Punchbowl Trail begins near the picnic area.

The Hike: From the parking area below South Fork Campground, join the signed trail. Almost immediately you'll reach a trail junction. (The steep South Fork Trail follows the canyon cut by the South Fork of Big Rock Creek up to the Angeles Crest Highway at Islip Saddle. Save this fine trail, which ascends from cactus to pine, from desert to alpine environments, for another day.) Stay on the Punchbowl Trail and boulderhop across the creek. (If your imagination has already run away from you, pehaps Charon the Ferryman will convey you across the watercourse.) The trail climbs through manzanita and heat-stunted pinyon pine to a saddle, where there's a view of the park and its faults. Descend

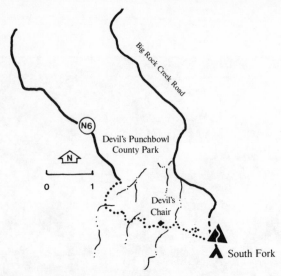

from the saddle, down chaparral-covered slopes and over to Holcomb Canyon. Along the way, notice the strange dovetailing of three plant communities: yucca covered hills, oak woodland, and juniper and piney woods.

You may wish to take a break near Holcomb Creek crossing. Oaks and big cone spruce shade the creek.

From Holcomb Creek, the trail ascends steeply up another ridge through a pinyon pine forest to the Devil's Chair. From a distance, those with fanciful imaginations can picture the devil himself ruling over this kingdom of fractured rock. Below the chair, there's an awesome panorama of the punchbowl and its jumbled sedimentary strata. The somersaulted sandstone formation resembles pulled taffy. If you look west to the canyon wall, you can see the vertical crush zone of the fault, marked by white rocks.

The Punchbowl itself may have been the work of the devil or more likely it was a deep canyon cut by streams running out of the San Gabriel Mountains. Over millions of years, the streams tore at the sedimentary rock and eroded the steep and cockeyed rock layers of the Punchbowl formation. Originally horizontal, these layers of siltstone and sandstone were folded into a syncline (U-shaped fold) by the pincer action of earthly forces.

While visiting the Devil's Chair, stay behind the protective fence; people have taken a plunge into the Punchbowl. Return to the trailhead the way you came or continue on the Punchbowl Trail to county park headquarters.

Above Devil's Chair, the trail contours west and offers good close-up views of the Punchbowl. 1½ miles from the Chair, your route crosses Punchbowl Creek, briefly joins a dirt road, then bears right on the trail leading to the Punchbowl parking area.

 64

Ryan Mountain Trail

Sheep Pass to Ryan Mountain
4 miles RT; 700′ gain.

This day hike tours some Joshua Trees, visits Indian Cave and ascends Ryan Mountain for a nice view of the rocky wonderland in this part of the National Monument. Ryan Mountain is named for the Ryan brothers, Thomas and Jep, who had a homestead at the base of the mountain. Their ranch was used as a water source for the Lost Horse Mine (See Hike 65).

The Joshua Tree is said to have been given its name by early Mormon immigrants because it heralded their approach to the promised land with limbs raised heavenward and the bearded appearance of biblical Joshua.

Despite its harsh appearance, the Joshua Tree, *Yucca brevifolia*, belongs to the lily family. Like lilies and other flowers. it must be pollinated to reproduce. The Tegeticula Moth does the job for the Joshua Tree, which in turn provides seeds for the newly hatched larvae of the moth. Long, long ago, during the evolutionary history of the Mojave Desert, the Joshua Tree and the moth joined together to produce more Joshua Trees and more moths, a partnership that continues to this day.

The Joshua Tree is a small world unto itself and gives life to a number of creatures. A multitude of insects swarm in and on the tree. Birds nest in its limbs and feed on the insects. Lizards take shelter under the fallen trees and limbs. Termites break down dead Joshuas to dust and the tree returns to the earth from which it sprung.

Joshuas are found almost exclusively in the Mojave Desert between 2,500 and 5,000 feet. The higher elevations, (relatively) cooler temperatures and more northerly latitude of the Mojave suits the Joshua better than the lower, dryer, hotter Colorado Desert. The trees grow at the foot of mountain slopes and capture the surface and groundwater draining from higher elevations. Once in awhile you'll see a Joshua Tree clumsily embrace one of its fellows but, generally, its water requirement keeps it distant from other trees.

The view from atop Ryan Mountain is to be savored and is one of the finest in the national monument.

Directions to trailhead: From the Joshua Tree National Monument Visitor Center at Twenty-Nine Palms, drive 8 miles south on Utah Trail Road (the main park road), keeping right at Pinto "Y" junction and continuing another 8 miles to Sheep Pass Campground on your left. Park in the campground, but don't take a camping space. You may also begin this hike from the Indian Cave Turnout just up the road. Be sure to visit Indian Cave. A number of bedrock mortars found in the cave suggests its use as a work site by its aboriginal inhabitants.

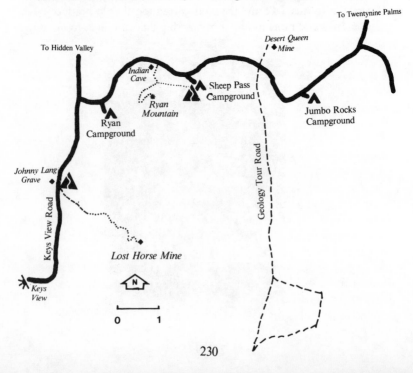

The Hike: From Sheep Pass Campground, the trail skirts the base of Ryan Mountain and passes through a lunar landscape of rocks and Joshua Trees. The Joshua is categorized as an evergreen, though each year much of its foliage withers, dies, and falls off. The ones near the trail would be better described as "everlasting" rather than evergreen.

Soon you intersect a well-worn side trail coming up from your right. If you like, follow this brief trail down to Indian Cave, typical of the kind of shelter sought by the nomadic Cahuilla and Serrano Indian clans that traveled through here.

Continuing past the junction, Ryan Mountain Trail ascends moderate-to-steeply toward the peak. En route you'll pass some very old rocks which make up the core of this mountain and the nearby Little San Bernardino range. For eons, these rocks have, since their creation, been metamorphosed by heat and pressure into completely new types, primarily gneiss and schist. No one knows their exact age, but geologists believe they're several hundred million years old.

Atop Mount Ryan (5,470') you can sign the summit register, located in a tin can stuck in a pile of rocks that marks the top of the mountain. From the peak, you're treated to a panoramic view of Lost Horse, Queen, Hidden, and Pleasant Valleys. There's a lot of geologic history in the rocks shimmering on the ocean of sand below. Not all the rocks you see are as ancient as the ones on Ryan Mountain. Middle-aged rocks, quartz monzonite predominating, are found at Hidden Valley, Jumbo Rocks and White Tank. Younger rocks, basaltic lava—mere infants at less than a million years old—are found in Pleasant Valley.

When you've enjoyed the rock show, return the same way.

Season: All year, but
very hot in summer
Topo: Lost Horse Mountain
See map p. 230

65
Lost Horse Mine Trail

Parking Area to Lost Horse Mine
3½ miles RT; 400′ gain.

Lost Horse Mine was the most successful gold mining operation in this part of the Mojave. More than 9,000 ounces of gold were processed from ore dug here in the late 1890s. The mine's 10-stamp mill still stands, along with a couple of large cyanide settling tanks and a huge winch used on the main shaft. The trail to the mine offers a closeup look back into a colorful era and some fine views into the heart of the Joshua Tree National Monument.

Many are the legends that swirl like the desert winds around the Lost Horse Mine. As the story goes, Johnny Lang was in 1893 camping in Pleasant Valley when his horse got loose. He tracked it onto the ranch belonging to Jim McHaney, who told Lang his horse was "no longer lost," and threatened Lang's health and future.

Lang wandered over to the camp of fellow prospector Dutch Diebold, who told him that he too had been threatened by McHaney and his cowboys. A pity too, because he, Diebold, had discovered a promising gold prospect, but had been unable to mark his claim's boundaries. After sneaking in to inspect the claim, Johnny Lang and his father George purchased all rights from Diebold for one thousand dollars.

At first it looked like a bad investment because the Langs were prevented by McHaney's thugs from reaching their claim. Partners came and went and by 1895, Johnny Lang owned the mine with the Ryan brothers, Thomas and Jep.

Peak production years for the mine were 1896-1899. Gold ingots were hidden in a freight wagon and transported to Indio. The ruse fooled any would-be highway men.

But thievery of another sort plagued the Lost Horse Mine. The theft was of amalgam, lumps of quicksilver from which gold could later be separated. Seems in this matter of amalgam, the mill's day shift, supervised by Jep Ryan, far outproduced the night shift, supervised by Lang. One of Ryan's men espied Lang stealing part of the amalgam. When Ryan gave Lang a choice—sell his share of the mine for $12,000 or go to the penitentiary—Lang sold out.

Alas, Johnny Lang came to a sad end. Apparently, his stolen and buried amalgams supported him for quite some time, but by the end of

Lost Horse Mine

1924 he was old, weak, and living in an isolated cabin. And hungry. He had shot and eaten his four burros and was forced to walk into town for food. He never made it. His partially mummified body wrapped in a canvas sleeping bag was found by prospectors alongside present day Key's View Road. He was buried where he fell.

Directions to trailhead: From the central part of Joshua Tree National Monument, turn south from Caprock Junction on Keys Road and drive 2½ miles. Turn left on a short dirt road. Here you'll find a Park Service interpretive display about Johnny Lang's checkered career. (You can also visit Lang's grave, located a hundred feet north of the Lost Horse Mine turnoff on Keys Road.) The trail, a continuation of Lost Horse Mine Road, begins at a road barrier.

The Hike: The trail, the old mine road climbs above the left side of a wash.

An alternative route, for the first (or last) mile of this day hike, is to hike from the parking area directly up the wash. Pinyon pine and the nolina (often mistaken for a yucca.) dot the wash. Nolina leaves are more flexible than those of yucca and its flowers smaller. The wash widens in about ¾ mile and forks; bear left and a short ascent will take you to the mine road. Turn right on the road and follow it to the mine.

A few open shafts remain near the Lost Horse, so be careful when you explore the mine ruins. Note the stone foundations opposite the mill site. A little village for the mine workers was built here in the late 1890s. Scramble up to the top of the hill above the mine for a panoramic view of Queen Valley, Pleasant Valley, and the desert ranges beyond.

Return the same way.

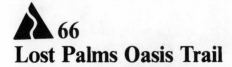

66
Lost Palms Oasis Trail

Cottonwood Springs Campground to Lost Palms Oasis
  8 miles RT; 300' gain.

Compared to a redwood or Ponderosa pine, the fan palm is a flimsy-looking thing but it's a tough tree, resistant to wind and fire, and it's been around a long time—about 10,000,000 years. These relics of Miocene times once ranged as far north as Oregon, but climatic and geologic changes forced their retreat to the oases of Southern California. One of the most beautiful of these oases is Lost Palms in Joshua Tree National Monument. The palms are retreating quickly so you'd better hurry and visit the oasis. In another 10,000,000 years it may be too late.

The Lost Palms Oasis Trail passes through a cactus garden, crosses a number of desert washes, and takes you to the two southern oases in the National Monument: Cottonwood and Lost Palms.

Directions to trailhead: Joshua Tree National Monument is reached off Interstate Highway 10 east of Indio. Enter the south end of the monument, follow the park road 8 miles to Cottonwood Spring Campground, and park your car at the campground. The trailhead is at the end of the campground.

The Hike: Leaving Cottonwood Spring Campground, the trail ambles through a low-desert environment of green-trunked palo verde trees, ironwood and cottonwood trees, spindly ocotillo plants and cholla cactus. Park service identification plaques describe the area's flora and fauna. The trail, a bit difficult to follow through the sandy wash, brings you to Cottonwood Spring oasis in ½ mile. The largely man-made oasis

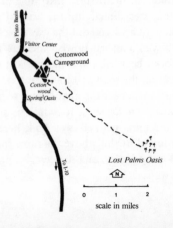

to Pinto Basin

Visitor Center

Cottonwood
Campground

*Cotton
wood
Spring Oasis*

To I-10

Lost Palms Oasis

0   1   2

scale in miles

Lost Palms Oasis

was once a popular overnight stop for freight-haulers and prospectors during the mining years of 1870 to 1910. Travelers and teamsters journeying from Banning to the Dale Goldfield east of Twenty-nine Palms, rested at the oasis. Teamsters planted the trees that gave this oasis its name. Cottonwood Spring is home to a wide variety of birds and a large number of bees.

From Cottonwood Spring, the trail marches over sandy hills, past heaps of huge rocks and along sandy draws and washes. A number of Park Service signs point the way at possible confusing junctions. Finally, you rise above the washes and climb to a rocky outcropping overlooking the canyon harboring Lost Palms Oasis. From the overlook, descend the steep path around the boulders to the palms.

Over one hundred palms are found in the deep canyon whose steep igneous walls sparkle in the desert sun. Little surface water is present at Lost Palms Oasis, but enough is underground for the palms to remain healthy. Lost Palms remained relatively untouched throughout the mining years, though some of its water was pumped to settlements eight miles to the south at Chiriaco Summit. Adjacent to Lost Palms Canyon is a handsome upper canyon called Dike Springs.

The sheer tranquility of this oasis often lulls tired hikers to sleep. Hikers who are insomniacs might try counting sheep. Shy and reclusive Desert Bighorn Sheep are often seen around this oasis—particularly in hot weather when they need water more often. If there aren't any sheep at the oasis, try counting palm trees, woodrats, or tarantulas.

After enjoying a peaceful nap, return the way you came.

67

Borrego Palm Canyon Trail

Borrego Campground to Falls
    3 miles RT; 600′ gain.
Borrego Campground to South Fork
    6½ miles RT; 1400′ gain.

Borrego Palm Canyon is the third largest palm oasis in California and was the first site sought for a desert state park back in the 1920s. It's a beautiful, well-watered oasis, tucked away in a rocky V-shaped gorge.

The trail visits the first palm grove and a waterfall. A longer option takes you exploring farther up-canyon. In winter, the trail to the falls is one of the most popular in the park. In summer, you'll have the oasis all to yourself. Watch for bighorn sheep, who frequently visit the canyon.

Directions to trailhead: The trail begins at Borrego Palm Canyon Campground located 1 mile north of Anza Borrego State Park Headquarters. Trailhead parking is available at the west end of the campground near the campfire circle.

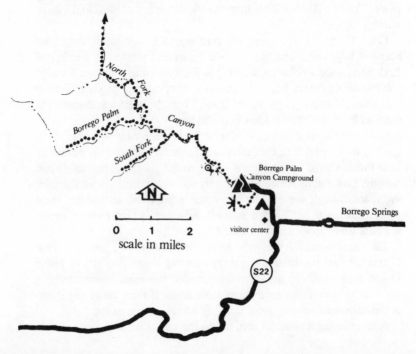

The Hike: Beginning at the pupfish pond, you walk up-canyon past many desert plants used by the Indians for food and shelter. Willow was used for house building and bow making, brittle bush and creosote had healing qualities, honey and mesquite and beavertail cactus were food staples. You might also notice shallow Indian grinding holes in the granite and find a fragment or two of reddish pottery.

The broad alluvial fan at the mouth of the canyon narrows and the sheer rock walls of the canyon soon enclose you as the trail continues along the healthy, but seasonal stream. Already surprised to learn how an apparently lifeless canyon could provide all the Indians' necessary survival ingredients, you're surprised once more when Borrego Palm Oasis comes into view. Just beyond the first group of palms is a damp grotto, where a waterfall cascades over huge boulders. The grotto is a popular picnic area and rest stop.

From the falls, you may take an alternate trail back to the campground. This trail takes you along the south side of the creek, past some magnificent ocotillos, and gives you a different perspective on this unique desert environment. By following the optional route, you can continue hiking up the canyon. Hiking is more difficult up-canyon after the falls, with lots of dense undergrowth and boulders to navigate around.

Option: To South Fork. From the "tourist turnaround" continue up the canyon. The creek is a fairly dependable water supply and is usually running late in the fall. The canyon is wet, so watch your footing on the slippery, fallen palm fronds. The canyon narrows even further and the trail dwindles to nothing. Parallel the stream bed and boulderhop back and forth across the water. The canyon zigs and zags quite a bit, so you can never see more than a few hundred yards ahead. The hike is well worth the effort though, because most of the 800 or so palms in the canyon are found in its upper reaches. Sometimes you'll spot rock climbers practicing their holds on the steep redrock cliffs above you.

The canyon splits 1¾ miles from the falls. Straight ahead, to the southwest, is South Fork. The rocky gorge of South Fork, smothered with bamboo, is in possession of all the canyon's water. It's quite difficult to negotiate. South Fork ascends to the upper slopes of San Ysidro Mountain (6,417'). The Middle Fork (the way you came) of Borrego Palm Canyon in dry and more passable. It's possible to hike quite a distance first up Middle Fork then North Fork of Borrego Palm Canyon, but check with the rangers first. It's extremely rugged terrain.

Return the same way.

68

Rockhouse Canyon Trail

**Bow Willow Campground to Rockhouse
7 miles RT; 700′ gain.**

A turn-of-the-century miner, Nicolas Swartz, boasted he took $18,000 worth of gold from his remote desert mine. In the great tradition of Lost Mine Legends, he died without leaving a map. In 1906, Mr. Swartz built a rock house in an anonymous canyon that soon picked up the name of his structure. History is a muddled affair. There are *two* rock houses in the state park and there's some question as to which actually belonged to Mr. Swartz. Lately, local historians say Swartz located his house in Nicholas Canyon on the other side of the park. They say the Darrel McCain family built the rock house in Rock House Canyon as a line shack for a cattle operation.

This looping day hike takes you climbing through a single palm canyon, visits the rock house and its canyon and returns via the wash on the bottom of Bow Willow Canyon.

Directions to the trailhead: From Interstate Highway 8 in Ocotillo, take County Road S-2 16 miles to the turnoff for Bow Willow Canyon and Campground. Follow the good hardpack sand road 1½ miles to the campground. Park in the campground, but don't take a campsite someone could use.

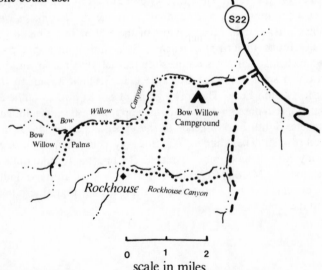

scale in miles

The Hike: Hike up Bow Willow Canyon on the signed jeep trail. Before you get much past the campground, make a 90-degree left turn (south) across a few hundred yards of wash to pick up the foot trail. One quarter mile up the trail is a beleagured young palm tree. You begin climbing steadily through a desert garden of granite boulders, agave and cholla cactus. As you near Rockhouse Canyon, the trail descends briefly and intersects Rockhouse Canyon Jeep Trail. Follow the Jeep Trail west for one mile to Mr. Swartz's abandoned rock house. We can only pray that Swartz was a better prospector than architect. However, it's the only shade around, so this is no time to quibble over aesthetics.

From the rockhouse, you follow a tentative foot trail that drops down into Bow Willow Canyon. The wash on the canyon floor makes a unique hiking experience. In the wash, there's less of that relentless creosote that gives so much of the desert its monotonous look. Water, scarce as it is, is the dominant force working here. Flash floods carry great chunks of rock down to the canyon bottom. Water sculpts the cliffs and has carved the great "V" you're hiking in. Coyote melons, bitter-tasting to humans and to the coyotes as well, dot the wash. The melons dry in the sun and the gourds blow about the wash. I'm often seized with the urge to bat them around with a stick and play some kind of prehistoric ballgame.

Spring scatters color in the wash. Monkey flowers and desert stars and a host of wildflowers brighten the sands and gravel bars. Even ocotillo changes its fit-only-for-firewood appearance and displays its new green leaves and flaming red flowers.

Before long you'll come to a barrier across the wash preventing dirt bikers from ascending into the upper reaches of the canyon. Past the barrier, the canyon widens and it's an easy 2-mile hike over soft sand back to Bow Willow Campground.

239

69

Calcite Canyon Trail

County Road S-22 to Calcite Mine
4 miles RT; 500′ gain.

Nature's cutting tools, wind and water, have shaped the ageless sandstone in Calcite Canyon into steep, bizarre formations. The cutting and polishing of the uplifted rock mass has exposed calcite crystals. Calcite is a common enough carbonate and found in many rocks, but only in a few places are the crystals so pure.

It was the existence of these crystals, with their unique refractive properties that brought man to this part of the desert. The jeep trail was built in the mid 1930s for miners to gain access to Calcite Canyon, as it came to be called. Because of their excellent double refraction properties, calcite crystals were useful in the making of bomb sights. Mining activity increased during World War II.

The calcite was taken from the canyon in long trenches, which look as if they were made yesterday. The desert takes a long time to heal.

This day hike takes the jeep road to its dead end at the mine. You'll see the Calcite Mine Area up close and get a good overlook of the many washes snaking toward the Salton Sea. A return trip through Palm Wash and its tributaries lets you squeeze between perpendicular sandstone walls and gives a unique perspective on the forces that shape the desert sands. The awesome effects of flashflooding are easily discerned by the hiker and suggest a narrow wash is the last place in the world you want to be in a rainstorm.

Directions to the trailhead: Follow County Road S-22 west from Highway 86, or 20 miles from the Christmas Circle to Calcite Jeep Road. The jeep road is just west of a microwave tower.

The Hike: Follow the jeep road, which first drops into the south fork of Palm Wash, then begins to climb northwest. Along the road you'll see long, man-made slots cut into the hillsides for the removal of calcite. Calcite Jeep Road dips a final time then climbs a last ½ mile toward the mine. Two miles from the trailhead, the road deadends at the mining area.

Calcite crystal fragments embedded in the canyon walls and scattered on the desert floor glitter in the sun. Behind the mining area, to the northeast, is a gargantuan hunk of white sandstone dubbed Locomotive Rock. The imaginative can picture a great Baldwin locomotive chugging

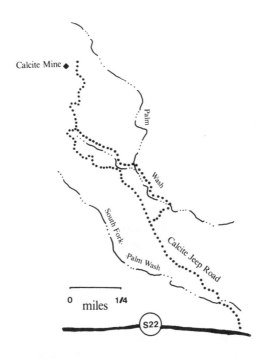

Calcite Mine

Palm

Wash

South Fork

Palm Wash

Calcite Jeep Road

0   miles   1/4

S22

up a steep grade. If you look carefully, you'll be able to see Seventeen Palms and some of the palms tucked away in Palm Wash in a bird's-eye view of the east side of the state park.

You can return the same way or descend through tributaries of the middle fork of Palm Wash. Take a last look at the steep ravines and washes to get your bearing. Middle Fork is but a hop, skip, and a jump from the mine, but the jump's a killer—a fifty-foot plunge to a deep intersecting wash. To get into the wash, you need to descend a half mile down Calcite Road to a small tributary wash. Descend this wash, which is fairly steep at first. The sandstone walls close in on you. One place, "Fat Man's Misery" allows only one fat truckdriver (or two skinny day hikers) to squeeze through at a time. When you reach the middle fork, a prominent canyon, follow it about ¼ mile to the brief jeep trail connecting the wash to Calcite Road. Hike back up Calcite Road 1/10 mile to the parking area.

Doane Valley, Palomar Mountain State Park

Chapter 13

PALOMAR MOUNTAINS

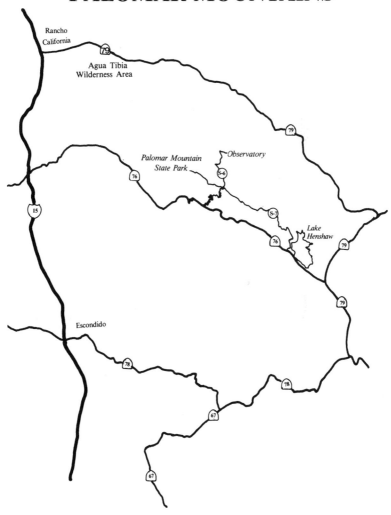

"Nothing prepares one for the surprise of Palomar. There it stands, a hanging garden above the arid lands. Springs of water burst out of the hillsides and cross the road in rivulets. The road runs through forests that a king may covet—oak and cedar and stately fir."

—Professor W.J. Hussey
while scouting for a telescope site

Palomar Mountains

THE PALOMAR MOUNTAINS, extending twenty-five miles along the northern boundary of San Diego County, are one of the few Southern California mountain ranges *not* bordering the desert. The range is an uplifted block with distinct fault lines on both the north and south sides. The north and south slopes are quite precipitous as a result of these faults. Three major ridges make up the Palomars. A long ridge near the Observatory rises to the range's highest point, unimaginatively named "High Point" (6,126'). A western ridge, protected by a federal wilderness area is called Agua Tibia and the rocky ridge east of High Point is Aguanga Mountain.

Indians called the Palomars, "Pauuw," which means quite simply, "mountains." The Spanish nóticed a large number of band-tailed pigeons in the area and named the mountains Palomar, "pigeon roost."

In the 1890s the Palomars were a popular vacation spot. Hotels and a tent city welcomed mountain lovers. When automania took hold in the teens and twenties, vacationers were lured to farther and more exotic locales. The Palomars reverted to semi-wilderness, undeveloped land thick with private property signs.

The Palomars were dubbed the "Mystery Mountains" because few people lived there when plans for the Observatory were formulated. Access to the range was difficult. Cars had to climb up a steep, nerve-wracking route called Nigger Grade. Motorists descending the grade tied trees to their car bumpers to slow their descent. Trees discarded at the bottom of the hill supplied local Indians with firewood for a long time. A new south grade road, the "Highway to the Stars," was built to the observatory site and opened up the mountains to visitors.

The beauty of the Palomars is entrusted to Palomar State Park and the Cleveland National Forest. Considering the mountains' pristine beauty and popularity with visitors, it's surprising there are so few miles of trail. These trails take the hiker through diverse ecosystems. Moist high altitude environments characteristic of coastal ranges much farther north are found on upper Palomar slopes. Lower, sun-drenched slopes host a chaparral community typical of Southern California mountains. Whether you hike through blue lupine on sunny slopes or tiger lilies in the shade, manzanita on dry slopes or azalea in damp canyons, a hike in San Diego County's "Mystery Mountains" is a memorable event.

70

Season: Nov.-June
Topo: Vail Lake
Wilderness permit required

Dripping Springs Trail

Dripping Springs to Giant Chaparral
7 miles RT; 1200′ gain.
Dripping Springs to Palomar Divide Truck Trail
13 miles RT; 2800′ gain.

Agua Tibia, place of tepid waters, refers to a warm spring at the foot of the mountains used by the Indians for their health. Today, Agua Tibia is the name given to a mountain and a wilderness on the border of Riverside and San Diego counties in the Cleveland National Forest.

The Agua Tibia Wilderness Area is on the northwest crest of the Palomar Mountains. The rugged area, three by five miles, seems inhospitable at first or even second glance. The slopes are covered with thorny chaparral. Stream erosion has carved deep and precipitous canyons. Temperatures exceed 100 degrees in summer and as much as two feet of snow may fall on open ridge in winter. Despite outward appearances, this land of radical temperatures and odd foliage has much to offer the hiker. The Dripping Springs Trail takes you to an area of giant chaparral. Huge manzanita have miraculously escaped the ravages of fire for over a hundred years. Following the Dripping Springs Trail all the way to the abandoned Palomar Divide Fire Road brings you to oak- and pine-dotted upper slopes that give you a panoramic view of the San Jacintos and San Bernardinos.

Directions to the trailhead: From Interstate Highway 15, exit east on Highway 79. Proceed 10 miles to the Dripping Springs Campground on your right. The signed Dripping Springs Trail begins at the south end of the campground. Near the entrance to the campground is a Forest Service station, where you may obtain a wilderness permit.

The Hike: Dripping Springs Trail immediately crosses the only water en route, Arroyo Seco Creek. It climbs south and southwest, switchbacking forever and ever up one false summit after another on the north side of Agua Tibia Mountain (4,779′). Look over your shoulder and you'll see Vail Lake and the mighty San Jacintos. Only the buzzing banter of a multitude of bees breaks the silence. In this land of little shade, uninterrupted views are provided of San Jacinto Peak to the northeast, San Gorgonio Peak to the north, and Mt. Baldy to the northwest.

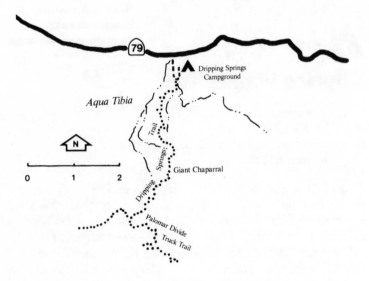

You arrive at the Giant Chaparral 3½ miles from the trailhead. Twenty-foot manzanita reside in an area watered by a seasonal, undependable spring. Usually, when you look at manzanita, you have difficulty deciding whether it's a tree or a shrub. Botanists say it's officially a shrub, but these specimens in the Agua Tibia Wilderness Area are tree-sized and shaped. In winter, white flowers tinged with rose decorate the red-brown bark. It's a tree. . .er, shrub that's particularly well adapted to its environment. In hot weather, the simple oval leaves turn on their sides, pointing their edges at the sun. In this way, the manzanita keeps its water supply from evaporating.

Return the same way or continue on the Dripping Springs Trail to higher and greener Agua Tibia slopes.

Option: To Palomar Divide Truck Trail. A half mile beyond the Giant Chaparral, the trail descends and you get a view southeast over the Palomars. Crowning a far-off ridge, the silver dome of Palomar Observatory sparkles in the sun. You begin switchbacking again and rise above the chaparral to oak and pine dotted slopes. Three miles from the Giant Chaparral, the Dripping Springs Trail intersects the Palomar Divide Truck Trail. From the truck trail, you can look over distant peaks and valleys and occasionally glimpse the Pacific Ocean, forty miles away. If you turn left at the truck trail and walk yet another mile, you'll reach a primitive campsite, just as the truck trail begins to head west.

Return the same way.

71

Observatory Trail

Observatory Campground to Palomar Observatory
4 miles RT: 800′ gain

Astronomer George Hale will be remembered both for his scientific discoveries and his vision of constructing great observatories. His first vision materialized as the Yerkes Observatory with its 40-inch telescope, his second as Mount Wilson Observatory with its 60-inch and 100-inch telescopes, and finally Palomar Observatory with its 200-inch telescope. The Great Glass at Palomar is the most powerful telescope in America and has done more to increase our knowledge of the heavens than any other instrument.

Most visitors traveling to Palomar drive their cars all the way to the top, visit the observatory, and drive back down. Too bad! They miss a nice hike. Observatory Trail roughly parallels the road, but is hidden by a dense forest from the sights and sounds of traffic.

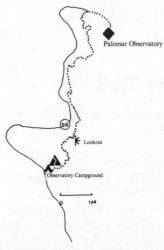

Palomar Observatory

Lookout

S6

Observatory Campground

0   1/4

Palomar Mountain doesn't have the distinct cone shape of a stereo-typical mountain top. It soars abruptly up from the San Luis River Valley on the south, but flattens out on top. Atop and just below the long crest, are oak valleys, pine forests, spring-watered grasslands and lush canyons. All the great views from the top do not come from the Hale telescope! Palomar Mountain provides a bird's eye view of much of Southern California. Miles and miles of mountains roll toward the north, dominated in the distance by the San Bernardino Mountain peaks. Southward, Mount Cuyamaca is visible and even farther south the mountains of Baja California. On the western horizon, orange sunset rays floodlight the Pacific.

Observatory Trail, designated a National Recreation Trail by the Forest Service, is a delightful introduction to the geography of the Palomar Mountains. It takes you from Observatory Campground to the peak, where you can learn about the geography of the heavens.

Directions to trailhead: From Interstate Highway 15, exit on Highway 76 east. Proceed to Rincon Springs. For a couple of miles, S6 joins with Highway 76. Continue on S6, forking to the left at South Grade Road (Highway to the Stars). South Grade winds steeply to Observatory Campground and up to the Observatory. Turn right into Observatory Campground. The Forest Service charges a day use fee. The camp-ground closes in mid-December for the winter. Follow the campground road until you spot the signed trailhead between campsites 19 and 20. The Forest Service booklet, "Guide to the Observatory Trail," which highlights flora and fauna found along the trail, is available at the trailhead.

You could just as well hike the Observatory Trail from top to bottom and have a friend or family member pick you up at the bottom. To reach

Mendenhall Valley from Observatory Trail

the upper trailhead, simply continue up the road to the Observatory parking area. The top of the trail is just outside the gates of the Observatory grounds (open daily 9 a.m. to 4:45 p.m.)

The Hike: The signed trail begins at the edge of the campground. You begin climbing over wooded slopes and soon get a grand view of Mendenhall Valley. You continue ascending over slopes watered by the headwaters of the San Luis Rey River. As the legend goes, young Indian girls visited one of the trickling mountain springs whose waters rushed over beautiful slender stones. The maidens would reach into the water to gather these stones, the number found indicating the number of children she would bear.

The last part of the trail climbs more abruptly up manzanita covered slopes. Soon you see the silvery dome of the 200-inch Hale telescope. This obelisk of symmetry and precision dwarfs nearby trees. Ever-changing patterns of sunlight and shade play upon the top of the dome.

Visit the observatory gallery to see the great telescope. And take a look at the nearby museum whose exhibits explain some of the mysteries unraveled by the 200-inch lens.

Return the same way.

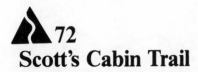

72
Scott's Cabin Trail

Silver Crest Picnic Area to Scott's Cabin
Cedar Grove Campground, Boucher Lookout
3½ mile loop; 800′ gain

Palomar Mountain is a state park for all seasons. Fall offers dramatic color changes, and blustery winter winds ensure far-reaching views from the peaks. In spring, the dogwood blooms and in summer, when temperatures soar, the park offers a cool, green retreat. People-size bracken ferns line trails and meadows.

A mixed forest of cedar, silver fir, spruce and black oak invites a leisurely exploration. Tall trees and mountain meadows make the park especially attractive to the Southern California day hiker in search of a Sierra Nevada-like atmosphere.

The discovery of bedrock mortars and artifacts in Doane Valley indicate that Indians lived in this area of the Palomars for many hundreds of years. The mountains' pine and fir trees were cut for the construction of Mission San Luis Rey. Remote Palomar Mountain meadows were a favorite hiding place for cattle and horse thieves, who pastured their stolen animals in the high country until it was safe to sneak them across the border.

This day hike, a 3½-mile loop, is a *grande randonnée* of the park, a four-trail-sampler that leads to a lookout atop 5,438-foot Boucher Hill.

Directions to trailhead: From Interstate 5 in Oceanside, drive northeast on State Highway 76 about 30 miles. Take County Road S6 north; at S7, head northwest to the park entrance. There is a day use fee. Park in the lot at Silver Crest Picnic Area just inside the park. Scott's Cabin Trail takes off from the right side of the road about 20 yards beyond the lot entrance.

The Hike: A trail sign points the way to Scott's Cabin, ½-mile away. Noisome Steller's jays make their presence known along this stretch of trail. Scott's Cabin, built by a homesteader in the 1880s, is found on your left. The crumpled remains aren't much to look at.

You'll descend steeply through a white fir forest and reach the signed junction with the Cedar-Doane Trail, which heads right, east. (This steep trail, formerly known as the Slide Trail because of its abruptness, takes the hiker down oak-covered slopes to Doane Pond. The pond is stocked with trout and fishing is permitted. A pondside picnic area welcomes the hiker.)

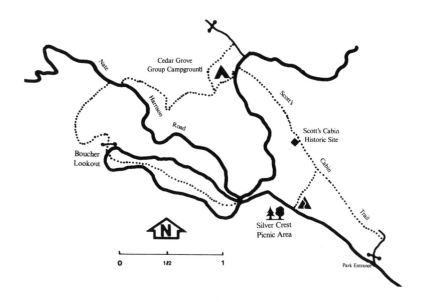

Continue past the Cedar-Doane Trail junction a short distance to Cedar Grove Campground. Follow the trail signs and turn left on the campground road and then right into the group campground. Look leftward for the signed Adams Trail, which cuts through a bracken fern-covered meadow. Once across the meadow, you'll encounter a small ravine where dogwood blooms during April and May. The trail winds uphill past some big cone spruce and reaches Nate Harrison Road.

The road is named in honor of Nathan Harrison, a southern slave, who followed his master to the California gold rush—and freedom—in 1849. Harrison laid claim to a homestead on the wild eastern edge of what is now state parkland, and had a successful hay making and hog raising operation, despite numerous run-ins with bears and mountain lions.

Across the road, your path becomes Boucher Trail, which ascends a north facing slope through white fir, then through bracken ferns and black oaks, to the summit of Boucher Hill.

Atop the hill is a fire lookout and microwave facility. From the summit, you get a view of the surrounding lowlands, including Pauma Valley to the west.

Return to the parking area via the Oak Ridge Trail, which descends one mile between the two sides of the loop road that encircles Boucher Hill. The trail heads down an open ridgeline to a junction of five roads, where it's a mere hop, skip and a jump back to the Silver Crest Picnic Area.

251

Stonewall Peak, Cuyamaca Rancho State Park

Chapter 14

CUYAMACA MOUNTAINS

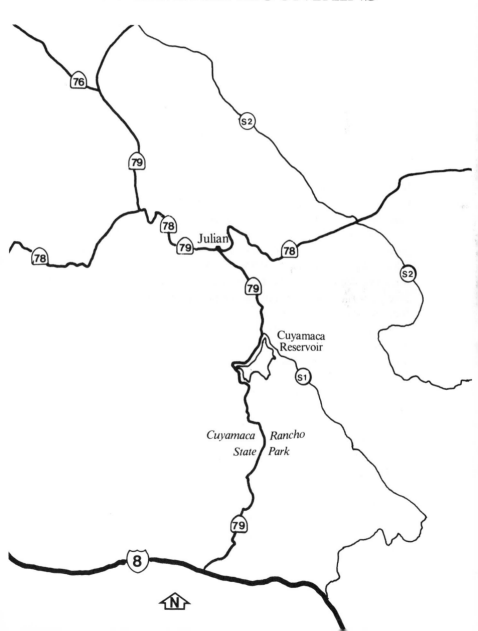

CUYAMACA MOUNTAINS

DIEGUEÑO INDIANS called the range "Ah-ha Kwe-ah-mac," which meant "no rain behind." The ancients were accurate observers, for the Cuyamacas seem to gather all storm clouds around their summits and then ration the rain among themselves. Residents on the desert side of the mountains can only gaze forlornly up at the thunderheads; the Cuyamacas see to it that not one drop falls on the vast sandscape to the east.

Plentiful rain and the Cuyamacas' geographical location between coast and desert make these mountains a unique ecosystem. The 4,000 to 6,500-foot peaks host rich forests of ponderosa and Jeffrey pine, fir and incense cedar, as well as some wonderful specimens of live and black oak. In lower elevations, broad grasslands stretch toward the horizon. The Cuyamacas are a delight for birdwatchers because desert, coastal, and mountain species are all found in the range.

In 1845, the Mexican government deeded Rancho Cuyamaca to Don Augustin Olvera (the same Spanish don of Olvera Street fame in L.A.). Olvera sold the rancho in 1869 for $1,000. Unfortunately for him, gold was discovered on the land a year later. Hundreds of Yankee and Chinese prospectors poured into the mountains. The Americans forced the Indians to move onto a reservation and give up their ancient ways. The Stonewall Mine near Cuyamaca Lake was one of the most successful hardrock mines. It produced over $2,000,000 worth of gold. The gold boom lasted only a decade; most prospectors moved on to Tombstone in 1888.

The rancho property passed through the hands of banks and businessmen before being purchased by Mr. and Mrs. Ralph Dyar. During the Depression, the Dyars generously sold their rancho to the state for half its appraised value, thus founding Rancho Cuyamaca State Park. Today, most of the Cuyamaca Mountains are protected within the 25,000-acre park.

More than a hundred and ten miles of hiking trails pass through the old rancho. The Cuyamacas offer four-season hiking at its colorful best: fall with its brown, yellow, and crimson leaves; winter snows on the higher peaks; spring with its wildflowers; and sudden summer thunderstorms.

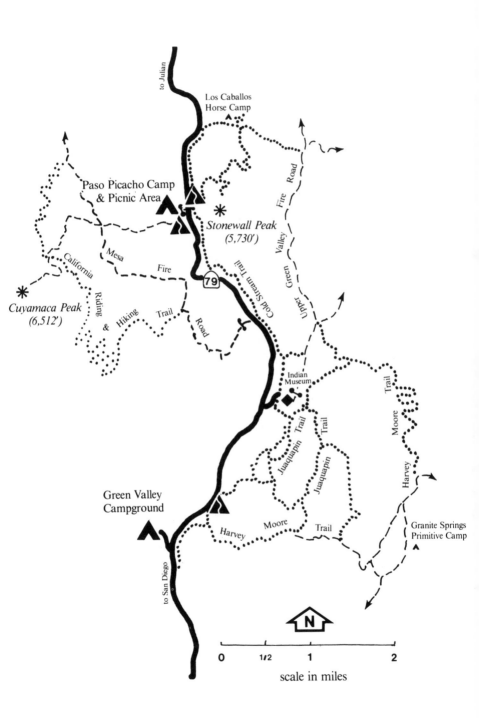

to Julian

Los Caballos
Horse Camp

Paso Picacho Camp
& Picnic Area

✳ Stonewall Peak
(5,730')

Green Valley Fire Road

Upper

✳
Cuyamaca Peak
(6,512')

California

Mesa

Fire

Cold Stream Trail

79

Riding

& Hiking

Trail

Road

Indian
Museum

Moore Trail

Juaquapin Trail

Juaquapin Trail

Juaquapin Trail

Moore

Harvey

Green Valley
Campground

Harvey

Moore

Trail

Granite Springs
Primitive Camp

to San Diego

N

0   1⁄2   1   2

scale in miles

255

▲ 73

Cuyamaca Peak Trail

**Paso Picacho Campground to summit
6 miles RT; 1600′ gain**

Of the more than one hundred miles of trails in Cuyamaca Rancho State Park, the route offering the most spectacular views is surely the 3-mile long Cuyamaca Peak Trail, which climbs through a forest of oak, pine and fir past Deer Spring to the summit. From the 6,512′ peak, the hiker has an open view from the Pacific to the Salton Sea.

Most day hikers are surprised to find such a densely forested mountain in Southern California. Encircling Mount Cuyamaca are silver fir and cedar, plus Coulter, sugar, ponderosa and Jeffrey pine.

The name Cuyamaca is believed to have been derived from the Indian word, *ekui-amak,* variously meaning "rain from above," "rain from behind," and "place beyond rain." Mission padres called the mountain "Sierra de Cuyamat" and American mapmakers later recorded it as Kyamanc, Quiamac and even as Queermack.

Indian legend has it that many more high peaks were once in the Cuyamaca Range, but the peaks took to quarreling amongst themselves. One troublemaking peak, *Hilsh-ki-e* (Pine Tree), battled the rest, who belched rocks upon his head. In the heat of battle, *Hilsh-ki-e* twisted the neck of *Pook-k-sqwee,* which acquired the name of Crooked Neck during this battle and is now known as Mount Cuyamaca. *Hilsh-ki-e* retreated and was exiled to lower elevation.

The trail, Cuyamaca Peak Fire Road, is a paved one lane road (closed to public vehicle traffic) that winds slowly to the summit. While this guide and its author generally avoid pavement like the plague, an exception has been made for this road; it offers a most enjoyable hike and a memorable view.

Directions to trailhead: You may begin this hike from two places, neither of which has good parking. The Cuyamaca Peak Fire Road intersects Highway 79 just south of the park interpretive center. Look for a legal place to park along Highway 79. Or you can pick up the trail at the southernmost campsites in Paso Picacho Campground. There's a state park day use fee.

The Hike: The ascent, shaded by oaks, is moderate at first. Look over your shoulder for a fine view of Stonewall Peak. After passing the junction with the California Riding and Hiking Trail, the route grows steeper. Pine and fir predominate high on the mountain's shoulders.

Just about at the halfway point, the road levels out for a short distance and you'll spot Deer Spring on the left (south) side of the road. Cool and delicious water gushes from a pipe.

The road passes through an area that was scorched in 1950 and 1970 by two severe forest fires. Quite a few tall trees were lost in the blazes. As you near the top, better and better views of Cuyamaca Reservoir and the desert are yours.

The road veers suddenly south, passes junctions with Conejos Trail and Burnt Pine Fire Road, and arrives at the summit.

The peak, located nearly in the exact center of San Diego County, provides quite a panorama—though because of the fire lookout, antennas and trees on top, you'll have to walk around the peak a bit and get your panoramic view in pieces. Some of the highlights include the Santa Rosa Mountains and Laguna Mountains. You can look across the desert into Mexico and westward over to Point Loma, the Silver Strand and the wide Pacific. Atop Mount Palomar, the white observatory can be seen sparkling in the distance.

Return the same way or perhaps improvise a return route back to Paso Picacho Campground via the California Riding and Hiking Trail and the Azalea Glen Trail.

74

Stonewall Peak Trail

Paso Picacho Campground to summit
4 miles RT; 900′ gain
Return via California Riding &
Hiking Trail, Cold Stream Trail
5.5 miles; 900′ gain

The forested shoulders of Stonewall Peak offer fine fall hiking. "Leaf peekers," as autumn tourists are called in New England, will enjoy viewing the brown, yellow, and crimson leaves of the Cuyamaca high country.

In 1870, Confederate General Stonewall Jackson had a Cuyamaca Mountains gold mine named in his honor. The name immediately caused trouble. Although the War Between the States had been over for five years, miners were ready to resume hostilities over the mere mention of the General's name. In the interest of harmony and high productivity, the mine's name was shortened to Stonewall, thereby identifying the mine with the prominent stony peak on the skyline above it.

Rounded Mount Cuyamaca (6,512′) is the highest peak in the range, but Stonewall Peak is more prominent. "Old Stony" is about a thousand feet lower, but its huge walls of granite and crown of stone make it stand out among neighboring peaks. The popular Stonewall Peak Trail will take you to the top of the peak (5,730′) and give you grand views of the old Stonewall Mine site, Cuyamaca Valley, and desert slopes to the east. An optional route lets you descend to Paso Picacho Campground via the California Riding and Hiking Trail and the Cold Stream Trail.

Directions to trailhead: From San Diego, drive east on Interstate Highway 8. Exit on Highway 79 north. The highway enters Cuyamaca Rancho State Park and climbs to a saddle between Cuyamaca and Stonewall peaks. Park near the entrance of Paso Picacho Campground. There's a state park day use fee. The trail to Stonewall Peak begins just across the highway from the campground.

The Hike: From Paso Picacho Campground, the trail ascends moderately, then steeply through oak and boulder country. The black oaks wear vivid colors in fall.

The trail switchbacks up the west side of the mountain. Hike through a thick cluster of incense cedar and when you emerge from the spicy smelling trees, views from the north unfold. Cuyamaca Reservoir is the most obvious geographical feature. Before a dam was built, creating the reservoir, Cuyamaca Lake, as it was called, was a sometimes affair. The Indians never trusted it as a dependable water source and the Spanish referred to it as *la laguna que de seco* or "the lake that dries up." During dry years, the cows enjoy more meadow than reservoir and during wet years, have more reservoir than meadow.

Vegetation grows more sparse and granite outcroppings dominate the high slopes as the trail nears the top of Old Stony. A hundred feet from the summit, a guardrail with steps hacked into the granite helps you reach the top. Far-reaching views to the east and west are not possible because a number of close-in mountains block your view. You can, however, orient yourself to Cuyamaca geography from atop Stonewall Peak. Major Cuyamaca peaks, from north to south, are North Peak, Middle Peak, Cuyamaca Peak.

It's exciting to be atop Stonewall Peak when a storm is brewing over the Cuyamacas, but wear your lightning rod. The peak has been known to catch a strike or two. Black clouds hurtle at high speed toward the peak. Just as they are about to collide with the summit, an updraft catches them and they zoom up and over your head.

You may return the same way.

Option: Return via California Riding and Hiking Trail. Backtrack 100 yards on the Stonewall Peak Trail to an unsigned junction. From here, bear right (north). The trail descends steeply at first, then levels off near Little Stonewall Peak (5,250'). It then descends moderately to the California Riding and Hiking Trail, a long trail that runs through San Diego and Riverside Counties. This trail traverses the west side of the park. You travel for 1 mile on the California Riding and Hiking Trail, which is actually part of the Stonewall Peak Trail. It forks to the right and crosses Highway 79. Don't take the fork, but continue ½-mile down the Cold Stream Trail, paralleling the highway, back to Paso Picacho Campground.

Season: All year
Recommended map: brochure,
California State Parks Guide
Topo: Cuyamaca Peak

 75

Harvey Moore Loop Trail

Sweetwater River—East Mesa—Harper Canyon
12 miles RT; 1000′ gain

Harvey Moore Trail honors a twentieth-century cowboy, who became the first superintendent of Cuyamaca Rancho State Park. Moore cowboyed all over the West before becoming foreman for Mr. and Mrs. Ralph Dyar who owned the Cuyamaca Rancho from 1923-1933. When the Dyars sold the rancho to the state in 1933, they insisted that Moore be made the first superintendent. It's easy to see why Moore and other cowboys loved this idyllic cow country. The Cuyamacas differ from other Southern California mountain ranges in one aspect; instead of being an elevated tumble of boulder-strewn peaks and steep canyons, they are grassy rolling hills where boulders are the exception, not the rule.

The Harvey Moore Trail is a tour of the park's life zones; rolling chaparral, manzanita groves, oak woodlands, grass prairies, lush meadowland. Not only are the zones readily apparent, but the way the landscape changes in response to sunlight and shade, wind and water, is clearly observable from the trail. Traveling the Harvey Moore Trail is like walking through a living ecology guide.

Directions to trailhead: From San Diego, drive east on Interstate Highway 8, taking Highway 79 north. The trailhead is 1 mile south of Cuyamaca Rancho State Park Headquarters (where you can pick up a map) or ½-mile north of Green Valley near the Sweetwater Bridge on the east side of the Highway. Another way: From Interstate Highway 5 in Oceanside, take Highway 78 and head east through Ramona and Santa Ysabel to Julian. Take Highway 79 south to the park.

The Hike: The signed trail begins just above the parking area. Since this is a loop trail, you may hike it either way; the climb is more gradual if you begin to the right (south). I recommend the counterclockwise route; the trail heads south, then west through rolling chaparral and continues a gradual climb through an oak woodland. Keep an eye out for the colorfully deciduous California black oak. In winter, its very dark bark and almost barren branches stand in majestic silhouette against the gray sky. In early spring, the first young shoots are pink or crimson. In summer, the mature leaves are bright green and with the coming of fall they glow yellow and red.

After 2 miles you pass the junction with the Dyar Springs Trail. The junctions along this hike are very well marked with handsome Harvey Moore Trail signs emblazoned in split logs. A half mile past this first junction you reach another. Bear right toward Granite Spring. Shortly, you arrive at Granite Springs Primitive Camp, one of the two trail camps in the state park. This shady spot is perfect for a picnic. Tasty spring water comes from an old hand pump.

Beyond Granite Spring, you rejoin the main trail, actually the East Mesa Fire Road. The East Mesa country that you'll be walking in for the next several miles is well-watered upland hosting wild oats, mustard, and in spring, splashes of wildflowers. In the morning and late afternoon, deer move silently through the tall waving grasses. Several Indian villages were once in the East Mesa area.

The Harvey Moore Trail leaves behind the East Mesa Fire Road, continues north through lush meadowland, then begins to climb up mixed pine and oak slopes. The trail zig-zags steeply down to Harper Creek, crosses the creek, and heads down-canyon. It then drops down the canyons and in a mile joins the creek, where there's a junction. The Harvey Moore Trail goes to the right and soon arrives at a main road just north of park headquarters. Bear left on the East Side Trail, cross the creek, and begin hiking through the grassy Sweetwater River basin. The grassland is cut with numerous minor trails, but you really can't get lost if you remember to keep the river on your right. It's easy, nearly level hiking back to the trailhead.

Escape to a California you only thought you knew...

California State Parks Guide

by the editors of Olympus Press

"Anyone into tent or RV camping amid beautiful scenery, special trails or wilderness will enjoy the 'California State Parks Guide.' It's a large-size compendium of 250 parks with 150 maps, 125 photos and lots of information that includes historical data, facilities and reservation details."
—Los Angeles Times

Day Hiker's Guide to Southern California
by John McKinney

- -

ORDER FORM

Quantity

—————— California State Parks Guide   **$12.95** ——————
ISBN 0-934161-01-1

—————— Day Hiker's Guide to Southern
California   **$10.95** ——————
ISBN 0-934161-02-X

Tax & Shipping ___$2.00___

($1 each additional book) ——————

Total enclosed ——————

Name _____

Address _____

City/State/Zip _____

Make checks payable to:
OLYMPUS PRESS
P.O. Box 2397
Santa Barbara, CA 93120